Evang

Evangelical Feminism

A History

Pamela D. H. Cochran

NEW YORK UNIVERSITY PRESS
New York and London

NEW YORK UNIVERSITY PRESS
New York and London
www.nyupress.org

Library of Congress Cataloging-in-Publication Data
Cochran, Pamela.
Evangelical feminism : a history / Pamela Cochran.
p. cm.
Includes bibliographical references and index.
ISBN 0–8147–1636–9 (alk. paper) —
ISBN 0–8147–1650–4 (pbk. : alk. paper)
1. Bible—Feminist criticism—History.
2. Evangelicalism—History.   I.   Title.
BS521.4.C63   2004
230'.082—dc22   2004015011

New York University Press books are printed on acid-free paper,
and their binding materials are chosen for strength and durability.

Manufactured in the United States of America

c 10 9 8 7 6 5 4 3 2 1
p 10 9 8 7 6 5 4 3 2 1

Contents

Acknowledgments   vii

1   Introduction   1

2   We're on Our Way, Lord!
    The Birth of Biblical Feminism, 1973–1975   11

3   All We're Meant to Be:
    The Early Years of Biblical Feminism, 1975–1983   32

4   Is the Homosexual My Neighbor?
    The Crisis in Biblical Feminism, 1984–1986   77

5   Empowered by the Word, I:
    Theological Changes in Biblical Feminism, 1986–   110

6   Empowered by the Word, II:
    Organizational Changes in Biblical Feminism, 1986–   149

7   Conclusion   190

    Notes   195

    Bibliography   225

    Index   235

    About the Author   245

Acknowledgments

This book has benefited from the input, encouragement, and support from numerous people and organizations. James Davison Hunter deserves particular credit for being an excellent adviser, mentor, and friend. He encouraged my research and challenged my thinking from the first day we met. Heather A. Warren shared her extensive knowledge of American religion and critical writing skills. My fellow graduate students in the religious studies department at the University of Virginia and the Institute for Advanced Studies in Culture graciously read portions of this manuscript while I was writing it or sat through presentations of portions of this material. In addition, the institute provided funds that allowed me to focus on my research during my final year of graduate studies. I also am grateful for the support of a Harvey fellowship while I was writing my dissertation.

As a young faculty member, I have continued to benefit from the feedback of colleagues. I especially want to thank Chuck Mathewes, Wallace Best, members of the Southeast Colloquium on American Religion, and my fellow participants at the Manuscript Workshop sponsored by the Center on Religion and Democracy at the University of Virginia: Chuck Mathewes, Ann Mongoven, Paul Lichterman, Eric Gregory, Brett Wilmot, and the ever present "Catherine." Who would have thought that such a diverse group of scholars would have so much in common? Your input was invaluable. My thanks also go to my editor, Jennifer Hammer, for her comments and patience.

My research could not have been accomplished without the assistance of the staff at the Interlibrary Loan department at the University of Virginia or the archivists for the various collections I used. Cathie Kroeger, at whose family home the Christians for Biblical Equality papers are housed, went above and beyond the duties of an archivist by housing and befriending me during my visit. I will never forget our swims in the pond and the ocean on the Cape. Sue Horner, who was the archivist for the Evangelical and Ecumenical Women's Caucus when I saw its papers, did the same for me in Chicago, although we exchanged the outdoor swims for coffee indoors. Robert D. Shuster and Paul A. Ericksen, archivists at the Billy Graham Center for the Study of Evangelicalism, although more traditional, were just as helpful, as were Claire McCurdy and Elizabeth Russey, archivists at Burke Library, Union Theological Seminary, where the Evangelical and Ecumenical Women's Caucus's records now are held. In addition to financial support, the Center on Religion and Democracy and the Institute for Advanced Studies in Culture have provided a vital intellectual home. I am grateful for the help and encouragement of their fellows, staff (especially Suellen Hill and Nicole Martin), and my research assistants, Susan Daughtry and Kristine Harmon.

My greatest appreciation goes to the many women of the Evangelical and Ecumenical Women's Caucus and Christians for Biblical Equality who very generously talked with and e-mailed me. I owe particular thanks to Nancy Hardesty, Letha Scanzoni, and Ginny Hearn, who always were quick to respond to yet another question and make helpful suggestions to various drafts of my writing. Ginny also taught me a lot about grammar through her skills as a copy editor. Although I know that none of these women agrees with all my conclusions, I hope that they will see in these pages my respect for them and their contribution to American religion.

Finally, I dedicate this book to my husband, Joseph, and son, Sampson, whose dedication to me cannot be bound within the pages of a book and for which I am eternally grateful.

1

Introduction

> Feminist theology cannot be done from the existing base of the Christian Bible.
> —Rosemary Radford Ruether, *Womanguides*, p. ix

On a rainy afternoon in the spring of 1982, a young pregnant woman visited the headquarters of Campus Crusade for Christ, a conservative Christian ministry to college students. Anne Eggebroten was dressed in one of her cutest pregnancy dresses (despite her disdain for typically feminine attire). She hoped that her outfit would help convey that she was "a good Christian woman" at the same time that she was trying to communicate a feminist message. Armed with bookmarks advertising a conference later that summer, her goal was to "reach the female employees [of Campus Crusade] with the good news of Jesus' freeing women."[1] Eggebroten was told that she would need the president's personal approval to hand out her advertisements, which "was unlikely for your organization," the Evangelical Women's Caucus. Eggebroten reported that less than twenty-four hours later, she received the bookmarks back in the mail. She concluded that "you'd probably have better luck smuggling Bibles across the Iron Curtain" than to interest a traditional, evangelical organization like Campus Crusade in an event sponsored by a feminist organization, even an evangelical one.

At the time of this incident, Eggebroten was teaching English full time at California State University at San Bernardino and was a member of NOW, a local church, and the Evangelical Women's Caucus, an evangelical feminist organization. For most people today, much less in the early 1980s, the terms *evangelical* and *feminism* are contradictory. *Evangelicalism* refers to a nondenominational coalition of conservative Christians known for its strict, or "literal," interpretation of the Bible. *Evangelical* also conjures up images of right-wing politics and social conservatism, including support for "traditional" gender roles. So how could an evangelical also support feminism, a movement that seeks, at its most basic level, to redress the inequalities, injustice, and discrimination that women face because of their sex? Surely a person cannot hold true to a feminist ideology and social agenda and a conservative theology at the same time?

Nonetheless in 1973, at a gathering of young evangelicals concerned about the dearth of conservative Christians working toward social justice, the seeds of "evangelical feminism" were sown. In that year, the Evangelicals for Social Action (ESA) convened a conference in Chicago to discuss social concerns, to which only a few women were invited. As a result of the discussions at that meeting, a second conference held in the following year involved a larger number of women and included a special seminar on the topic of women's equality. This seminar led to the emergence of an "evangelical women's caucus" and a concomitant "biblical" or "evangelical feminist" movement characterized by the belief that when interpreted correctly, the Bible teaches the equality of women and men.[2] The Evangelical Women's Caucus (EWC) maintained a unified front for more than a decade until a resolution recognizing a lesbian minority in the organization revealed fundamental differences among the members over the role of biblical authority that led to emotional tensions and, ultimately, schism. What was the social and religious context that enabled the development of an "evangelical feminism"? And what were the theological issues it had to confront?

What follows is the story of the emergence and theological development of biblical feminism, why the members of the movement split, the results, and what all this reveals about conservative Protestantism and religion generally in contemporary America. At the heart of this engagement among evangelical feminists was a negotiation over the nature, meaning, and scope of biblical authority, the end result of which was a weakening of scriptural authority, a change that had been taking place not just among evangelical feminists but throughout American religion. My account reveals a shift from inerrancy (the belief that the Bible is inspired by God and is entirely without error) to hermeneutics (methods of textual interpretation) as the means of establishing evangelical identity and the general weakening of authority located beyond the self. As such, the history of evangelical feminism is more than just a narrative of events. It also is a kind of "color commentary" on the struggles over authority in American evangelicalism and religion more broadly and thus has important lessons to teach us about American evangelicalism, American religion generally, and the nexus between religion and public life.

Central to the question of authority in American Protestantism is the biblical text itself. It is the Bible, unmediated through the institutional church or authoritative leaders, that directs the beliefs and actions of the believer. At the heart of the issue of scriptural authority is the trustworthiness of the source. Does the biblical text reliably reveal divine will? Is it historically accurate? Even if one finds it reliable and accurate, how does one apply it to one's own life in contemporary America, given that it was written in very different social and historical contexts?

Such issues are crucial to biblical feminists because as evangelicals, they believe that the Bible—not progressive revelation or traditions as they developed through communities or were constructed through philosophy—is God's revealed truth. As such, to these women, the Bible, and the faith it reveals, is central to solving the problem of women's oppression in the home, church, and society. In coming to this conclusion, biblical feminists have employed modern, and contested, methods of biblical interpretation. Central to the altercation in the EWC was a disagreement over which methods were acceptable and, therefore, what conclusions could be drawn. To some, condoning lesbianism in their organization clearly indicated a shift in the basis of religious authority away from the Bible toward a greater emphasis on the outside culture, both secular and religious (i.e., liberal). Yet even the women who opposed recognizing lesbianism in their movement altered their conception of biblical authority. These changes in their hermeneutics and concept of biblical authority caused biblical feminists to play an important role in shifting the boundaries of American evangelicalism. Accordingly, the story of evangelical feminism clarifies and addresses trends visible in American religion and culture since the 1960s.

Within conservative Protestantism, evangelical feminists helped reshape how evangelicals defined themselves through their use of modern hermeneutical methods and acceptance of a limited definition of inerrancy. Prior to the 1970s, American evangelicals defined themselves by their adherence to the belief that the Bible contains no errors and teaches God's truth on every topic on which it touches, from faith to science to psychology. Beginning in the 1970s, however, based on modern methods of biblical interpretation, some evangelicals began to limit the infallibility of scripture to the topic of faith and its practice, thereby contesting the foundation of the movement. By using a more limited definition of inerrancy and modern hermeneutical methods in their interpretations of scripture relating to women's roles, evangelical feminists helped shift evangelical boundaries away from inerrancy to the rules of engagement, that is, the methods of interpretation. In this, the history of evangelical feminism reveals a surprising theological rigor among conservative Protestant women that has not previously been recognized.[3]

The debate among biblical feminists further reveals the impact on evangelicalism and American religion of an increasing rise in individualism in American culture. It is not news to say that individualism is on the rise in liberal Protestantism, in which personal experience and social justice long have been interpretive keys. In addition, since the 1960s, spirituality—personal faith that is not tied to a particular institutional religious form—has become more popular.[4] Many of the same scholars who have chronicled the rise of personal faith have also documented the numerical growth of conservative American Protestantism. In large part, this increase can be attributed to a relationship to the text of scripture as authoritative that has kept the symbolic boundaries of evangelicalism largely intact. That is, American evangelicalism has remained largely exclusive in its faith claims. It has not become inclusive or tolerant of a broad range of theological or social views in the way that many mainline churches have. Many scholars of American religion thus have been content to argue that evangelicalism is thriving in a modern—some might say postmodern—environment.

What is interesting in the account of evangelical feminism is that it indicates that although American evangelicalism may continue to survive and grow, it may not be thriving after all. A deeper analysis shows the increasing encroachment of a more individualized, therapeutic, and consumerist society on conservative Protestantism, one in which moral agency is determined by individual preference rather than by a transcendent point of reference and in which individuals have a "religious preference" rather than a "confession of faith." This can be seen most clearly among the more progressive evangelical feminists who have come to rely on personal experience as authoritative in their interpretation of scripture, thereby weakening their commitment to external, transcendent authority. They have incorporated a broader array of theological, social, and faith perspectives, and their organization, the Evangelical Women's Caucus, is more inclusive. The more traditional evangelical feminists also have been affected by secular American culture, though more subtly. They remain more exclusive in their faith beliefs and maintain a strong conception of biblical authority. In doing so, the more traditionalist evangelical feminists have provided a genuine, alternative, feminist theory to secular feminism, one based on a preestablished, external moral order. Still, the impact of a consumerist, therapeutic culture can be seen in the heavy weight these traditionalists place on the ability of individual reason to correctly understand the words of scripture unaided (which deemphasizes the traditional authority of the institutional church) and in their focus on using the Bible to meet the perceived needs of the individual. Such trends, which stress individual preference and reason, among evangelical feminists indicate that the modern ideals of pluralism and individualism have made a greater impact on American religion than previously acknowledged, thereby reducing the scope and force of religious authority in America.

What is more, the story of evangelical feminism suggests that evangelicalism may have inadvertently contributed to the loss of its own dominance in American society because it does not challenge the increasingly consumerist culture. For as evangelical feminists illustrate, evangelicalism—with its voluntary nature, democratic tendencies, anti-institutionalism, use of modern tools, and cultural relevance—fits quite well in an increasingly consumerist American culture. Precisely because of this, it has helped shape a new pluralization in America. As many scholars have argued, America has always been pluralist. Along with the pilgrims in Massachusetts, there were Quakers, Baptists, and Jews in the religiously free Rhode Island; Catholics in Maryland; and Anglicans in Virginia.[5] But since the time of the First Great Awakening beginning in the 1730s, evangelicalism has been the dominant faith and influence, and pluralism referred to religious people identifying themselves with a particular faith tradition to which they were bound, with rules and behaviors they tried to maintain. Today's situation, however, involves faith practitioners choosing among religious beliefs and practices, rather than between them, which is substantively different from the past. Today's progressive biblical feminist, for example, may combine in her "evangelical feminism" some Buddhist, some Daoist, New Age, Jewish, and Christian beliefs. Pluralization is now the dominant fact of American religion. As such, religion and faith are not at risk of being destroyed by modernism in American society. However, the binding nature of those faiths is at risk, and evangelicalism, despite its own apparent health, has participated in the destruction of the acceptance of faith (of all kinds) as binding.

Definition of Terms

Several historians have told the history of American evangelicalism, beginning with its roots in nineteenth-century revivalistic religion and the modernist-fundamentalist controversy. Ernest Sandeen, George Marsden, Virginia L. Brereton, and Joel Carpenter, among others, have recounted this story compellingly.[6] It is not my intention, therefore, to retrace their steps but merely to provide enough clarity to help those readers unfamiliar with these histories. In sum, most scholars generally agree that what now is referred to as *evangelicalism* arose after World War II among a group of believers who subscribed to the basic doctrines of fundamentalism but rejected its lack of theological sophistication and its cultural excesses. These reformers, called *new* or *neo*-evangelicals, hoped to bring fundamentalism out of its intellectual isolation, broaden its evangelistic appeal, and return it to its revivalistic roots. They maintained a high view of biblical authority, including the Princeton definition of inerrancy and a belief in the "fundamentals of the faith," such as the virgin birth, substitutionary atonement, Jesus' bodily resurrection, the second coming, and the need for a personal salvation experience. A crucial change that new evangelicals made to achieve their goals, however, was to use modern theological methods, including some aspects of higher criticism.

I use the term *evangelicalism* with two connotations in mind. The first is a historical definition that takes into consideration the historical situation of American evangelicalism as a pietistic, revivalist movement embedded in the American milieu of democracy, individualism, and capitalism.[7] In this sense, evangelicals are those who shared the Reformation tradition of the Pietists, Puritans, Methodists, Baptists, Presbyterians, Wesleyans, and the Holiness movement.[8] Evangelicals are those who are following in the path of their historical forbears and who share similar beliefs and characteristics. Accordingly, Presbyterians, Congregationalists, Wesleyans, and the Holiness churches in the later nineteenth and early twentieth century are seen as heirs to the evangelicals of the earlier revivalist movements, whereas Unitarians are not. Later, fundamentalists acceded to the label of evangelical, and their modernist opponents became the "liberal" mainstream church. In contemporary America what was known as the *neo-evangelical* movement in the 1950s and 1960s (along with pentecostals and, often, fundamentalists) is known now simply as mainstream *evangelicalism.*

Part of what marked all these disparate groups as evangelical was a common set of beliefs, such as the authority of scripture, the efficacy of Christ's atonement on the cross, the necessity of a personal salvation experience, and the importance of evangelism and a transformed life.[9] But they also had a similar style or character. Across all these time periods, evangelicals have been marked by certain affinities. Thus, evangelicalism has been democratic in the way it has stressed individual agency in conversion, popular preaching, and a lack of respect for tradition, authority of the clergy, and institutional organization. Evangelicals tend to lack denominational loyalty, follow charismatic teachers, and be innovative organizationally, whether that has been in splitting and forming new denominations or through parachurch groups to promote missions or a particular issue. The desire to be culturally relevant is another characteristic that has marked evangelicalism across historical periods. Evangelicals have used the tools of modern technology and the marketplace to spread the good news of the gospel, by way of circuit riders, television preachers, and megachurches. They also have been willing to use the philosophical ideas of their day to reach nonbelievers, in their desire to be culturally relevant. This has led evangelicals to make rational arguments for the reliability of the biblical witness and to incorporate the latest scholarship into their methods of biblical interpretation.

The second connotation of the term *evangelicalism* is a sociological one. In this sense, the definition is about who is inside and who is outside the evangelical fold.[10] For this reason, such a definition is more precise than the historical one and more debated among sociologists and historians of religion. It is for sociological reasons therefore that historians such as George Marsden and Virginia Brereton and sociologists like Christian Smith have struggled with defining evangelicalism.[11] For it is whom you study that determines what you will find. For example, evangelicals from the Holiness and Reformed traditions look quite different from each other. They share a commitment to the basics of the faith and theological conservatism, but those from a Holiness background appear to be more emotional. Conversely, those from a Reformed background appear more rational. The charismatic women of the Women's Aglow Fellowship, studied by R. Marie Griffith in her book *God's Daughters*, with their ties to the Full Gospel Businessmen's Association, look quite different from the mostly male theologians of Marsden's study of the Fuller Seminary and the women in this book.[12]

I begin by using Marsden's sociological definition of evangelicals as those who are consciously evangelical, that is, that community or coalition rooted in a commitment to a transdenominational infrastructure of institutions, including churches, schools, colleges, parachurch organizations, and the media. I also use the insight of Jon R. Stone, who, building on Marsden, focuses on the coalitional nature of evangelicalism.[13] Stone concentrates on the role of social issues in evangelicals' attempts at self-definition during the post–World War II years, the immediate historical context of my study.[14] According to Stone and Marsden, the early leaders of postwar evangelicalism (neo-evangelicalism) were concerned with making evangelicalism a theologically conservative movement that would apply faith to a broad range of social issues affecting American life. Neo-evangelicals desired to reclaim the center of nineteenth-century American evangelicalism, positioning themselves as its true heirs and bringing about the kind of social reforms seen in that era of American Protestantism. As such, postwar evangelicalism became coalitional in nature, incorporating a variety of groups with disparate special interests.

It is here that the story of evangelical feminism fits into the sociological and historical definition of evangelical. Biblical feminism was one of those "disparate" special interests that made up the neo-evangelical coalition in the 1970s and 1980s. It began among a group of well-educated, upper-middle-class women (and a few men) who believed that women suffered injustices and discrimination because of their sex and that the Bible offered a viable solution. As one evangelical feminist argued, "The real hope for humanity lies not in discarding the Bible but in coming to a more profound understanding and implementation of it."[15] The individuals who made up the movement were self-consciously evangelical and were associated with a variety of evangelical organizations, including the journals *Eternity* and *Christianity Today*, Trinity Evangelical Divinity School, Fuller Seminary, Northpark Theological Seminary, Gordon College and Gordon-Conwell Seminary, Word Books publishing, the National Association of Evangelicals, the Evangelical Theological Society, and a variety of evangelical churches and denominations (including the Wesleyan, Baptist, and Reformed traditions). They also adhered to the basics of evangelical theology. Biblical feminism was distinct from the rest of (neo-)evangelicalism, however, because of its social progressivism on the issue of women's equality, and at the same time it distinguished itself from secular feminism "by its insistence on the centrality of biblical authority on the issue of women in church and society."[16]

Method and Organization

At the center of my study are the two leading biblical feminist organizations—the Evangelical Women's Caucus (EWC) and Christians for Biblical Equality (CBE)—and the women and men who have articulated their theologies.[17] Because questions of authority are addressed in theology, this book looks first at the intellectual history of evangelical feminist theology (principally on the view of biblical authority) and second at the history of its leading institutions—the Evangelical and Ecumenical Women's Caucus and Christians for Biblical Equality—and their social agendas. I am not trying to prove that every member of the two groups subscribes to every theological or social position of their leading spokespersons. I am arguing, however, that the ideas and positions of those leaders have filtered down to influence their organizations' structure and membership, both socially and theologically.

Most of the women in the organizations that represent evangelical feminists—women like Anne Eggebroten, Nancy Hardesty, Ginny Hearn, Catherine Clark Kroeger, Alvera Mickelsen, and Virginia Mollenkott— are unknown to most evangelicals and scholars of evangelicalism. Several recent studies have assessed women's power within evangelicalism or documented women's contributions to evangelicalism, revealing that gender issues and women's work in missionary and benevolence societies and in Sunday schools have played an important role in shaping its churches. But no study as yet has analyzed the history and theology of contemporary evangelical feminists to discover what impact they have made and how they might illuminate the situation of contemporary American religion. I hope this book will help give the women in evangelicalism their due, not just as majority members in the pew and service societies, but also as intellectuals and leaders. I hope, too, that this information will serve as a resource for those evangelicals who may want to consider the influence of the contemporary milieu on the future of their movement. For in many ways, this is a story about unintended consequences.

I have structured my writing around four periods in the history of evangelical feminism. Chapter 2 begins with the development of biblical feminism as an organized movement and its first theological forays. This chapter also sets the movement in the context of American evangelical religion and the secular women's movement. Chapter 3 describes the early years of biblical feminism, between 1975 and 1984, in which the movement grew amid apparent unity, and its early theology. The next, chapter 4, addresses the explosion of diversity among evangelical feminists. Those years, from 1984 to 1986, were a watershed for evangelical feminists as they addressed divergent views on biblical authority, precipitated by the issue of homosexuality in the EWC.

In the next two chapters I examine the period from 1987 to the beginning of the new millennium. The theological consequences of these different views of biblical authority are covered in chapter 5, in which two distinct biblical feminist theologies are described. This chapter is devoted to evangelical feminists' biblical interpretations of passages traditionally seen as limiting women's leadership in the church and the home. The institutional consequences of the disagreement over biblical authority, including the split into two separate biblical feminist organizations, the Evangelical Women's Caucus and Christians for Biblical Equality, is the focus of chapter 6. Here I assess the shifts in biblical feminist theology, especially in relation to views of biblical authority, and look at those changes in relation to American evangelicalism. In these last two chapters, I consider two separate groups of biblical feminists: the traditionalist evangelical feminists, who still believe that the Bible is the ultimate authority in matters of faith and practice, and progressive evangelical feminists, who consider reason and experience to be sources of authority equivalent to scripture.

Chapter 7 summarizes my findings and looks at the importance of the story of evangelical feminism to American religion in general and to religious ideas on public culture, in order to consider the effect of biblical feminism on American public culture.

2

We're on Our Way, Lord!
The Birth of Biblical Feminism, 1973–1975

In 1969 Nancy Hardesty, an assistant editor of *Eternity*, a Christian magazine, left her position and moved to the Chicago area to teach English at Trinity Evangelical Divinity School. During her first month there, Hardesty received a letter from a writer, Letha Scanzoni, with whose work she was familiar from *Eternity*. Scanzoni remembered Hardesty because she had sent her a supportive note after one of Scanzoni's articles challenging traditional evangelical views of women's roles received a lot of criticism. In the letter, Scanzoni invited Hardesty to join her in writing a book on women's liberation from a Christian perspective. Hardesty accepted.

Scanzoni lived in Indiana at the time, a five-hour drive from Chicago. Nonetheless, the two women frequently visited each other and sometimes communicated every day. The interaction changed both women's lives. Scanzoni found in Hardesty a "writing partner," "friend," and "sister" and credited Hardesty with helping her juggle family, career, and school.[1] Hardesty called their collaboration "a union of two souls."[2] Scanzoni gave her "acceptance, empathy, and love," according to Hardesty, at a time when she was "bitter, lonely, insecure, frustrated, and troubled." Without intending it to, their partnership became an illustration of the kind of community that feminism advocated.

Their collaboration changed other lives as well when *All We're Meant to Be: A Biblical Approach to Women's Liberation* was finally published in 1974. In 1971, when Scanzoni and Hardesty finished writing the book, no publisher thought that women's liberation would interest conservative Christian women, despite the growing women's liberation movement. They were wrong. *All We're Meant to Be* was a publishing hit, winning awards and going through at least five printings. More significantly, it helped show evangelical women around the United States that they could be both evangelicals and feminists. The book, along with the Evangelical Women's Caucus, also was instrumental in initiating a biblical movement for women's rights in the church, home, and society.

The Founding of the Evangelical Women's Caucus

In the summer of 1973, Ron Sider, acting director of the Philadelphia campus of Messiah College, sent a letter of invitation to a select group of approximately sixty evangelicals to a workshop on the topic of evangelicals and social concern to be held at the YMCA hotel in Chicago on November 23 through 25, Thanksgiving weekend. Sider, Jim Wallis (editor of the *Post-American*, a socially conscious, politically left-leaning, evangelical journal), and several others connected to the *Post-American* formed a planning committee consisting of progressives from a variety of evangelical institutions.[3] The goal of the 1973 conference was to determine specific ways in which evangelicals could express their concern for social justice and make an impact on the political arena. The issues in which these evangelicals expressed interest included U.S. militarism, economic justice, racism, and women's liberation, a topic to which the fall 1974 edition of the *Post-American* was dedicated.

Few women were invited to this first gathering of socially conscious evangelicals. Although the planning committee tried to include women, they came up with a list of only eight, not all of whom attended. Several wives, however—who themselves were not invited but whose husbands were—did attend the conference. Their presence increased the number of women participating to approximately seven. Among the invited women who came were Sharon Gallagher, coeditor of *Right On* (which later became *Radix*), and Nancy Hardesty.

The conferees were informed that the purpose of the conference was to foster discussion, prayer, and planning, eschewing formal paper presentations. Although no specific topics were mentioned, Hardesty quickly accepted the invitation and submitted proposals on women's rights, abortion, and pornography. She also suggested discussing the following:

All persons, male and female, are created in God's image and are thus equal.

All persons are given equal responsibility by God for the propagation of the human species and for the preservation of the earth.

Thus women must be treated equally with men. In the church women should be allowed to exercise fully whatever gifts the Holy Spirit has endowed them with, including public leadership in worship and administration on both local and national levels.

In the home women should exercise equal rights and responsibilities with their husbands in the marital relationship and in regard to any children. A woman's homemaking should be considered of equal value with other work outside the home and compensated accordingly.

In the business world, women should be given equal pay and equal benefits commensurate with their training and experience without regard to sex or marital status. This includes so-called "Christian" organizations.

In education, women should be given equal opportunity to pursue their goals without discrimination in admission, course offerings, financial aid, athletic facilities, faculty appointments, promotions, etc.[4]

Hardesty indicated that the Christian community needed to "clean up their own houses" before they could speak to the secular world, especially about women's rights. This meant that women needed to be given equal access to jobs, pay, and education in Christian organizations. In regard to abortion, Hardesty suggested a prochoice stance that promoted a woman's right to choose to terminate a pregnancy, especially in the case of rape, incest, or when it threatened the health of the mother. She added, however, that the church should urge women to deliberate carefully before opting for abortion while offering objective counseling, support, and assistance to pregnant women and single mothers. Her main concern regarding pornography was that Christian organizations should be careful not to violate freedom of speech or advocate censorship.[5]

The organizers allocated much of the time at the conference to drafting a declaration on social concerns, but there also were small group meetings, whose purpose was to suggest concrete proposals for action. According to Gallagher, participants in the women's task force were united by their shared feelings of isolation as feminists within the Christian community. Participants in this small group meeting approved a resolution calling for the condemnation of the improper exegesis of biblical passages and encouraged new hermeneutical studies of scriptures regarding women.[6] Another statement concerning women that came out of the conference appeared in the final draft of the "Chicago declaration" (as it became known), along with ten other statements on topics ranging from forgiveness to poverty and racism. It stated: "We acknowledge that we have encouraged men to prideful domination and women to irresponsible passivity. So we call both men and women to mutual submission and active discipleship."[7]

After the conference, which became known as the Thanksgiving workshop, Sider and others circulated the declaration for more signatures via mail and in publications such as *Christianity Today*, which printed it along with an article about the Thanksgiving workshop. Additional endorsements were collected from William Starr, president of Young Life; Timothy Smith, professor at Johns Hopkins University; and James Sire, editor at InterVarsity Press. Encouraged by the success of their signature drive, a planning committee began to organize a second conference for 1974. This time, two women joined the committee: Hardesty and Cheryl Forbes, an editorial associate at *Christianity Today*. With their help, almost thirty women attended, including Anne Eggebroten, then a graduate student in English, and Letha Scanzoni, author of several of the earliest articles on feminism from a Christian perspective and Hardesty's coauthor of *All We're Meant to Be*.[8]

The format of the second gathering was similar to that of the first and included plenary sessions. But most of the proposal work took place in smaller groups. The women's task force, which Hardesty chaired, came up with a number of concrete ideas. Some of these urged their Christian brothers and male leaders to be more sensitive, to affirm women, and to provide avenues for women to participate and lead. Specifically, the women appealed to husbands for help with child care so as to give mothers some free time. They urged the church to support and affirm nontraditional families, such as singles, the elderly, and one-parent households. They also asked churches to evaluate their educational materials for evidence of sexism.

The women did not leave all the responsibility for change in the hands of pastors and husbands but set ambitious goals for themselves. The women planned to organize Bible studies on women in the family, church history, the contemporary church, and the working world. They intended to develop criteria for churches to help evaluate their educational materials for sexist views and then called on conference attendees to use this material in their own churches. They made plans to contact every evangelical college and seminary to encourage offering women's studies programs. On an individual level, the women were encouraged to attend consciousness-raising workshops and to think of ways to live as role models of gender equality. They called for women in hiring positions to promote qualified women and made Cheryl Forbes a contact point for women seeking employment. They also suggested readings on the use of nonsexist language for personal development and recommended establishing a committee to evaluate translations of the Bible for their use of sexist language.

A great deal of unanimity was necessary for so many proposals to be accepted in such a short time, although there was some disagreement. A large minority of women dissented from a proposal that approved women's ordination and affirmed solidarity with the eleven women ordained by the bishop of the Episcopal Church in Philadelphia (against the bylaws of the denomination) in July of that year. Some men at the conference complained that the women were mimicking the secular feminist movement and were fighting too hard for their proposals, one of which was to endorse the equal rights amendment, which included a pledge to work for its passage. The black women at the conference were not enthusiastic about aligning themselves with white women's causes, deeming race a more important issue for them. Therefore, they eschewed the women's task force to attend the African American caucus, which drew up strong statements about the white evangelicals' lack of concern for black issues. (As a result, a third Thanksgiving workshop addressed those complaints.)

Still, at least two of the projects proposed at the second Thanksgiving workshop materialized, and they were significant to the future of biblical feminism. The first was that *Daughters of Sarah* agreed to act as a clearinghouse to coordinate many of the proposals from the Thanksgiving Day conference. *Daughters of Sarah*, a journal dedicated to biblical feminism, was not itself an outgrowth of the meeting, as the first edition was published just prior to the second Evangelicals for Social Action conference in November 1974. Its founders were academically oriented women in the Chicago area involved with Evangelicals for Social Action, including Hardesty. Lucille Sider Dayton, the assistant director of the Urban Life Center in Chicago (also sister of Ron Sider, wife of Donald Dayton, and one of the "uninvited" wives to attend the first conference), was the first editor of *Daughters of Sarah*. She stated that the periodical's aim was a modest one. The staff wanted to establish a network of women and men who shared a concern for Christian growth and wanted to explore the historical tradition of women in Christianity and how faith was relevant to all areas of women's lives. The inaugural issue included an historical article by Sider Dayton, an exegetical article by Hardesty that looked at the creation accounts, a gender-neutral parenting article, and a suggested reading list. With their skeletal organization already in place, *Daughters of Sarah* gave the biblical feminists at the second conference a central place to coordinate materials and information.

As part of its coordination role, *Daughters of Sarah* agreed to maintain the address list for the second significant action of the women's task force, the development of the Evangelical Women's Caucus to coordinate and implement the workshop proposals. Sider Dayton, Gallagher, Forbes, and Pat Ward, a professor of French at Penn State University, were among those listed as contact persons for the new organization. Ward compiled the names, addresses, and interests of women who wished to participate, and by January 1975 a steering committee was formed. The committee recommended a national conference, to be held in November, and hired a staff person. They also suggested organizing in local chapters, much like those of the National Organization for Women. Already Maryland, New York, Massachusetts, Illinois, Michigan, California, and Minnesota had several groups beginning to coalesce. Thus, within two months, the first biblical feminist organizations were born.

Historical Context

What prompted fifty-three men and women to declare at the first Thanksgiving workshop in November of 1973 that men and women are called to mutually submit to one another? The impetus for the gathering that resulted in this statement was a presumed resurgence of conservative theology within evangelicalism. Events at "Explo '72," a conference sponsored by the Campus Crusade for Christ and focused solely on training in personal evangelism, illustrate the lack of social concern and evangelicalism's return to conservatism that Sider, Wallis, and others deplored. During "Explo," Wallis and a few others attempted to promote an antiwar agenda by distributing literature and carrying placards. Initially, officials from the Campus Crusade expressed concern about the demonstrators' political agenda in protesting the war but allowed the group to continue its activities. But when Wallis and his friends, who called themselves the People's Christian Coalition, began demonstrating behind the speaker's platform during a flag ceremony by military personnel (replete with signs stating "Cross or Flag" and "Christ or Country" and chants of "Stop the War"), the officials silenced them. This lack of left-wing social concern seemed to be proof to Wallis and Sider of a new conservatism in evangelical ranks, reminiscent of an earlier, more militant fundamentalism. In the letter of invitation to the first Chicago conference on social concerns, Sider explained:

> A development of historic significance has occurred in the last decade. Eight years ago the "Death of God" theology captured national headlines; today Key '73 [an event similar to "Explo '72," also sponsored by the Campus Crusade] and the Jesus People have replaced that deceased fad. A conservative religious tide is sweeping the country. Will evangelicals meet the challenge and take advantage of this historic opportunity by proclaiming the biblical message of concern for the whole man? Or will one-sided evangelicalism help to provide an excuse for a revival of theological liberalism by proclaiming and living a truncated message?[9]

In offering this challenge, Sider was appealing to larger, more enduring themes in American Protestantism than the shorter-lived, liberal "Death of God" or the conservative "Jesus People" movements. Sider was reminding his readers of the ongoing struggle between liberalism and conservatism in American evangelicalism.

At this time, those struggles revolved around the issue of biblical inerrancy. In brief, biblical inerrancy is concerned with the issue of scriptural authority. Those who subscribe to this doctrine believe that the Bible is the inspired Word of God, completely true and faithful in all matters on which it touches. In the early 1970s, evangelicals were not far removed from their fundamentalist heritage and thus were struggling to both identify with and separate from their forefathers, who formed one branch of the successors to nineteenth-century evangelicals. Contemporary evangelicals attempted to maintain theological continuity through their adherence to the fundamentalists' "fundamentals of the faith."[10] In their behavior, however, evangelicals in the 1970s had more in common with the

Protestant liberals, the mainline heirs of nineteenth-century evangelical-ism, as seen in their commitment to social activism, ecumenicism, intel-lectualism, and modern social mores. Thus, the energy expended by evangelicals debating inerrancy served the purpose of delineating bound-aries between themselves and American Protestant liberals, on the one hand, and their fundamentalist ancestors, on the other.[11]

The historian Martin Marty observed that in particular, the younger evangelicals significantly parted company with the fundamentalist pat-tern. He singled out the Chicago declaration, the statement released by the participants of the 1973 Chicago workshop, as an obvious example of this.[12] The difference between the older and younger evangelicals was significant, as illustrated by father and son in the Fuller family. The first generation of contemporary evangelicals, like Charles Fuller, had origi-nally been fundamentalists. Hence they well remembered the struggle against modern liberalism. The next generation of new evangelicals, typ-ified by Dan Fuller (a professor at Fuller Theological Seminary) and his younger colleagues, were influenced more by the contest against funda-mentalism on the right. Biblical feminism was born out of the social ac-tivism and openness to the modern theological methods of these younger, more progressive evangelicals. Biblical feminism highlights this second generation's struggle over biblical interpretation and accommodation to modern culture, both intellectually and socially.

"Neoevangelicalism"

The beginning of contemporary evangelicalism, known as "new" or "neo-evangelicalism," can be traced to the founding of the National As-sociation of Evangelicals in 1942 and Fuller Theological Seminary in 1947.[13] It was not until the 1950s, however, with the publication of *Christianity Today* in 1956, that evangelicalism could be distinguished from fundamentalism. These new evangelicals still accepted the funda-mentals of the faith and emphasized the need for a personal salvation ex-perience. They still firmly held to the authority of scripture. But as they sought to move beyond the cultural and intellectual isolation of the fun-damentalist movement, they began to engage with nonevangelicals and consider what they could learn from contemporary thought. One in-stance of an evangelical attempt to broaden this cultural horizon was

Billy Graham's 1957 New York City crusade. As was his habit, Graham came at the joint invitation of local churches. But in this case, Graham refused to work only with fundamentalist churches and came instead at the invitation of the Protestant Council, a consortium of nonevangelical, liberal churches. This event caused an uproar among fundamentalist churches, many of which refused to cooperate with the liberals. To expand their intellectual framework, many new evangelicals also returned to the tradition of earning degrees from nonevangelical institutions.[14] Daniel Fuller, son of the radio evangelist and Fuller Seminary founder Charles Fuller, initially attended Princeton Theological Seminary, despite his parents' suspicion that it had become theologically liberal.[15] Later he even studied neo-orthodoxy with Karl Barth in Switzerland. In 1956, the cultural and intellectual changes among some fundamentalists led *Christian Life*, itself a fundamentalist magazine, to laud the younger generation and declare that "fundamentalism has become evangelicalism."[16]

Young Evangelicals and Theological Reform

This willingness to engage contemporary thought created tension not only between fundamentalists and evangelicals but also between the first generation of evangelicals and their younger colleagues. Younger scholars like Bernard Ramm, Edward J. Carnell, and Daniel Fuller were willing to use modern theological methods to reconsider the traditional conception of the inspiration of scripture, an issue at the heart of evangelical theology. In 1954 Bernard Ramm, a Baptist teaching at Baylor University, caused a stir in evangelicalism by challenging the notion that a high view of biblical inspiration necessarily implied biblical reliability in science as well as in faith.[17] By 1958 Edward J. Carnell, then the president of Fuller Seminary, was selected by Westminster Press to write a book on the case for orthodoxy. In it, Carnell took pains to distinguish his evangelical theology from fundamentalism even more than from neo-orthodoxy or liberal theology. Some of the aspects of fundamentalism that Carnell challenged were its separatist tendencies and the theological influence of dispensationalism that caused many fundamentalists to ignore current social problems.[18] He also decried the intellectual stagnation that an emphasis on the classic Princeton view of inerrancy (called this because it was developed by leading Princeton theologians) had caused, that is, that the only things worth knowing were in the Bible. Dan Fuller maintained his strong commitment to a commonsense reading of scripture but believed that this meant the Bible could be upheld according to the intellectual standards of the day. In particular, then, evangelicals needed to review their defense of the Bible as being without error "in whole and in part."

The younger evangelicals believed that intellectual honesty required a reconsideration of the old Princeton definition of biblical authority because they found it exceedingly difficult to claim that no errors existed in the biblical record. From Switzerland, Dan Fuller sent a letter explaining to his parents that some biblical chronologies were simply wrong.[19] Other scriptural inaccuracies included numerical errors (such as the discrepancy between Numbers 25:9, which states that 24,000 died in a plague and 1 Corinthians 10:8, which states that 23,000 died), phenomenological errors (when Jesus called the mustard seed the smallest of all seeds), and differing accounts of the same event in the four gospels. For example, three gospels had Jesus saying that Peter would deny him three times before the cock crowed; the fourth records that Jesus said Peter would deny him three times before the cock crowed twice.

Ramm, Fuller, and Carnell did not believe that these errors in any way limited biblical authority but saw them as minor discrepancies, "bookkeeping errors." None of the mistakes was in an area essential to the faith. But it made evangelicals look foolish to the outside world to claim that scripture was entirely without error. Thus the Bible was still inerrant, but not "in whole and in part." The more progressive evangelicals preferred to limit biblical inerrancy to matters of faith and practice or to say that the Bible was the only infallible guide to faith and practice. Their goal was to reform the concept of inerrancy, not to abandon biblical authority. As Fuller pointed out to his parents, he and the others wanted to strengthen it by making it more intellectually credible.

The younger generation of evangelicals believed they could make biblical authority more convincing by applying the hermeneutical skills they had learned from Protestant liberalism in a more traditional way. One of those tools was the use of higher criticism. Higher criticism (called this to distinguish it from textual—or "lower"—criticism, which attempts to restore the language of the original texts) was concerned with evaluating the literary structure, date, and authorship of biblical texts. By uncovering possible sources of a biblical author's text and thus imputing creativity to human authors, conservative Protestants feared that higher criticism could be used to dispute traditional authorship of biblical passages or dating, thereby undermining biblical authority. The young evangelicals, however, did not use higher criticism to test the genuineness of a text but continued to subscribe to the doctrinal approach to biblical interpretation, which assumed that scripture was divinely revealed. In using this new theological tool, the theologian's goal was to uncover God's eternal principles and apply them to everyday life, not to find the most authentic and objective texts. Evangelical scholars used higher criticism to reveal historical information that added understanding about the context in which a text was written. By using higher criticism in this way, the young evangelicals did not destroy the authority of the text. Instead, they gained a better understanding of the circumstances surrounding its composition and, in doing so, helped make the Bible more credible.

By the mid-1970s, however (around the time of the first Thanksgiving Day workshop), the disagreement among evangelicals on the topic of inerrancy had taken a toll. At Fuller Theological Seminary, the faculty had split along the lines of conservative and progressive evangelicals over the issue. Fuller's original statement of faith read much like the Westminster confession used by the Presbyterians: the scriptures "are the Word of God, the only infallible rule of faith and practice." But as the controversy over biblical authority grew, Fuller's creed was changed in 1949 to state: The original autographs of scripture "are plenarily inspired and free from error in the whole and in the part."[20] This satisfied conservative evangelicals that inerrancy was still a part of Fuller's statement of faith. After many years and further struggles, though, the progressives won control of the seminary.[21] Dan Fuller was appointed dean of the faculty, and in that position he played a crucial role in establishing David Hubbard, a graduate of Fuller and a progressive evangelical, as Fuller's president. In the wake of these changes, many of the conservative evangelicals left Fuller. One of these was Harold Lindsell, a founding faculty member and later vice president, who took a position at *Christianity Today*. Later, Lindsell played a leading role in the ongoing inerrancy controversy with his book *The Battle for the Bible*. In 1972 Fuller finally adopted a new statement of faith that removed the word *inerrancy* and the premillennial clause. (Premillennialism, although not always tied to dispensationalism, was the aspect of dispensationalism that gave it its otherworldly focus.) Also, in keeping with progressive evangelicalism's commitment to social activism, Fuller began to emphasize spiritual formation and added two schools of practical ministry in the areas of psychology and world missions. The first female faculty member, Roberta Hestenes, joined the school at this time, and Jack Rogers, who was soon to play a leading role in the inerrancy debates, was hired as a professor of the philosophy of religion.

Young Evangelicals and Social Reform: Initial Forays into Biblical Feminism

In addition to reforming evangelical theology, progressive evangelicals hoped that they could improve biblical credibility by reconsidering what the Bible said about contemporary social issues. With its growing impact on American society, women's equality was an obvious question to address. As early as 1966, Letha Scanzoni warned conservative Christians that in an age of enlightenment when women were educated and aware of other cultures, questions about the status quo were bound to arise.[22] In 1973, when the first Thanksgiving workshop occurred, secular feminism was an active and vocal movement.[23] In 1963, Betty Friedan's *Feminist Mystique* appeared and roused American housewives to action with its critique of their domestic role and complicity in the U.S. consumer economy. The National Organization for Women (NOW) was founded in 1966, and *Ms.* magazine began publishing in 1972, just one year before the Evangelicals for Social Action gathering. In the same year as the Chicago workshop, the Supreme Court ruled in *Roe v. Wade* that state antiabortion laws violated women's right to privacy. Also by this time, both houses of Congress had passed the equal rights amendment, though it still needed to be ratified by the states.

Women in the church, too, were struggling with how to achieve equality. Several denominations, primarily from Wesleyan and Holiness traditions, already regularly ordained women as pastors,[24] and the United Methodist and Presbyterian U.S.A. churches had been ordaining women for almost twenty years. Yet in 1975 women still made up less than 1.5 percent of ordained ministers in the Presbyterian Church, and of those, only about thirty were head pastors of their own congregation.[25] Two Lutheran denominations, the Lutheran Church in America and the American Lutheran Church, began ordaining women in 1970. That same year, the Episcopal Church U.S.A. recognized women as deacons for the first time, the first step toward ordination in that denomination; but in 1973, Episcopalians again voted to refuse ordination to the priesthood to women. Despite this, or rather because of it, in 1974 three former bishops ordained eleven women in Philadelphia's Church of the Advocate. The ordinations were declared invalid, but by 1976, the General Convention of the Episcopal Church approved women for ordination.

During this period, female theologians from the mainline churches based their arguments for women's equality largely on the charge of "androcentrism" and on liberation theology. In 1960, Valerie Saiving published an article in which she contended that the theologian's sexual identity had a large influence on perceptions of the divine. Historically, she argued, theology had been conceived through a male lens, which ignored women's experience and thus relegated women to a subordinate position. Theology had been "androcentric," meaning that as the traditional interpreters of biblical texts, men put male experience at the center of their hermeneutic. In the late 1960s into the 1970s, Mary Daly, Letty Russell, and Rosemary Radford Ruether all published books critical of androcentric theology and proposed a feminist liberation theology instead.[26] Based on South American liberation theology, they each began their theological reflections from the experience of women's oppression rather than from traditional (male) dogma or biblical interpretation.

By contrast, socially conscious evangelicals hoped to make the Bible more relevant to Americans' lives by addressing issues related to women's equality from a biblical perspective. They were not merely conceding to the secular and more liberal Protestant cultures around them; young theologians began with the Bible, using contemporary hermeneutics to reinterpret traditional understandings of women's roles in the church and home. From the beginning, Scanzoni and other evangelical feminists paid more attention to historical argumentation and biblical exegesis than to arguments from secular culture. In "The Feminists and the Bible," Scanzoni describes the historical connections between women's rights and American Christianity—especially in the Quaker, Methodist, and Holiness churches—before proceeding with the argument that Paul had been misinterpreted as teaching women's subordination. By arguing both theologically and historically that the call to use women's gifts in leadership was an important part of authentic Christianity, Scanzoni hoped to divert complaints that she was just adding a feminist veneer to Christianity.[27]

The use of Genesis 1 and Ephesians 5 is another example of the way that progressive evangelicals and conservative theologians reinterpreted scripture differently. Traditionally, conservative Protestants believed that Genesis taught that God created women to be submissive to men. Man was created first; Adam was commanded to subdue the earth; and woman was told that man would rule over her. Ephesians 5:21–22 states: Submit "yourselves one to another in the fear of God. Wives, submit yourselves unto your own husbands, as unto the Lord" (King James Version).[28] Traditionalists emphasized verse 22 and wifely submission. Many conservative ministers failed even to refer to verse 21. Progressives instead pointed to the earlier verse and the larger context of the passage—a calling to live in the power of God's spirit—inviting men and women to submit to one another in love. Thus, young evangelicals assumed that both men and women were equally created in the image of God and were given equal responsibility to steward the earth. This is why in the press statement from the Evangelicals for Social Action's first Thanksgiving conference, both women and men were called to "active discipleship" and "mutual submission."

By the early 1970s, a number of younger evangelicals were applying modern hermeneutical methods to the issue of women's roles. In 1971, Nancy Hardesty published an article in *Eternity*, and in the same month, Ruth Schmidt, a professor of Spanish at the State University of New York at Albany (who later served as president of Agnes Scott College from 1982 to 1994), wrote an article for *Christianity Today* proposing that the Christian community reexamine all scripture dealing with women's roles. Nor was it only women who held these convictions. In a series in the *Post-American*, Donald W. Dayton argued along much the same lines as Scanzoni had earlier, suggesting that a hierarchical view of male and female relationships was based more on Neoplatonic misreadings of the text than on scriptural teachings. He contended, too, that American evangelicalism had a long tradition of social activism and women's equality.[29]

The most prominent theologian to use modern hermeneutical methods to help correct past interpretations was Paul K. Jewett, who focused on the writings of the apostle Paul. His conclusions and the fact that his was the first book-length reinterpretation questioning the biblical status of women gave needed theological weight to the evolving women's movement within evangelicalism. In 1975 when he published *Man as Male and Female*, Jewett was a professor of systematic and historical theology and a close friend of Dan Fuller. In that book he addressed the problems of dualism and patriarchalism found in traditional interpretations of Paul. Jewett was convinced that those passages relating to the role of women in the church were among the least understood in the Bible because the historical context had been ignored. To gain insight into the cultural and historical setting in which the texts were written, Jewett turned to historical-cultural criticism. Other advocates of women's equality suggested that Paul meant something other than it appeared or that Paul's statements were culturally limited. Jewett drew the still more radical conclusion that Paul was mistaken in his statements suggesting women's subordination to men based on his (Paul's) misinterpretation of Genesis. This caused an uproar in the evangelical community because many people thought he was undermining the authenticity, and therefore the inerrancy, of the scriptures. In the end, the seminary censured Jewett for his hermeneutical approach to the Pauline texts, but it remained convinced of his commitment to biblical authority, and no other action was taken against him.

All We're Meant to Be

The most influential work in helping launch the evangelical feminist movement was Scanzoni and Hardesty's book *All We're Meant to Be*. When it came out in 1974, Scanzoni and Hardesty received a hailstorm of appreciative letters from women at seeing their feelings and opinions in print. In 1975, based on a survey of 150 evangelical leaders, *All We're Meant to Be* received *Eternity* magazine's book-of-the-year award, placing it ahead of George Eldon Ladd's *A Theology of the New Testament* (Ladd was a preeminent New Testament scholar) and Paul K. Jewett's *Man as Male and Female*. According to many biblical feminists, it also helped raise their consciousness to the possibilities and responsibilities for women in the evangelical church.

Before *All We're Meant to Be* was published, evangelical feminists used a variety of theological methods to make a biblical argument for the liberation of women. Often this focused on those theological traditions that emphasized the leading of the Holy Spirit (such as the Methodists, Quakers, and Holiness churches) over systematic doctrine (such as the Presbyterians). For example, most evangelical feminists read the curse in Genesis 3 ("Your desire will be for your husband, and he will rule over you") as descriptive, not prescriptive. They then pointed out that Christ came to relieve the penalty of the curse. At Pentecost, the prophecy was fulfilled, demonstrating this reversal:

> This is what was spoken by the prophet Joel: "In the last days, God says, I will pour out my Spirit on all people. Your sons and daughters will prophesy, your young men will see visions, your old men will dream

dreams. Even on my servants, both men and women, I will pour out my Spirit in those days, and they will prophesy." (Acts 2:16–18)

Increasingly, however, biblical feminists were relying on evangelicalism's younger New Testament and biblical scholars to give them the means to uphold a high view of scriptural authority while reinterpreting passages traditionally understood to teach women's subordination. Scanzoni and Hardesty represented this new approach. For example, they used a course outline from Jewett's systematic theology class at Fuller to help them interpret the creation accounts and drew on neo-evangelical methods of biblical interpretation that relied on historical-cultural criticism to help them place documents in context. By using these methods, Scanzoni and Hardesty could show that many of the passages traditionally seen as limiting women's roles were situationally limited and still maintain a strong view of biblical authority. For a text to be situationally limited means that its teachings are not intended to be normative commands for all people at all times but are provisional principles given to a specific church to deal with a particular situation.

In addition to the younger evangelical scholars, Scanzoni and Hardesty studied nonevangelical theologians popular with progressives, such as Dietrich Bonhoeffer and Helmut Thielicke, and they followed their mentors' model by interacting with the contemporary broader intellectual culture. They drew on feminist (Germaine Greer, Simone de Beauvoir, Kate Millett, Betty Friedan), psychological (Eric Fromm, Sigmund Freud, Abraham H. Maslow, Erik Erikson), sociological (Max Weber, Mircea Eliade), anthropological (Margaret Mead), and scientific (Masters and Johnson) sources to help them address issues of sexual roles, gender, and their cultural formation.

In contrast to others in their current intellectual milieu, however, Scanzoni and Hardesty accepted the authority of the Bible. Their theology began with scripture and what it said about God and women, not with their feminist convictions or personal experience. Their aim was to show that biblical Christianity liberated, rather than oppressed, women. To do this, they had to show that the prevailing teaching of the church stemmed from misunderstanding the scripture. Thus, the defining chapter of their book explains their biblical hermeneutic and highlights it as central to the issue of women's equality.

The authors begin their discussion of biblical interpretation with a quotation from G. C. Berkouwer, the theologian to whom many progressive evangelicals turned when they became dissatisfied with the fundamentalist conception of scriptural authority.

> The Word has to be free to remake and reform the Church over and over again. The moment the Church loses interest in working the mines of the Word because it thinks it has seen all there is to see, that moment the Church also loses its power and its credibility in the world. When the Church thinks it knows all there is to know, the opportunity for surprising discovery is closed. The Church then becomes old, without perspective, and without light and labor and fruitfulness.[30]

This serves notice that from Scanzoni and Hardesty's perspective, a high view of biblical authority is not inconsistent with the use of new hermeneutical methods as they become available, including, in this case, historical and cultural criticism. In the rest of the book, Scanzoni and Hardesty apply these methods to the creation accounts and, primarily, to the Pauline corpus to reinterpret common conservative readings of those texts.

Scanzoni and Hardesty first examine the creation accounts, since it was on these passages that traditional scholars based their belief in women's subordination. This was both because the creation accounts supposedly revealed God's intended relational order and because the apostle Paul often appeared to use Genesis to support his view of women. Traditionalists focused on Genesis 2 and 3: Eve's creation out of Adam's rib and the fall. They based their view on chapter 2, verse 18, in which God says he is making for man a "helper," *ezer k'neged*, and chapter 3, verse 16: "Your desire will be for your husband; and he will rule over you." Conservatives believed that these passages taught a created order in which women are subordinate to men. They then used this to interpret Paul's statement in 1 Timothy 2:12–14 that women are prohibited from teaching in church because "Adam was formed first, then Eve" and because "Eve was the one deceived," not Adam. Traditionalists claimed that Paul's reference to the order of the creation and fall proved that the apostle intended his injunction against teaching to be normative for all times and places.

Scanzoni and Hardesty suggest that this logic is fundamentally flawed, since the creation accounts, including Genesis 1, do not teach a divine relational order in the first place. They believe that the essential unity of men and women with God is the main lesson of Genesis 1: "And God created them male and female, in God's image God created them" (1:27). The primary teaching is not that God is male or that men are intended to rule over women in a divine relational order. Also, in verse 28 (which is addressed to *h'adam*, "humankind," not only to males), men and women are given equal responsibility to care for the earth: "Rule over the fish of the sea and the birds of the air and over every living creature that moves on the ground." This further illustrates the essential unity of woman and man, not man's superiority to woman.

In regard to the fall, Scanzoni and Hardesty argue that just as men and women were given equal responsibility to care for the earth, they also were assigned equal blame for their sin. Looking at scripture as a whole clearly shows that both Adam and Eve were at fault for sin, not that Eve was more at fault, since she was deceived first. Scanzoni and Hardesty point out that scripture never uses *ezer k'neged* to refer to a subordinate helper. Instead, it is most commonly used to refer to God. Finally, Scanzoni and Hardesty agree with earlier analyses of Genesis 3:16 that the curse "he will rule over you" represents a perversion of God's intended relational unity, which Christ came to redeem.

After reexamining the creation accounts, Scanzoni and Hardesty could finally deal with Paul's statement in 1 Timothy. A survey of the historical situation at Ephesus (the city where Timothy was pastor of the church) reveals a congregation that faced unique problems owing to female, ecstatic religious practices. The church was struggling to maintain its Christian witness in a pagan society that included women's being led astray by false prophets. When combined with the proper understanding of Genesis, that historical context, Scanzoni and Hardesty insist, proves that Paul did not prohibit all women for all time from teaching based on their role in the fall; rather, it indicates that the prohibition on women's teaching is situationally limited. Paul intended to limit the teaching of women, who were new to the faith and who could have been led astray by false teachers, at that time and in that place only, to preserve the witness of the church.

Scanzoni and Hardesty proceed to exegete other "problem passages" (i.e., those that had been traditionally interpreted to teach that women's roles in the church, home, or society were limited) using historical studies to set the cultural context for how women were treated in the biblical world. In each analysis, they determine that in the New Testament, only Galatians 3:28 makes a theological statement about women. Since a part of their biblical hermeneutic is that theological passages should be used to interpret situational passages, Scanzoni and Hardesty conclude that all other New Testament passages on women should be read in light of Galatians. Adding to this their corrected reading of Genesis, which undermined its use to support women's subordination in the New Testament, they conclude that the "problem passages" were situationally conditioned.

Not only did Scanzoni and Hardesty's hermeneutics in *All We're Meant to Be* push the limits of evangelical reforms, so too did their social practice. Along with being prochoice regarding abortion, they advocate shared parenting and egalitarian marriages in which the husband is not the hierarchical "head" of the household. In the chapter on singleness, in which Hardesty deals with the sexual needs of single women, she rules out adultery for the single Christian, but she approves of masturbation and leaves open the possibility of lesbianism. Hardesty points out that even though the scripture prohibits homosexual acts, "neither Paul nor any other biblical writer speaks of a 'homosexual orientation' or of an attraction for members of one's own sex."[31]

Despite some of these controversial suggestions, reviews of the book in the evangelical press were almost unanimously favorable. Even *Christianity Today*, a less progressive evangelical publication than *Post-American* or *Eternity*, whose editor and publisher at the time was Harold Lindsell, a strict inerrantist, ran a very positive review written by Cheryl Forbes.

Still, the negative comments that the book did receive often were related to the authors' hermeneutics. A review in the *Journal of the Evangelical Theological Society* praised *All We're Meant to Be* as a "fine work" but still asked how theologians could determine when a biblical passage was culturally limited. The reviewer was not convinced that Scanzoni and Hardesty had used the best method, and thus he was not sure they had proved their claim.[32] It is important, though, that no reviewer criticized *All We're Meant to Be* for moving beyond the boundaries of evangelicalism in its view of biblical authority, a common criticism of Jewett's *Man as Male and Female*. Thus, despite some controversial ideas, Scanzoni and Hardesty were able to locate themselves—and therefore, biblical feminism—within the broader evangelical coalition.

Such positioning could not have been possible without shifts in evangelicalism on the issue of biblical authority. It was the increasing acceptance of new hermeneutical methods and a limited definition of inerrancy that enabled biblical feminism to convince a growing number of evangelicals over the next ten years that their movement was, indeed, "biblical," that it held itself under the authority of God through his revealed word. In turn, evangelical feminists helped foster these changes through their widespread use of new interpretive methods. One theologian, Gerald T. Sheppard, contemplating the role of progressive evangelicals, including biblical feminists, and the role of the inerrancy debates in neo-evangelicalism concluded:

> Perhaps the most significant threat to the older hermeneutical language of evangelicalism arises from an articulate feminist position being explored by young evangelicals. As set forth by Paul Jewett and Virginia Mollenkott, the issue centers on whether or not certain of Paul's statements about women are "culturally conditioned." Once again the function of biblical hermeneutics as the social contract of evangelicalism becomes obvious.[33]

Sheppard is specifically referring to Paul Jewett's book *Man as Male and Female*, to which Mollenkott wrote the foreword. Sheppard's point is that the hermeneutical differences within evangelicalism correspond better to sociological than to theological realities. Hermeneutics operated as a means of maintaining symbolic boundaries for the community. Evangelicals may have disagreed with fundamentalist excesses, but they agreed about the tendency in modern liberal thought toward epistemological relativism. Inerrancy began to serve as a way to limit how far toward liberalism the fundamentalist reforms would go. As a boundary, it could guard against both witting and unwitting accommodation to outside influences.

Others agreed with Sheppard. Historian George Marsden argued that in their efforts to redefine fundamentalism intellectually and culturally, evangelicals had put themselves in an ambiguous middle ground, needing to define themselves on both the left and the right:

> Having broken with fundamentalism, the conservative wing of the new evangelicals needed a meaningful test to limit how far reforms of fundamentalism might go. Inerrancy could play that role. It was distinctive of the fundamentalist movement, yet shared by some other conservative traditions. Since fundamentalist evangelicals usually lacked authoritative church bodies, inerrancy was an effective tool for drawing a boundary for the movement.[34]

In their effort to promote women's equality, feminist evangelicals began to play a crucial role in the changing nature of American evangelicalism by changing the way it understood biblical authority. And despite the controversy within the broader American evangelicalism that they helped foster, the productivity and impact of the burgeoning biblical feminist movement continued to grow over the next decade. But it was also during this period that the apparent unity among evangelical feminists began to break up, and again, biblical authority played a pivotal role in their disagreements.

3

All We're Meant to Be

The Early Years of Biblical Feminism,
1975–1983

As biblical feminism developed and expanded, the movement continued to be plagued by controversy, both inside and out. As the movement grew theologically and organizationally, a fissure within the fledgling organization developed. At first, the fracture was not very visible, since some evangelical feminists wanted to maintain a united front for effectiveness and credibility, and others simply were not aware of disagreements stirring beneath the surface. Although the differences in theology and politics were not evident yet in the organizational structure of biblical feminism, they nonetheless could be seen in the publications, politics, and theology of those in the movement. This tension within biblical feminism had much to do with what was occurring in the broader evangelical movement as the battle over the meaning and scope of biblical authority, particularly as defined by the doctrine of inerrancy, heated up. Biblical feminists based their struggle for women's equality on the Bible, helping push forward the evangelical boundaries set by the meaning and scope of biblical authority.

Still, by outward appearances, biblical feminism was a healthy movement, and any weakness or division was not apparent to most people, whether outside or inside the movement. It was growing numerically, organizationally, and in theological sophistication and inspired dedication and loyalty from its members.

The Women of the Evangelical Feminist Movement

Who were these evangelical feminists? On the cover of the first few issues of *Daughters of Sarah*, they described themselves in this way:

We are Christians; we are also feminists. Some say we cannot be both, but Christianity and feminism for us are inseparable.

DAUGHTERS OF SARAH is our attempt to share our discoveries, our struggles and our growth as Christian women. We are committed to Scripture and we seek to find in it meaning for our lives. We are rooted in a historical tradition of women who have served God in innumerable ways and we seek guidance from their example. We are convinced that Christianity is relevant to all areas of women's lives today. We seek ways to act out our faith.[1]

This manifesto must have struck a chord with conservative American Protestant women, for within two years, *Daughters of Sarah* had a mailing list of approximately one thousand, and in less than four years, by early 1978, it had twelve hundred subscribers.[2]

Who were the subscribers to a journal on evangelical feminism? Periodically, *Daughters of Sarah* surveyed its readership to obtain a general profile. The first poll was in 1976. At that time, 90 percent of its readers were women; 83 percent were between the ages of twenty-three and thirty-four, and 63 percent had done some graduate study. These statistics are not too surprising, since most of the women in the original Chicago group were associated with colleges and universities. These women made the point, however, of asserting that their intent was not to make biblical feminism the province of only middle-class professional women; rather, they wanted their ideas to go beyond that circle.[3] Nonetheless, two years later, a second *Daughters of Sarah* survey revealed that its readers were still primarily well-educated, middle-class, urban, or suburban-dwelling women with a postgraduate education. An important change between the 1976 and 1978 surveys would be easy to miss, however, because *Daughters of Sarah* had changed the age categories. In 1978, 82 percent of the respondents were between twenty-three and forty-five years old, whereas in 1976 virtually the same percentage was between twenty-three and thirty-five. It seems fair to conclude that the change in categories was due to an aging readership.[4]

In 1980 and 1984, *Daughters of Sarah* surveyed its readers yet again.[5] The percentage of readers who had done some graduate study continued to increase (from 63%, 65%, 63%, to 70%). By 1984, a full 54 percent held a graduate degree. Most (69%) still lived in urban or suburban areas. For the first time, income level was included. Forty-one percent of the respondents had a household income above $30,000, and 70 percent had a family income above \$20,000.[6] Once again, though, the magazine editors shifted the age groups they measured. When seen this way, it appears that the *Daughters of Sarah* audience was steadily aging, but the magazine was definitely adding to its subscription base. In 1978, circulation stood at approximately one thousand, and in 1984, it was approximately three thousand. Thus, the aging process was not merely because the original subscribers were getting older. It appears instead that *Daughters of Sarah* attracted primarily the same generation of readers, a generation that was aging. Hence, despite Hardesty's assertion in the second, revised edition (1986) of *All We're Meant to Be*, biblical feminism—at least in this earlier time—did, indeed, seem to be a mostly white, middle-class, middle-aged American phenomenon.[7]

These statistics tell only a little about the women of evangelical feminism, though. The women of the Evangelical Women's Caucus described themselves best, and they had many opportunities to recount their spiritual and social pilgrimages. One such forum was the newsletter, *Green Leaf*, of the California Bay Area's chapter. First edited by Anne Eggebroten, Virginia Hearn took over in 1981, and it was she who named the newsletter. In doing so, she had both feminist and biblical allusions in mind. Green was the color of the American woman's movement, symbolizing life and hope, and these are the same connotations implied in Isaiah 17:7–8: "Blessed is the person who trusts in the Lord, whose hope the Lord is. For that person shall be as a tree planted by the waters, and . . . her leaf shall be green" (*Green Leaf*, spring/summer 1981; King James version). Hearn had been an assistant editor at HIS magazine (a publication of the InterVarsity college ministry) for seven years and the managing editor of the publications of the Christian Medical Society before she and her husband decided to move to Berkeley. When Walter and Virginia Hearn first experienced Berkeley in 1968/69 during a year-long sabbatical, he had been a professor of biochemistry at Iowa State University. Impressed by the political activism of the younger new evangelicals in the community, especially the Christian World Liberation Front (CWLF), they decided to begin new careers as a freelance writing/editing team in the Bay Area. Virginia Hearn's career had a lasting influence on the EWC. From 1981 to 1983 and again from 1985 to 1988, Hearn edited *Green Leaf*, and from 1985 through 1989, she edited *Update*, the national newsletter for the EWC.[8] In addition, she published two series of articles on biblical feminism and edited *Our Struggle to Serve*, a volume of testimonies from women in the biblical feminist movement.[9]

Hearn understood the power of women gaining a voice, and so under her leadership, both *Green Leaf* and *Update* gave Evangelical Women's Caucus members a forum in which to talk about their pilgrimages into evangelical feminism. During these early years (1981–1983), most of the women wrote about their childhood faith in Christ, in which they were not overly concerned about women's oppression. For some, they were blissfully unaware of the sexism in their church. Others were aware of women's subservient role but were encouraged by loving parents or allowed to use their gifts "under the head" of a man so that they did not encounter personal limitations. The women testified, however, that as they matured and desired to serve in a particular function (such as a teacher in an adult education class or a leader in a religious organization), they did encounter the church's oppression. One woman's awakening occurred when she was not allowed to lead the singing for her college youth group at a church meeting because she was female. The testimonials continued along lines similar to this by Ann Moor:

> It is no exaggeration to say that EWC has changed my life. Through it I have found a network of . . . women who have known the pain and injustice of being pushed toward confining boxes for which they were not made; but they refused to accept an inferior definition of themselves. Nor did they stop searching until they saw a face of God seldom illumined in conservative churches."[10]

A number of these women went on to seminary and became pastors. Others decided to return for further education, several in counseling. Many of these women were "firsts": the first female pastor in their congregation, the first female head of a denominational ministry division, and the first female editor of a religious organization or journal.

Anne Eggebroten, who was first mentioned in the introduction, related her story in several publications over many years.[11] She was a participant at the second Evangelicals for Social Action Thanksgiving workshop and a founding member of the Evangelical Women's Caucus and served as a model for the commitment of women to the EWC, the type of activities in which they engaged, and their high level of involvement.

Eggebroten wrote that she became a Christian in 1962 and a feminist later in the 1960s when she was an undergraduate at Stanford. Shortly after graduating, she joined the National Organization for Women (NOW). Eggebroten then attended graduate school at the University of

California at Berkeley, studying medieval English literature. She received her degree and accepted a nontenure track position at California State University at San Bernardino after nine years of graduate study.

As a young married woman, Eggebroten admitted struggling to integrate marriage, academics, and eventually motherhood with her feminist ideals. Keeping her maiden name was one way she attempted to preserve her individual identity; using her degree was another. But after one year of teaching and an offer to continue at Cal State, she chose—in her own words—"to compromise my career in favor of motherhood." Her daughter, Roz A. Eggebroten, was born in 1982, at which time Eggebroten's husband took four months of paternity leave, a move so startling that an article about it appeared in the local paper. That helped Eggebroten through her second semester of teaching at San Bernardino, but by the summer, she was worn out from coping with a full-time job and family. She found, she explained, her theory about "keep[ing] career to preserve identity" to be exhausting. Thus, the next fall, Eggebroten agreed to move back to the Bay Area for her husband's job. Instead of working full time, she taught grammar courses part time at the City College of San Francisco, in order to avoid putting her child in day care. In another testimonial, Eggebroten admitted that turning down a job did not fit her own picture of who she was, but "'baby' and 'image' are abstract, whereas my R.A.E./E.R.A. baby is concrete . . . and I find myself loving her a great deal and sacrificing my dearest things for her."[12] In 1985, Eggebroten and her husband had another child. This time she took a maternity leave that lasted several years.

Eggebroten's personal struggles to integrate career and family did not mean that she was abandoning her feminist ideals. She remained active in the local and national Evangelical Women's Caucus, rallied for the passage of the ERA, wore a prochoice button during her pregnancy ("Prochild, Pro-family, Pro-choice"), and initiated a project in which the EWC ran ads in *Ms.*, *Family Circle*, and *Woman's Day*.[13] Eggebroten also initiated a picket of a "Fascinating Womanhood" seminar that she saw advertised on her pastor's bulletin board at church. She asked her friend Ginny Hearn to join her. As a result, Eggebroten, Hearn, and eighteen others picketed the seminar with signs declaring "Jesus Was a Feminist" and "Worship God, Not Your Husband." They also handed out flyers with the contact numbers of the Bay Area Evangelical Women's Caucus. Eggebroten and another woman, Edie Black, even signed up and paid for the seminar in order to attend and ask difficult questions of the presenters. Later, Eggebroten, joined by Hearn and Sharon Gallagher, helped launch the Bay Area Evangelical Women's Caucus chapter (BAEWC).

Organizational Growth

Over the next ten years, through the work of dedicated women like Eggebroten, Hearn, and Gallagher, biblical feminism continued to grow and develop into a recognizable movement within evangelicalism. The Evangelical Women's Caucus also grew in size and complexity as women in all parts of the country became active in local chapters. The local movements provided a community in which to practice biblical feminist ideals, and the national office played a coordinating role. Not long after the second Thanksgiving workshop in 1974, at which the Evangelical Women's Caucus was formed, the steering committee began working on bylaws and an organizational structure. They quickly set up a system based on local chapters, similar to NOW's, began fund-raising, and planned for biennial conferences to gather its members together in one location.[14]

Like the Evangelicals for Social Action conferences from which they sprang, the Evangelical Women's Caucus's first gathering was held on Thanksgiving weekend of 1975 in Washington, D.C. The event, entitled "Women in Transition: A Workshop in Biblical Feminism," attracted 360 women and men to discuss the topic of women's liberation in the church. Conference planners formulated ambitious goals, from facilitating mutual support and communication to assertiveness training and negotiation skills, as well as reporting on the status of proposals from the Thanksgiving Day workshop.[15] A varied program was planned. Virginia Mollenkott gave the keynote address, at which she called for the "de-absolutizing" of biblical culture, by which she meant the need to recognize that the patriarchal culture of biblical times was not authoritative for the present day. Letha Scanzoni and Lucille Sider Dayton also were plenary speakers. Almost thirty workshops were offered on topics ranging from "Paul and Jesus and Feminism" by Mollenkott (one of the most popular) to "Models for Marriage" and "Woman to Woman Relationships," led by both Nancy Hardesty and Virginia Mollenkott. Attendees also formed six-person "discovery groups" that met for discussion throughout the conference and attended an introductory session at which they drew pictures to represent their core thoughts and values. At the business meeting, participants passed a resolution in support of the equal rights amendment and voted to send a telegram affirming their solidarity with their Catholic sisters, who were meeting in Detroit to discuss women's ordination.

These national gatherings would not have been possible without the work of volunteers at the local level. It was local groups that sponsored and did most of the coordinating work for the next four conferences. The California chapters, in the Bay Area (BAEWC) and the Southwest, were particularly strong. By 1980, the Bay Area chapter had seventy members and a mailing list of 320 for its newsletter, and the Southwest chapter played host to the second national conference. Washington, D.C., had another strong chapter At least five separate study groups met in different parts of the metropolitan area, sponsoring events such as a panel discussion on women in ministry, lectures, and one-day conferences. They also rented an exhibit booth at the National Organization of Women annual convention held in Washington in 1978. That summer, at the invitation of the national ERA, the Washington Evangelical Women's Caucus coordinated an interdenominational worship service that featured a liturgical dance and the choir from the Sojourners fellowship. Other active chapters formed in New Jersey; Michigan; Seattle; Albany, N.Y., and Minnesota, where, under the leadership of Catherine Kroeger, this chapter created its own resource room and state conference and participated with other local agencies to combat the problem of spousal abuse.

In addition to organizing the first conference and the local chapters, the national steering committee began publishing a national newsletter, whose purpose was to keep members across the country in touch with one another. It was filled with news from local chapters, conference reports, and information pertaining to the EWC's elections and bylaws. Under the leadership of Ann Moor, who became editor in 1978, it increasingly included editorials, book reviews, and even poetry and officially became known as *Update*. Still, through the late 1970s and early 1980s, the focus of the newsletter remained on connecting far-flung, often isolated members. Sometimes it announced someone had entered seminary, received a graduate degree, or a promotion. Other times it publicized awards, lectures, and books. In a survey Moor took of her readers, they indicated that the main purpose for which they read *Update* was for assurance that they were not alone.

In spite of several active chapters, dedicated members, and a mailing list of fifteen hundred, the EWC struggled to survive at a national level during its early years. In 1977, a shortage of funds led to organizational cutbacks on a national level. The national steering committee disbanded, and the full-time staff member was replaced with a part-time secretary. Also, many of the same women participated on the national council for years, such as Joyce Erickson (an associate professor at Seattle Pacific University), who remained chairperson of the EWC from the time the position was established in 1978 until 1982. This indicated that the number of committed volunteers may have been limited. In her first editorial in *Update* in 1978, Moor expressed uneasiness about the caucus's health. She praised the EWC's numerical growth and psychological support of women, but she complained that "some of us my have forgotten the debt we owe EWC for helping us become who and what we are. Others may simply feel 'burned out' after having expended so much effort building up chapters and encouraging struggling sisters."[16] Perhaps the EWC was only surviving but not thriving after such an auspicious beginning.

The conferences, too, were affected. Originally intended to be annual, EWC members found it was too taxing to try to obtain the necessary resources, both physical and financial, to stage a national conference every year. Three years thus elapsed before the second gathering in 1978. The EWC's second national conference took place over a four-day period on the grounds of Fuller Theological Seminary. Through the office of faculty member Roberta Hestenes (director of the ministry division of Fuller's communication and educational ministries department and an ordained Presbyterian minister), Fuller, the flagship seminary of new evangelicalism, cohosted the conference in association with the EWC's Southwest chapter. Many members of Fuller's faculty led seminars, including the president, David Hubbard. Other speakers from Fuller's faculty were Paul Jewett, Jack Rogers, Paul Hiebert, William Pannell, Don Williams, and Glenn Barker.

Attendance soared above that at the first national conference. Approximately one thousand people came, to choose from ninety-five workshops, twelve continuing-discussion groups, and dozens of seminars on topics covering the theological foundation for women in ministry, egalitarian perspectives on women in ministry, marriage and family issues, and issues of justice, language, and liturgy. Dozens of people participated as speakers or leaders of the workshops and seminars. Other leading evangelicals who participated were Julie Anderton, the associate dean of students at Westmont College; Gary Demarest, the pastor of La Cañada Presbyterian Church and founder of Fellowship of Christian Athletes;

and Berkeley Mickelsen, a professor of New Testament interpretation at Bethel Theological Seminary, and his wife, Alvera, a writer and teacher at Bethel College.

The success of this second national event revived the far-flung organization. Finances, which had been depleted, quickly recovered. The conference presaged the importance that national conferences, which took place in the summer, would have for the EWC. They became a time for caucus members to hear from leading writers and theologians, offer organizational advice at the business meeting, and gather for fellowship with like-minded people. (The active but geographically separated members of the EWC began to refer to themselves as "the sisters of summer.")[17] Between these national gatherings the local chapters were the focal point of the EWC's activities. In fact, the ability to proceed with annual gatherings, beginning with the Pasadena conference at Fuller in 1978, was due in large measure to the strength of these local chapters. It is not coincidental that the oldest and most established chapters hosted the next three meetings. Michigan was the site of a regional event in 1979; the Albany chapter sponsored the 1980 conference in Saratoga Springs, and Seattle welcomed the EWC in 1982.

The revival of the EWC's spirits could be seen in *Update*. Starting in the 1980s, the organization began to move away from its survival mentality (of supporting beleaguered, isolated biblical feminists) toward an activist orientation. This shift was most apparent when *Update* became the organ for the EWC's support of the equal rights amendment (ERA). The ERA was first introduced in 1923 as the twenty-seventh amendment to the Constitution, but it was not until NOW took up its cause in 1970 that Congress considered it. By 1972, both the House and the Senate had approved the amendment, and it was given a ratification deadline of March 1979. In 1978, this was extended to June 1982.

As *Update* reported, the EWC found itself in the thick of the fight for the ERA's passage in this countdown period. In 1981, NOW sponsored another ERA rally in Washington, D.C., and Virginia Mollenkott was chosen by the National Council of Churches to represent Protestants at the event. Sharing the platform with Alan Alda, NOW president Ellie Smeal, and others, Mollenkott delivered a three-minute speech. *Update* had a lengthy account of the event and reprinted the entire text of Mollenkott's speech. The same issue also warned readers that time was running out for ratification. Readers were urged to wear buttons declaring "People of Faith for ERA" and to put pro-ERA stickers on their cars or to write to an editor or legislator. A year later, *Update* reported that the national coordinator for the EWC, Florence Brown, and EWC member Britt Vanden Eykel lobbied legislators in Oklahoma to seek its ratification there. As a result, Vanden Eykel was hired by NOW's national office to rally evangelical support for the ERA's passage.

In addition to a more proactive orientation after the 1978 conference, the EWC added more chapters and affiliate groups. In 1982, the caucus's bylaws were changed to allow for affiliate chapters, groups that consisted of only three or more national members. Although they had to accept the statement of faith, they were not subject to other caucus bylaws. Hence, they did not need to meet twice a year, but they also were not able to send a chapter representative to the national council, as the full chapters did. Creating the affiliate chapters allowed the EWC to grow organizationally while recognizing those areas with fewer members. Both full and affiliate chapters coalesced in California's Central Valley, the Greater Boston area, Oklahoma, Portland, Indiana, and Toronto.

The Evangelical Women's Caucus seemed to be on an upswing: the local chapters and affiliates were healthier financially, with a surplus for several years in a row; the conferences were well attended; members were progressing in their personal and career objectives; and biblical feminists were publishing books and articles with leading Christian journals and publishing houses. But this seemingly unambiguous success hid a growing theological rift within biblical feminism that later divided the organization. Still, in 1978 through 1983, finances were healthy, membership was steady, and the 1978 Pasadena conference set the tone for a biblical feminist agenda, practically and theologically, for the next five years.

Early Biblical Feminist Interpretation

Through 1978, most biblical feminists held a similar theological perspective. They wanted to prove that traditional interpretations, especially those of the apostle Paul, were misinterpretations. Paul was not sexist; he was misunderstood. Roberta Hestenes's background article for the 1978 conference, "Scripture and the Ministry of Women within the Christian Community," describes this kind of biblical feminist theology, which she situates squarely in the center of evangelicalism. In the very first sentence, she states that since biblical feminists are deeply committed to the authority of the scripture, it is there that they first need to look to settle the question of women's roles in the Christian community. Hestenes then lays out two competing theological paradigms for viewing women's ministry in the church. The traditionalist paradigm, she writes, has

> a tendency to say that while spiritual realities change (e.g., a new order in baptism or conversion) yet on earth in human relationships the old order remains. Kings and princes, masters and slaves, Jews and Gentiles, male and female may be transformed inwardly by the power of the gospel, but outwardly remain the same. Only in the final consummation, with the coming of Christ in power, will human society take the shape which God intends for it.

In the egalitarian paradigm, in contrast, a new church order has already begun: "Resurrection power is a present possibility (Ephesians 1:19–20). . . . We in the Church may rightly look to the liberating power of the gospel to be present here and now in all areas of human life."[18] Because this approach relates to relationships between the sexes, Hestenes specifically emphasizes the radical newness of Christian marriage in which believers submit to each other in love—a reference to Ephesians 5:21. In conclusion she writes: "All of the passages about women in Acts and the Epistles need to be read not only from the center of Jesus Christ but also in light of the New Testament teaching about the 'new creation' (2 Corinthians 5:14–21) —which is both individual and corporate."[19] Her point is that the egalitarian paradigm focuses not on the future transformation of male and female relationships but on an attempt to live out the liberating power of the gospel in earthly relationships at home and in publicly acknowledged leadership roles granted to women in the church.

Although Hestenes came from the Reformed tradition, a similarity to Wesleyan theology is noticeable in her argument, in part because of post-fundamentalist evangelicals' predilection for the Methodist emphasis on social change. Wesleyan theology took its name from John Wesley (1703–1791). After his own personal experience of conversion, Wesley began to preach that true faith restored the moral image of God in the believer. His intention was not to establish a new denomination, but later his followers—known as Methodists—split from the Anglican Church. Methodists insisted that believers' lives would look different from those of nonbelievers, that believers would show continual moral improvement and would act toward others out of God's love and grace. Wesleyan theology was broadly similar to Reformed theology in following the biblical pattern of creation, fall, and redemption. But whereas the Reformed tradition was often known for its emphasis on human sinfulness and God's sovereignty, the Wesleyan tradition was noted for its emphasis on the work of the Holy Spirit to bring the believer to righteousness, resulting in a changed life. These changes in individuals then would lead to corporate and even societal change. The eighteenth-century revivals in England—which led to reforms in prisons, child labor, and social services—exemplified what effect the Methodists thought God's love and grace would have on the present-day life of the church and the world.

With its focus on the Holy Spirit, Wesleyan theology naturally emphasized spiritual gifting as well. This allowed women and other marginalized groups to participate more in leadership, because Wesleyans believed that God distributed spiritual gifts equally without regard to race or gender. In another essay, Hestenes makes this the link between the Holy Spirit and women's leadership through 2 Corinthians 3:17–18, in which Paul states, "Now the Lord is Spirit, and where the Spirit of the Lord is, there is freedom. All we, who with unveiled faces all reflect the Lord's glory, are being transformed into his likeness with ever-increasing glory, which comes from the Lord, who is Spirit." Hestenes notes that all Christians, both men and women, are transformed by the Spirit and that this transformation brings freedom. Later Paul writes, "So from now on, we regard no-one from a worldly point of view. Though we once regarded Christ in this way, we do so no longer. Therefore, if anyone is in Christ, there is a new creation: the old has gone, the new has come!" (2 Corinthians 5:16–17). With this passage, Hestenes links individual renewal to a new task and a new relationship to the church and the world. In Christ's body, each member is given a manifestation of the Spirit for the common good (1 Corinthians 12:7). For this reason, Christian women have a responsibility to transcend and transform a culture that would hinder such a manifestation of the Spirit.[20]

With this background, what Hestenes called a "traditionalist" versus "egalitarian" paradigm looks much like a Reformed versus Wesleyan theological model. For example, Hestenes argues that traditionalists assumed that Christian transformation was to be a "spiritual" change. A Christian woman's external roles and relationships would not change. Therefore, they interpreted the term *headship* (in Ephesians 5:23) to mean authority and rule. Egalitarians, however, believe that the new spiritual relationship created by conversion brought help from the Holy Spirit to transform human, cultural institutions. Egalitarians interpret headship organically as an indication of the connectedness between men and women. Therefore, they do not conclude that headship indicated submission only of women to men.

The Wesleyan influence on early biblical feminist theology can be seen most directly in the work of Donald W. Dayton, Lucille Sider Dayton, and Nancy Hardesty. The Daytons and Hardesty were together in the Chicago area as colleagues at Trinity, in Evangelicals for Social Action, and at *Daughters of Sarah*. As early as 1974, this trio was writing about the evangelical heritage of the women's movement, asserting that Wesleyan Methodism and the Holiness movement nurtured and informed the nineteenth-century women's movement in America.[21] While historians might debate their singular focus on evangelicalism as the cradle of feminism to the exclusion of other forces, they did paint a rich portrait of Christians involved in the early women's movement.[22] This involvement came through individual men and women like abolitionists Angelina and Sarah Grimké; evangelist Charles Finney, who founded the first coeducational college in the world (Oberlin); Antoinette Brown, an Oberlin graduate and the first woman ordained in the Wesleyan Methodist Church; Luther Lee, the man who ordained her; and Frances Willard, a suffragette. Later Hardesty also wrote two books that reveal the formative influence of Wesleyan theology on her thinking. In *Women Called to Witness*, Hardesty studies the Finneyites, followers of Charles Finney's revivals in the 1820s and 1830s, and argues that the revivalists' theology and practice equipped evangelicals "to adopt a feminist ideology, to reject stereotyped sex roles, and to work for positive changes in marriage, church, society, and politics."[23] In a later volume, Hardesty organizes her argument around Finney's theology and illustrates how nineteenth-century feminists were influenced by it.[24]

Thus, many early biblical feminists, including the Daytons, Hardesty, and Hestenes, concluded that a Wesleyan theological basis gave evangelicals the best way to remain faithful to all of scripture and to the central thrust of the gospel. It gave biblical feminists the best method of holistically interpreting the creation accounts, the female prophetic tradition of women in Israel and the church, Jesus' treatment of women, the church as a spiritual community built by the Spirit, and the Pauline passages. These feminists acknowledged that the Pauline passages caused the most trouble for egalitarians but insisted that in a Wesleyan framework and with the aid of historical criticism, Paul could be seen as an example of a believer "seeking to proclaim the eternal gospel and to guide young congregations in a particular time and culture."[25]

The theological framework provided by Wesleyan theology—Christian women's freedom in the Spirit to use their gifts, the recovery of women's history in the church, reinterpretation of problem passages using historical and cultural analysis, and practical application—undergirded much of biblical feminist theological endeavors.

By the late 1970s and early 1980s, many articles and a number of books were published on the topic of biblical feminism. Two of the more prolific and well-read authors during this time were Patricia Gundry and Virginia Mollenkott. A look at their writings reveals that there were, even at this early date, two methodological approaches to biblical feminist theology. But at this time, both were still considered "evangelical" in the progressive sense. Because of the importance of biblical authority to evangelicalism, both Gundry and Mollenkott initially focused on the reinterpretation of those texts that were used to keep women submissive to their husbands and out of public positions of leadership. Both therefore also found it necessary to address the appropriate methods of biblical interpretation. It is in this second focus that the differences between the two types of biblical feminism become apparent. The issue boiled down to determining when a biblical text was culturally or situationally limited. Gundry and the more conservative evangelical feminists remained committed to a strict definition of biblical authority that did not allow them to ignore certain of Paul's statements on women, whereas Mollenkott argued that a commitment to biblical authority was not incompatible with the view that some of Paul's pronouncements were simply wrong because they were based on his limited human perspective.

Patricia Gundry: Representative of "Conservative" Evangelical Feminists

Pat Gundry[26] defined a biblical feminist as "one who is committed to the authority of the scriptures and whose feminism follows from that conviction."[27] She thus advocated the evangelical conviction that the Bible, not culture, is the ultimate guide for Christian action. This did not mean, however, that Gundry did not allow experiences with the culture of her day to suggest a critical reevaluation of unconsidered assumptions.

Augustine, Luther, and Calvin all had similar experiences, with the fall of the Roman empire, indulgences, and the sovereignty of God, respectively. In her case, Gundry admitted that secular feminism gave her the impetus to examine what the Bible said about women's roles. She began her reappraisal by asking pastors about the meaning of passages like 1 Timothy 2:11–15: "A woman should learn in quietness and full submission. I do not permit a woman to teach or to have authority over a man. . . . But women will be saved through childbearing" (NIV). She found that her query elicited only surly responses, which made her aware that most of her Christian information came from secondary sources: pastors, theologians, and, in the case of women's roles, from writers like Bill Gothard and Marabel Morgan.[28] So she began years of studying the Bible for herself.

Her conclusions appeared in 1977 as the book *Woman Be Free!* At the time of its release, Gundry's husband Stanley taught at the Moody Bible Institute, a conservative evangelical school in Chicago. According to Pat, people at Moody initially tried to ignore her book. Two years later, however, all that changed when she gave a lecture on women's rights in Glen Ellyn, a suburb geographically close to Moody. Conservative Christians sent scores of letters to Moody objecting that the wife of a Moody professor was speaking out for women's rights.[29] Eventually Moody banned Pat Gundry from its media and on August 1, 1979, asked Stan Gundry to resign, since he and his wife were an embarrassment to the school.

In *Woman Be Free!* Gundry communicates her "embarrassing" vision of Christian liberty for women. She points out that Christian women have been treated as second-class citizens in God's kingdom and admits that, yes, secular feminism helped raise her awareness of this. That does not mean, however, that the subordinate treatment of women is necessarily biblical. Gundry acknowledges that the evangelical church gives lip service to equality between men and women but qualified it as "equality of essence" not "position." That is like "saying the sun is shining but it's not day," she points out.[30] Equality of "essence" and "position" cannot be separated. Based on her own study, Gundry determines that the Bible teaches male and female equality in every way: "The ground at the foot of the cross is level."[31]

Gundry also exposes several "threats" that she claims conservative Christian men use to hold women down, such as women would lose their femininity, disrupt order, and destroy society. Gundry realizes that these alarms are not new. In an 1837 sermon, Pastor Jonathan F. Stearns expressed similar fears about the first feminist stirrings in America:

On you, ladies, depends, in a most important degree, the destiny of our country. . . . Yours it is to decide, under God, whether we shall be a nation of refined and high minded Christians, or whether, rejecting the civilities of life, and throwing off the restraints of morality and piety, we shall become a fierce race of barbarians, before whom neither order, nor honor, nor chastity can stand.[32]

Gundry believes that in her day, as in Victorian society, women are considered the guardians of societal morality. She realizes, though, that there might have been reasons beyond biblical culture that caused conservative Christian men to keep women in their place.

Through their studies of Victorian religion and culture, historians of American religion have helped elucidate some of these external influences. For example, Ann Douglas contends that in Victorian America, clergy and women evolved into becoming the custodians of the moral fabric of society in order to maintain an essential role in the working of a society in which they were becoming increasingly marginalized.[33] And historians Margaret Bendroth and Betty DeBerg help show that the fundamentalists supported inerrancy in the early twentieth century in large measure because it allowed evangelicals to distinguish themselves from secular piety. Because they were more rational and logical, inerrancy made men the guardians of faith and orthodoxy, whereas Victorian society, in which emotions and sentimentality reigned, made women, with their natural aptitude for religion, the keepers of morality.[34] Such historical arguments suggest that the main reason to keep conservative Christian women submissive might have been based on something other than biblical teaching.

In evangelical circles at the time of Gundry's writing, the accusation that feminists were denying the inspiration of scripture had the most impact. She called it "an all-purpose silencer."[35] Nonetheless, she refused to remain quiet:

We must not be confused by the words inspiration and interpretation. To claim inspiration of the Scriptures is to believe that what the Bible says is true—that it is God's written Word to us. Interpretation involves explaining what this Word means to us on a human level. Therefore, interpretation leaves room for human error, and we must recognize in others' pulling of spiritual or educational rank that they are not infallible in their interpretation of Scripture.[36]

Because Gundry was committed to the belief that all scripture was inspired, she needed to show that human error had led to misunderstanding the New Testament view of women and that new interpretations were needed.

The evangelical preoccupation with biblical authority stems from concern that the Bible remain the primary guide by which Christians determine how to act in the culture of their day. By not considering the historical context in which the texts were written, however, Gundry believes that evangelicals have done a disservice to biblical authority. She explains how: "We must use the principle illustrated even if the specific instruction is not transcultural . . . we have often denied many of those principles by insisting on a rigid, literal, transcultural application of these passages."[37] For example, by insisting that Paul teaches the subordination of women, evangelicals have failed to apply the true timeless principle: seeking to save the lost. She writes:

> We drive away unbelievers even now by some of our rigid rules regarding women. Women outside Christ are saying, "We reject a God who treats half His human creation as second-class creatures." They are taking our actions as representative of God's attitude. We, by our practices in the church, cause "the word of God [to be] dishonored."[38]

In this way, Gundry was able to maintain that the proper application of God's word is to include women in visible positions of leadership.

In her second book, *Heirs Together*, Gundry enumerated the principles, taken from Bernard Ramm, by which evangelicals could culturally interpret scripture while upholding biblical authority.[39] First, all scripture must be interpreted in its immediate context in a paragraph, passage, argument, and book. Second, texts need to be interpreted in light of what they meant to the original audience. Therefore, third, the interpreter should consider the customs and events of the time in which the text was written. Fourth, each passage should be interpreted in light of all other scripture. This means that texts of the Bible cannot be contradictory. To help interpret apparent contradictions, her fifth principle is that clear and obvious passages should be used to enlighten less clear passages. For example, the obtuse passage in 1 Timothy 2 ("woman shall be saved through childbearing") should not be used to interpret Paul's clear statement in Galatians 3:28 ("there is neither male nor female"), but vice versa. Sixth, interpretation should be based on the best available translation of the original language. Seventh, scholars should interpret social teachings in light of doctrinal ones. For example, texts that seem to teach segregation or slavery need to be considered in view of the larger doctrinal themes of the priesthood of all believers and freedom in Christ. Last, Gundry states that passages must be applied in a way that is harmonious with their original intention. The illustration she offers for this principle is 1 Corinthians 11. By insisting that women wear hats, scarves, or special caps to cover their heads, Christians have defeated the original principle that women should appear in a socially acceptable manner of dress.

The "Conservative" Feminist Reinterpretation

At this early stage in their theology, evangelical feminists were preoccupied with reinterpreting those texts used to keep women subordinate to men. Not unlike Mary Daly's early work, *The Church and the Second Sex*, conservative Christian women were seeking to recover a place for women in the church. For evangelical feminists this meant that they first had to establish principles for interpreting difficult texts and maintaining a high view of biblical authority. Their methodology was therefore more thoroughly explicated than it was employed. For example, in Gundry's first book, only one chapter deals with the application of her hermeneutics to the entire Pauline corpus and the creation accounts. Although the application of their hermeneutical principles progressed, the goal of the more conservative biblical feminists remained the same: to recover Paul's writings from androcentric interpretations and reconstruct them as feminist through the use of historical and cultural criticism. What follows are two examples of the way in which more conservative biblical feminists have interpreted biblical passages considered "problematic" for having women in leadership in the church and home.

1 Corinthians 11

1 Corinthians 11:2–10 states:

> I praise you for remembering me in everything and for holding to the teachings, just as I passed them on to you. Now I want you to realize that the head of every man is Christ, and the head of the woman is man, and the head of Christ is God. Every man who prays or prophesies with

his head covered dishonours his head. And every woman who prays or prophesies with her head uncovered dishonours her head—it is just as though her head were shaved. If a woman does not cover her head, she should have her hair cut off; and if it is a disgrace for a woman to have her hair cut or shaved off, she should cover her head. A man ought not to cover his head, since he is the image and glory of God but the woman is the glory of man. For man did not come from woman, but woman from man; neither was man created for woman, but woman for man. For this reason, and because of the angels, the woman ought to have a sign of authority on her head.

Gundry begins her interpretation of this scripture by observing that the context for this text starts in chapter 10 with Paul's discussion of freedom in Christ. Paul was responding to a specific question from the Corinthian church about eating meat offered to idols. His reply was that Christians need to use their best judgment; for "'everything is permissible'—but not everything is beneficial" (10:30). Paul then urges the Corinthians to follow his example in limiting their freedom so as not to hinder others from accepting the gospel message. In this context, Gundry argues, Paul was suggesting to the Corinthians that even though not every custom should be followed, the habit of women wearing a head covering—like eating meat sacrificed to idols—was important for its moral significance in that culture. Therefore, women should not use their freedom to pray with their head uncovered if it would hinder the proclamation of the gospel.

Although Gundry does not expand further on this interpretation of 1 Corinthians 11, other evangelical feminists have. Richard and Catherine Clark Kroeger studied the Greek view of sexuality to better understand the cultural and historical context at Corinth at the time that Paul was writing. Richard, a pastor, and Catherine, a graduate student in patristics, based their theory on the widespread homophilia and pederasty found in Greek society. They argue that the tendency to prefer one sex to the other led to the subjugation of women. Given this cultural situation, the Kroegers suggest that in 1 Corinthians 11, Paul was seizing the opportunity to promote women "as a gift from God and a treasure to man."[40] They claim that in the Greek and Roman eras, philosophers viewed woman's creation as a maleficent action by the gods. Paul countered this idea by declaring that the original purpose for woman was beneficial, that she was to be a blessing to man, not a bane. To bolster this contention, they explain that the phrase "woman [was created] for the man's sake"

(NAS) did not make her inferior to man. In other passages that use the same wording, 2 Corinthians 8:9 ("our Lord Jesus Christ, that though he was rich, yet for your sakes he became poor") and 1 Corinthians 4:6 ("I [Paul] have applied these things to myself . . . for your benefit") connote a positive, spiritual benefit, not one of subservience. Paul, therefore, was teaching the common humanity of male and female: "Woman was formed from the very substance of man and shares the same qualities of heart and mind."[41]

They contend that Paul could not have been teaching a divine order of creation when he wrote: "The head of every man is Christ, and the head of the woman is man, and the head of Christ is God." The Kroegers connect the idea of headship with the concept "glory of" found in verse 7: "He [the man] is the image and glory of God; but the woman is the glory of man." They observe that in other biblical texts Paul calls men "the glory of Christ" (2 Corinthians 8:23 and 1 Corinthians 11:7), and in 1 Thessalonian 2:20, he calls the Christians his glory. They conclude that Paul subscribed to the idea that believers were being transformed to reflect the glory of Christ (2 Corinthians 3:13). Thus he was highlighting the interrelation and continuity of man and woman in God's image. But that reflected image, or glory, needed to be veiled, a tradition that runs throughout the Old Testament (e.g., Exodus 13:21–22, 1 Kings 8:10–11, and Isaiah 4:5–6). Paul therefore advocated the custom of covering a woman's head not to signify woman's submission to man but as a symbol of honor and the independent nature of her relationship with God. The term *exousia*, translated as "a sign of authority," supports this explanation, they claim, since it was never used in the Greek to signify submission to the power of another but, rather, power exercised by the individual.

Ephesians 5

Whereas 1 Corinthians provides material for feminists' attempt to reinterpret a passage used to limit women's roles in the church, Ephesians 5:21–24 provides material for their effort to recover a text used to subordinate women in the home:

> Submit to one another out of reverence for Christ. Wives, submit to your husbands as to the Lord. For the husband is the head of the wife as Christ is the head of the church, his body, of which he is the Saviour.

Now as the church submits to Christ, so also wives should submit to their husbands in everything.

This was a key text that traditionalists used to construct the concept of a Christian marriage in which the husband is the head of the household. Other Pauline texts address the concept of male headship, but they are in passages that deal with little-understood cultural practices, in specific historical situations (1 Corinthians 11 and 14). Ephesians, as a more theological work, offers a more compelling argument for women's subordination to men in marriage.

Gundry, the Kroegers, and other feminists believed that the key to interpreting this passage in an unbiased manner was to translate correctly the term *kephale*, "head." Another husband and wife team, Berkeley and Alvera Mickelsen, professors of New Testament and journalism, respectively, addressed this question at a conference on Women and the Bible sponsored by Stan Gundry, Catherine Kroeger, and David Scholer. The Mickelsens began by searching the most complete English-Greek lexicon available, compiled by Liddell, Scott, Jones and McKenzie and first published in 1843. It is based on thousands of Greek writings covering nearly sixteen hundred years. This lexicon lists more than twenty-five possible figurative meanings for *kephale*. None of these listings includes the meaning of "authority," "superior rank," "leader," or any hierarchical connotation. The Mickelsens continued by refuting those scholars who translated *kephale* as "head." Some scholars improperly based their translation on only two examples of such a use in Greek writings, and these postdated the writing of the New Testament. Other traditional scholars argued for the meaning of "superior rank" in Paul's writing, based on the assumption that Greek translators of the Old Testament, the Septuagint, used *kephale* to translate *ro'sh*, which has a connotation of rank. The Mickelsens pointed out that only eight times, out of 180, did the Septuagint translators use *kephale* to translate *ro'sh* and that this was too small a percentage to be significant. They suggested instead, after looking at other New Testament passages that use the term, that *kephale* would best be translated as "source," "origin," or even "honor." Thus, Paul's statement that "the husband is the head of the wife" (NIV) cannot be read to advocate the husband as ruler over his wife. Instead, it indicates an organic unity, that the husband and wife are part of one body in which the husband's role is to nurture, love, and serve his wife.

Virginia Mollenkott:
Representative of the "Liberal" Evangelical Feminists

Virginia Mollenkott grew up in a strict fundamentalist (Plymouth Brethren) home. Despite being raised in a culture that prohibited divorce, her father left home when she was nine years old. When her mother found out that Virginia was sneaking out to meet her father, she was sent away to a private Christian school. She was ostracized and suffered extreme loneliness there after being falsely accused of "forcibly stripping" another girl. In the face of such traumatic experiences with a morally rigid belief system, Mollenkott found solace in memorizing scripture and became determined to be a missionary because she "would be allowed a fuller role in the life of the church (because most men were uninterested in being missionaries)."[42] After high school Mollenkott attended Bob Jones University, another fundamentalist institution, which had a strict dating policy. School policy allowed male and female students to see each other only several hours a week, and touching, of any kind, was forbidden. These "rules," Mollenkott complained, were "perfectly calculated to keep men and women from getting to know each other well."[43] Yet marriage was encouraged; so immediately after graduating, Mollenkott married her boyfriend. She later admitted being convinced within hours of her wedding ceremony that she had made a mistake. Still, she stayed with her husband for seventeen years.

From the first year of her marriage, Mollenkott worked part or full time while also earning master's and doctoral degrees. She graduated from Bob Jones in 1953. By 1955, she had her M.A. in English from Temple University and received her Ph.D. from New York University in 1964. She was an instructor at Shelton College in New Jersey and even chaired its English department from 1956 to 1963, while she pursued her doctorate. In 1963 Mollenkott moved to Nyack Missionary College. She described these early career years as "health-wrecking:"

> Taking care of a small son and being responsible for the washing, ironing, bed-making, cleaning, shopping, cooking—the works. I remember feeling it was unfair that my husband could get up from dinner and watch TV all evening while I washed the dishes, put the baby to bed, and then cleared a place for myself at the kitchen table to study for my graduate courses and prepare for my next day's classes. I frequently

worked until the wee hours, always struggling to shut out the sound of the incessant television.[44]

It was upon the completion of her doctorate that Mollenkott took stock of her life and, sensing that divorce was inevitable, left the Christian college where she taught and sought employment at a secular college. In 1967, she was hired by William Paterson College in New Jersey, where she remained until her retirement. In 1971, she divorced her husband after a lengthy separation.

Mollenkott began writing and speaking extensively on the topic of biblical feminism shortly after her divorce. A friend whom she had met on a Christian tour of Italy and who was an ardent feminist encouraged Mollenkott to read secular feminist literature. Around the same time, in the early 1970s, she read the articles written by Scanzoni, Hardesty, and others published in various Christian periodicals. When Denver Seminary hosted a theological conference on women, Mollenkott was invited to present an overview of the women's movement. It was there that she met Jewett, Hardesty, and Scanzoni. The result was her foreword to Jewett's *Man as Male and Female*, several articles, lectures, and, ultimately, her first book on biblical feminism, *Women, Men and the Bible*.

In these initial forays promoting feminism among evangelicals, Mollenkott called for the "de-absolutizing" of patriarchal culture in scriptural interpretation. She argued that Christians needed to recognize that even though patriarchy was an integral, accepted part of the biblical culture, God did not intend to enshrine it as a normative ideal for all cultures. Mollenkott pointed out that Christians had de-absolutized other cultural traditions found in the Bible, for example, the divine right of kings and slavery. In fact, Mollenkott continued, it was far less detrimental to biblical authority to admit that some of the apostle Paul's statements reflected his human limitations than to deny Paul's liberating vision of a "classless, nonracist, nonsexist" community.

As Paul Jewett did, Mollenkott believed that certain of Paul's writings were irredeemably influenced by his humanity. This was evident, according to Mollenkott, by obvious contradictions in Paul's writings:

The same Paul who praises Phoebe and tells the Roman church to give this outstanding leader all the help they can, the same Paul who praises Priscilla, who preaches to a congregation of women even though he had been taught that they couldn't form a quorum, this same Paul told women to keep silent in church. That's the problem.[45]

Mollenkott argued that these discrepancies were the result of rabbinical influences on Paul. Before following Christ, Paul had been a persecutor of Christians, educated as a rabbi in the leading Jewish school. This training taught him that woman was inferior to man because she was created after him and from him. Influenced by this misogynist teaching, Paul naturally struggled between the liberating theological message of the gospel and his rabbinical training. But Mollenkott did not like to call Paul's contradictions "errors." Instead, she described them as "just an honest record of a human being working through his conflicts," much like King David's imprecatory psalms in the Old Testament.[46]

Like most evangelicals, including those who held a verbal, plenary view of the inspiration of scripture, Mollenkott did not believe that God dictated the Bible to the New Testament writers as if in a trance. Rather, she believed that each of the biblical writers contributed some of their own personality and experience to what they wrote through their particular style, word choice, cultural background, and the like. For example, many evangelicals accepted that the four gospel accounts reveal the different influences of their human authors. The Gospel of Matthew reveals the imprint of a former tax collector through its parables relating to money and its Jewish emphasis; Mark is slanted toward a Roman audience; Luke is directed toward the Greeks; and John writes with a broader, more philosophical audience in mind, highlighting the personal nature of his close relationship with Jesus.

But questions arose about Mollenkott's hermeneutics because of her opinion that the Bible, though a divine book, came through fallible human channels and reflected their foibles. As John Alexander, editor of *The Other Side*, asked, How could one decide when the Bible was limited and when not? Or, put another way, were evangelicals simply letting American, instead of biblical, culture dictate their social practices? Mollenkott did not think so. Citing Matthew 19:3–9, she argued that even Jesus interpreted scripture with an awareness of culture. When Pharisees tried to trap Jesus by contrasting his view of divorce with Mosaic law, Jesus responded that Moses permitted divorce (Deuteronomy 24:1–3) "because your hearts were hard. But it was not this way from the beginning," referring to God's original intention for human relationships. Mollenkott concluded, "By playing off Deuteronomy against Genesis, Jesus is not impugning the inspiration of the Old Testament but is showing that certain passages were inspired to meet specific needs in response to human hardness, while other passages (recognizable by context) convey God's ultimate intentions for the human race."[47]

Mollenkott's Principles of Interpretation

Mollenkott enumerated several principles by which one could recognize which scripture could, and should, be limited. Most important was what she called "the analogy of faith." An argument by analogy reasons that if a principle is true in one area, it may well be true in another. So Mollenkott asked what the primary teaching was about faith in the New Testament and the example of Jesus' life. In her book *Women, Men and the Bible*, she studies the lives of Jesus, Paul, and Peter to see how they relate to others. She also considers the overall message of the New Testament epistles and concludes that the overarching principle of faith is of unity, love, and human justice. Thus, Christians should evaluate specific texts in light of their conformity to these ideals. No text should be read in such a way that it departs from those major themes of the Bible.

Closely related to this is the principle, already discussed, that clearly understood passages of scripture should always govern the interpretation of more obscure, difficult ones. Similarly, no teaching should be based on a brief scriptural reference. In 1 Timothy 2:11–15, Paul makes the convoluted argument that women should be submissive, learn in quiet, and not have authority over men, since Eve was deceived first and women will be saved through childbearing. Interpreters long have had difficulty in interpreting this passage. It seems to contradict salvation by faith; it is unclear what childbirth has to do with the argument; and it seems to base women's submission on Eve's gullibility. However, numerous passages clearly teach the doctrine of salvation by faith ("It is by grace you have been saved, through faith," Ephesians 2:8), and the Bible teaches just as clearly that both Adam and Eve were cupable for sin's entering the world. Thus, 1 Timothy 2:11–14 should not be read to contradict the major doctrine of salvation by faith alone or to teach that women are more sinful than men.

Context also sheds light on whether a particular passage was culturally or historically restricted. For example, evangelicals commonly accept that the New Testament helps clarify the Old. Thus, Christians reject "an eye for an eye" retaliation based on Jesus' Sermon on the Mount: "You have heard that it was said, 'Eye for eye, and tooth for tooth.' But I tell you, do not resist an evil person. If someone strikes you on the right cheek, turn the other cheek also" (Matthew 5:38–39). Another type of context involves considering the genre of a passage. Was the statement being evaluated made in a theological text, such as Galatians, or in a letter addressed to a specific audience and historical situation, such as 1 Timothy? Even closer study means determining the literary form of the specific passage, whether poetry, epistle, parable, history, or didactic. Last, a close study of the individual words used—their meaning, grammar, idioms, and historical background—should help the reader reach the proper interpretation, which, Mollenkott states, is to understand the literal meaning of the text as it was understood by the original hearers.

After the literal meaning is determined, Mollenkott advocates looking for a secondary meaning, one that is symbolic, spiritual, mystical, figurative, or allegorical. Consider, for example, Galatians 3:28: "There is neither Jew nor Greek, slave nor free, male nor female." Galatians was written as a theological statement, and its main theme is freedom in Christ. The major argument in Galatians 3 concerns whether new Christian converts had to conform to Jewish customs. Paul did not think so. Mollenkott concludes that Paul intended to teach that no artificial barriers (as opposed to ethnic or biological differences) exist in God's family. In the case of men and women, patterns of dominance and submission, which create relational barriers, are dissolved. Mollenkott argues that Paul was not speaking of some distant future, since he wrote in the past tense: "for all of you who were baptized into Christ have clothed yourselves with Christ" (3:27). She concludes that based on what God had already done (baptized all believers into Christ), there is a present mystical reality of unity within a diverse body. Mollenkott thereby asserts that Paul is calling Christians to live in a way that makes this mystical fact a living reality.

Many evangelicals questioned whether this hermeneutic for determining cultural limitations was legitimate and if it upheld biblical inspiration. Women in the biblical feminist movement disagreed on the answer. Sharon Gallagher, editor of *Radix*, was one who objected to Mollenkott's method. In a solicited letter to the editor of *Sojourners*, Gallagher wrote that Paul's teachings were uniquely inspired and transcended whatever cultural limitations he may have had. She complained that it was unfair to compare Paul's instructions to churches, which were deliberately didactic, with David's imprecatory psalms, which were personal prayers, not originally intended for instruction. Gallagher contended that Mollenkott's hermeneutic allowed the individual "to decide which mood (liberated or unliberated) Paul was in, in specific passages."[48] Thus Mollenkott was absolutizing modern American culture, in place of patriarchal culture, by putting it in the position of judging scripture rather than vice versa. Gallagher's alternative, much like those of other conservative biblical feminists, was to reclaim all Paul's writings as liberating for women. The apostle's words had been obscured by centuries of androcentric interpretation—"priestcraft" (a term Gallagher borrowed from Lucretia Mott)—and evangelical feminists needed to struggle to retrieve his original meaning.

In his interview with Mollenkott, the editor of *The Other Side* also questioned the hermeneutic that Mollenkott advocated. Admitting that he was persuaded by her argument, Alexander feared that he was opening the floodgates for relativism: "Maybe the domino theory is right in theology. If you give up inerrancy, everything else collapses around you." He added, however, that "on the other hand, perhaps my pursuit of an objective standard is itself culturally conditioned. Maybe I learned that from Occam and Descartes and Locke."[49] If he did end up accepting Mollenkott's hermeneutical method, he asked, should he resign from *The Other Side*, since he would no longer be able to uphold the mission of the magazine to "call Christians back-to-the-Bible?" She replied:

> I don't think you should do that [resign]. . . . Someone needs to teach evangelicals the difference between faith and fear. Maybe that's part of your job. Let the rest have their iron maiden definition of inspiration, which they use to oppress other people. Let them declare themselves as fundamentalists. Let's the rest of us get on with the job.[50]

Presumably, that job referred to the progressive evangelical attempt to offer intellectually credible biblical interpretation and to draw people into the church who had been alienated by fundamentalism's isolationist stance.

The "Liberal" Feminist Interpretation

Women, Men and the Bible was Mollenkott's attempt to "get on with the job" and give her view of what the scriptures had to say about relationships between men and women. She distinguished her position both from secular feminists who advocated for female supremacy and from traditionalists who taught a chain of command theory in which males represent God on earth. Mollenkott mainly focused on biblical doctrines important to defining a Christian way of relating and argued that a male bias was read into evangelical beliefs on the creation, Trinity, incarnation, and regeneration.

Creation and the Trinity

Like most biblical feminists, the first texts Mollenkott addressed were the creation accounts. Her goal was to refute the assumption of God's masculinity, not merely to show that woman was created equal to man. Genesis 1: 26–27 states:

> Then God said, "Let us make man in our image, in our likeness, and let them rule over the fish of the sea and the birds of the air, over the livestock, over all the earth, and over all the creatures that move along the ground." So God created man in his own image, in the image of God he created him; male and female he created them (New International Version).

Mollenkott first points out, as others had before her, that the word used for "man" in Genesis 1, *h'adam,* is a generic term meant to include all humanity, not just the male of the species. Second, both men and women are created in God's image: "In the image of God he created them; male and female he created them" (NIV, Inclusive Language edition). Since both sexes reflect God's image, men cannot claim that God is male, even though the first part of the Trinity is called "the Father." To bolster her argument, Mollenkott cites several places in the Old and New Testaments that use feminine images of God the Father. One example comes from Isaiah 42:14, in which God speaks as a woman in labor: "For a long time I have kept silent, I have been quiet and held myself back. But now, like a woman in childbirth, I cry out, I gasp and pant."

Mollenkott further presses her point that God is not male by arguing that just as the Father cannot be considered masculine, neither can the Son or the Spirit. Jesus is frequently depicted as having feminine traits, and since the time of the early church, some biblical scholars have argued that the Holy Spirit is feminine. Mollenkott does not agree with those who solved the problem of God's sex by assigning male and female gender to various persons of the Trinity, though. Instead, she maintains that God transcends all human limitations, including sexuality. Mollenkott insists that biblical evidence, beginning with the creation accounts, teaches this, by using both masculine and feminine imagery to depict God. Mollenkott acknowledges that the Bible uses predominately masculine images of God and that these representations have led both men and women to conclude that God is male. In a highly androcentric, patriarchal culture, however, Mollenkott maintains that the inclusion of any feminine picture of God is incredible—and significant.

After finishing *Women, Men and the Bible*, Mollenkott directed her literary skills to recovering the female imagery of God in the Bible. In an essay published in the *Christian Century* in 1982, Mollenkott states that she learned the importance of imagery and language from goddess worshipers. Up until that time, Mollenkott had given little attention to goddess worship because she assumed that it was separatist and disregarded men. But it was from goddess worshipers that Mollenkott came to realize that worship of a god who sounded exclusively male was conducive to male supremacy.[51] In her second book, *The Divine Feminine*, each chapter focuses on one of fifteen different Old or New Testament images, including God as midwife, mother bear, homemaker, and lady Wisdom. In addition, Mollenkott wrote several articles and participated in preparing the new inclusive-language lectionary for the National Council of Churches.

The Incarnation

The second doctrine that Mollenkott addresses is the incarnation. She observes that although Jesus did inhabit earth as a male, biblical writers do not refer to the incarnation as Jesus' becoming "male," *aner*, but of his becoming "human," *anthropos*, or "flesh," *sarx*. John 1:14 states, "The Word became flesh [*sarx*] and made his dwelling among us," and Romans 5:15 records that "the gift is not like the trespass. For if the many died by the trespass of the one man [*hice*, meaning "one"; *anthropos* is left unstated but implied], how much more did God's grace and the gift that came by the grace of the one man [*anthropos*], Jesus Christ, overflow to the many!" The emphasis in the incarnation is on God's becoming "enfleshed humanity," not on Jesus' maleness.

At this point, Mollenkott addresses two misconceptions about the incarnation. The first is that by feminists who blame women's oppression on the concept of Christ's submissive suffering. Mollenkott counters this misunderstanding by arguing that Jesus was of one being with God, who voluntarily chose, for a specific purpose, to submit. The second misconception is that by traditionalists who misapply Christ's submission only to the role of women in relation to the church and their husbands. (Mollenkott spends much more time on the traditionalist misconception than the feminist one.) She contends that Christ's submission was to be a model to all Christians, male and female, for how they should relate to God and one another. In fact, to make the analogy that the wife is to her husband as Christ is to the Father would be to make the male analogous to the first person of the Trinity, an idolatrous concept.

In this context, Mollenkott argues that Ephesians 5 is actually a model of voluntary submission in marriage. Like Christ, who voluntarily chose to submit to the Father, the husband, emulating Christ, should voluntarily submit to his wife. The wife's response to her husband's initiation would be a mutual, voluntary submission to him. The goal of the passage, then, is not to tell husbands how to persuade their wives to serve them without complaining; it is to teach all humans how to relate to one another. In this particular instance, the scripture deals with the relationship between husband and wife.

Regeneration

The last doctrine Mollenkott addresses is regeneration. She asserts that the equality of men and women is grounded in the doctrine of the new creation. According to Mollenkott's theology, creation has gone, or will go, through three stages: pre-fall, fall, and future perfection. Christians currently live in the fallen world and therefore are limited. But they already have experienced a part of the final phase of redemption by having the Holy Spirit within them. Thus, the final phase, future perfection, has already begun for those who are God's children, but it will not be fully completed until Christ returns again. The Holy Spirit helps Christians live out their calling now as a new creation, which is exemplified by a community in which there is no "Jew or Greek, circumcised or uncircumcised, barbarian, Sythian, slave or free, but Christ is all, and is in all" (Colossians 3:11). This scenario, Mollenkott explains, describes how all relationships are intended to be in future perfection. Christians are called to live this out on earth in their life. The relationships of dominance described in the fall are, according to Mollenkott, descriptions of an erroneous way to relate. Colossians 3 prescribes how Christians ought to behave.

The Response to Mollenkott's Theology

Like *All We're Meant to Be* and Gundry's books, *Women, Men and the Bible* generally was reviewed positively in the evangelical press. It is not surprising that it was warmly received in *Christian Century*, a mainline journal, and *Daughters of Sarah*, which was very complimentary of Mollenkott's book, finding her conclusions "quite sensible," despite "some minor questions" about her hermeneutics and stance on biblical authority.[52] But *Women, Men and the Bible* was just as favorably critiqued in *Christianity Today*. A close look at this review reveals why one evangelical scholar looked positively on Mollenkott's work despite some misgivings.

Philip Siddons, a Presbyterian pastor, outlined four methods for dealing with the difficult Pauline passages on women.[53] The first is to deny Paul's authorship and thus deny the passages' canonicity. The second is to limit the relevancy of Paul's words to the time in which he lived. The third, Mollenkott's method, is to emphasize that God spoke through limited human beings; thus although the passages were written to instruct Christians throughout the centuries, they still reveal incompleteness and a struggle for Christian perfection. The fourth method, Gundry and Gallagher's, uses literary context, historical context, and theological context to show that Paul, like Jesus, was actually egalitarian.

The differences between Siddon's second and third style of interpretation are important. The second approach denies that certain of Paul's writings have any relevance for Christians in the modern world. Hence the result is to ignore entire portions of scripture. For evangelicals, this would be a denial that all scripture is infallible and efficacious. The third approach still finds some redeeming value in scripture that reveals human weakness. Mollenkott believes that contemporary Christians can learn from seeing a godly person in process. For example, her interpretation of 1 Corinthians 11 and 14 (enjoining women to silence and submission, "as the Law says") stresses that Paul showed his Christian immaturity by being more concerned with custom than with promoting freedom in Christ. Mollenkott points out that the Old Testament "assumed female submission, but contained no law to command it."[54] Contemporary believers can learn from Paul's mistake not to be so wedded to tradition that they fail to proclaim the good news of the gospel. Despite Siddon's overall praise for *Women, Men, and the Bible*, he nonetheless criticized Mollenkott for being too quick to regard the clear meaning of the text as the product of cultural conditioning. He thought that it would serve Christians better to apply historical and literary criticism to difficult passages, and thereby reveal their consistency with the rest of Paul's writings, than to give them up too quickly as patriarchal.

A Summary of Evangelical Feminist Hermeneutics

In a comparison of the two evangelical feminist approaches to scripture, differences become evident. Both the more conservative and the more liberal biblical feminists' early work was praised for its biblical approach to the question of women in the evangelical church, and few progressive evangelicals questioned whether Gundry, Scanzoni, Hardesty, or Mollenkott were evangelicals. Most also approved of their overall hermeneutical methods, including the use of higher criticism. Aside from a few biblical scholars, most reviewers of Gundry's and Mollenkott's books did not distinguish between the two authors' interpretive methods. The husband and wife reviewers of Gundry's book, *Woman Be Free*, in the *Covenant Quarterly* are typical of this prevalent view. They commend Gundry for her "solidly evangelical examination" of women's roles and for addressing "head-on" the major biblical arguments used by traditionalists to limit women with the same kind of exegesis as that of Scanzoni, Hardesty, and Mollenkott. But some reviewers of Mollenkott's work, including Sharon Gallagher and Philip Siddons, did notice two distinct hermeneutical methods. According to them, Mollenkott was too quick to resort to cultural conditioning to deal with Paul's less palatable teachings to American ears. Thus, the hermeneutical question around which arguments about biblical authority arose was how to determine when a text was culturally conditioned.

At this time, the theology of biblical feminism was not a systematic but a popular one, mostly dependent on the interpretive methods of progressive evangelical scholars, but also drawing on the variety of American theological traditions such as Reformed and Wesleyan theology. Virginia Hearn, the editor of *Update* and *Green Leaf*, summarized evangelical feminist theology as being based on three principles: In creation, both men and women were created in God's image; Jesus' treatment of women was extraordinary; and, the gospel intended to abolish distinctions among people, which becomes evident when the New Testament is read correctly in its historical context.[55] By reaching a popular audience with newer methods of biblical interpretation, biblical feminists were influential in changing the definitional boundaries of evangelicalism. By focusing on a contemporary issue of widespread concern to modern Americans, they also have been instrumental in broadening the social coalition of evangelicalism through their focus on social issues as essential to a truly evangelical faith.

The Evangelical Identity Crisis and Inerrancy Debates

Not all evangelicals looked so benignly on the growth of a feminist movement within evangelicalism. One such progressive evangelical who did not was Richard Quebedeaux.[56] Quebedeaux was a freelance writer known for his inside analysis of the progressive evangelical subculture. In 1974 he wrote *The Young Evangelicals*, in which he predicted that the younger, more progressive evangelicals would become the mainstream of American Protestantism. His second book, *The Worldly Evangelicals* (1978), was more pessimistic. In it, Quebedeaux expresses his disillusionment with what he considers the progressives' faithlessness to the gospel, which has made them inconspicuous in secular society because they have become too much like the world.

Evangelical feminists illustrated what he meant. Quebedeaux based his opinions about biblical feminism on a master's thesis from the Pacific School of Religion, in which the author concluded that all evangelical feminists relativized orthodox doctrinal formulations, let personal experience inform their ethics, and learned their behavior from the world instead of from the church or the Bible.[57] According to Quebedeaux, evangelical feminists are "a profound instance of the world's setting the agenda for the church, rather than vice-versa," because they have allowed the secular feminist movement to dictate their agenda. His repugnance for evangelical feminist accommodation is evident in his writing. In one place he parenthetically notes, "Mutual submission has been used by evangelical feminists as a more pious and Christian-sounding substitute for the word equality."[58] His point is that "equality" is a secular, not a Christian, concept. Other evangelicals, especially more conservative ones, agreed with Quebedeaux's analysis.[59] The attacks often were two pronged: evangelical feminists did not take seriously the authority of scripture, and they were more influenced by the secular culture of feminism than by biblical Christianity.

"EWC is much more than a warmed-over, imitative, Christianized version of secular feminism," Scanzoni responded to the charge of secular influence. "We did not become feminists and then try to fit our Christianity into feminist ideology. We became feminists because we were Christians."[60] Such a response does not deny the importance of the historical moment. Scanzoni did not, for example, deny that feminist ideas spurred evangelical feminists' thinking on social issues pertaining to women. Scanzoni was arguing that the influence of her Christian faith was more fundamental to her biblical feminism than secular feminism was. She compared biblical feminists with prophets, whom God used to rouse the church from slumber over issues of mercy and justice. Evangelical feminists felt that the church had strayed from a correct understanding of God's will for women, and so they heralded the biblical ideals that could be found in the feminist movement. With such an argument, Scanzoni revealed biblical feminism's dependence on the rise of progressive evangelicalism. Had progressive evangelical theologians not primed evangelicals to accept both scriptural reinterpretation and social activism, biblical feminism could not have succeeded as it had thus far.

To the criticism that evangelical feminists had merely accommodated secular feminist ideas, Roberta Hestenes replied that the argument used against women in public church leadership was the same one used to maintain the practice of slavery before the Civil War: that redemption meant spiritual renewal without a corresponding renewal of institutions and relationships. Yet prophets, in the form of abolitionists, helped convince the church that this was a misinterpretation of the texts. It was time, evangelical feminists said, for the same kind of reconsideration of women's roles in the church and Christian family. Hestenes also commented that the issues with which women in the evangelical churches were struggling did not come from the women's liberation movement. Rather, they were the result of changes in lifestyles and life expectancies in modern society. She pointed out that the average woman in 1900 lived for forty-six years, whereas in 1978 she lived for seventy-eight years. That meant that at the turn of the century, a woman died not long after rearing her children to their teenage years. In 1978 a woman could expect to live thirty years after her children left home, a place in which she no longer worked alongside her husband for family sustenance. Hestenes noted, too, that families in modern, mobile American society were more isolated from one another. She argued that it was neither countercultural nor an accommodation to culture but biblical for women to look anew at scripture for answers to the dilemmas of modern life.[61]

As far back as 1957, Carl F. H. Henry—considered the founder of neo-evangelicalism—addressed questions of biblical authority and its role in establishing evangelical credentials. In his tract *Evangelical Responsibility in Contemporary Theology*, Henry describes how evangelicals can biblically address modern culture without becoming trapped in that culture. They should start with the supreme authority of scripture and then apply it to the current situation as a theological and spiritual resource. Sometimes, however, he acknowledges that the Bible is unclear. In this case, two principles should guide evangelicals: views that attempt to be faithful to scripture "should be honored as evangelical" even if this necessitates a plurality of opinions, especially when it is debatable how important an issue is, anyway. He warns, prophetically as it turned out, that "there is a real danger that evangelicalism, sensing the need for a distinct identity, will define itself over precisely, negatively or reactively . . . diversity within evangelicalism is to be tolerated where a corresponding diversity can be demonstrated within Scripture."[62]

By 1976, however, Henry was expressing disappointment that his prophecy was being fulfilled. After briefly outlining his dreams for evangelicalism and some of its successes, he wrote: "While he is still on the loose, and still sounding his roar, the evangelical lion is nonetheless slowly succumbing to confusion about its own identity. The cohesion that American evangelicals had shown in the sixties has been fading in the seventies through multiplied internal disagreements and emerging counterforces."[63] Henry complained, in particular, that evangelical energies were being dissipated by mounting internal tension from two sources: those who "have switched to a somewhat more critical view of Scripture" and those who deplored evangelicalism's lack of sociopolitical engagement.

Henry, himself a supporter of inerrancy, was frustrated nonetheless that the emphasis on inerrancy as an arbiter of evangelical identity squelched the coalition's ability to work together toward spiritual renewal and social reform. He complained that "the somewhat reactionary elevation of inerrancy as the superbadge of evangelical orthodoxy deploys energies to this controversy that evangelicals might better apply to producing comprehensive theological and philosophical works so desperately needed in a time of national and civilizational crisis." Henry was particularly disappointed with the editors at *Christianity Today* (Harold Lindsell, editor in chief) for making inerrancy "a theological weapon with which to drive those evangelicals not adhering to the doctrine into a nonevangelical camp."[64] He noted that reputable evangelicals were arrayed on both sides of the debate. He pointed to Bruce Metzger, a professor at Princeton Theological Seminary; George Ladd, a faculty member at Gordon-Conwell Seminary; and Jack Rogers, a faculty member at Fuller Theological Seminary, as credible scholars who did not support inerrancy and to Harold Ockenga, the president of Gordon-Conwell; Kenneth Kantzer, the dean and vice president of graduate studies at Trinity Evangelical Seminary; J. I. Packer, a professor at Trinity College, Bristol, England; and Harold Lindsell as supporters of inerrancy.

The most widely known supporter of inerrancy was Lindsell. In 1976, while an associate editor at *Christianity Today*, Lindsell published a fiery criticism of the progressive evangelical position, aptly entitled *The Battle for the Bible*. In it he claimed that "a great battle rages today around biblical infallibility among evangelicals. To ignore the battle is perilous. To come to grips with it is necessary. To fail to speak is more than cowardice; it is sinful." Lindsell did not sin in this regard. He argued that the clear tradition in the church for two thousand years had been that the Bible was completely infallible, in other words, "inerrant." Lindsell defined inerrancy as follows:

> The Bible in all of its parts constitutes the written Word of God to man. This Word is free from all error in its original autographs. . . . However limited may have been their knowledge, and however much they may have erred when they were not writing sacred scripture, the authors of scripture, under the guidance of the Holy Spirit, were preserved from making factual, historical, scientific, or other errors.[65]

According to Lindsell, those who hold a less strict definition of biblical authority are on a slippery slope that will lead to the denial of other orthodox doctrines. Traditional beliefs will be "tossed over, discarded with the doctrine of infallibility."[66] He points out that historically, the church excluded from its fold those who were not considered orthodox.

According to Lindsell's logic, anyone who does not hold to full verbal, plenary inspiration is no longer orthodox and should no longer be considered part of the evangelical church.

Lindsell seemed to be responding partly to his struggles while still on the faculty at Fuller Theological Seminary and that led to his, and fellow inerrantists, leaving Fuller. He appeared to be defining evangelicalism in a way that would excise the progressives and limit the movement's overall turn toward more theological openness and social activism. Many of his former colleagues at Fuller assumed that Lindsell was expanding the war against them to push them out of the broader evangelical movement. Lindsell may have lost the battle at Fuller, but he appeared determined to win the war for control of the evangelical coalition.

Many progressives publicly rebutted Lindsell's argument in *Battle for the Bible*. Jack B. Rogers, along with Donald K. McKim, published a lengthy historical study of how the church viewed biblical inspiration. In *The Authority and Interpretation of the Bible*, they agreed with Lindsell that the church had historically accepted the authority of scripture but concluded that Lindsell was anachronistically attributing his own understanding of inspiration to theologians whose comprehension was quite different.[67] Others argued against Lindsell's view on theological and philosophical grounds.[68] Henry refuted Lindsell's use of inerrancy as a theological litmus test of evangelical orthodoxy. In a review of *Battle for the Bible*, Henry made this analysis: "A Bible unencumbered with some of his [Lindsell's] theories and standing on its own invulnerable supports, may be far more powerful than one propped up by retaining walls engineered by resolute evangelicals."[69]

In 1979, Lindsell again took aim at progressives in the evangelical coalition with his next book, *The Bible in the Balance*. Similar to *Battle for the Bible*, in this work Lindsell repeats his contention that one cannot be an evangelical without adhering to inerrancy: "To deny inerrancy is to deny what Jesus believed, taught, and practiced. It is a denial of the lordship of Jesus Christ. And I do not think that he who denies the lordship of Jesus can be an evangelical."[70] Lindsell is careful to note that this does not mean that such people are not Christians as long as they accept other essentials of the faith. Lindsell's distinction between "evangelical" and "Christian" is revealing.[71] It shows that Lindsell was, indeed, using inerrancy as an easy guide to distinguish "evangelicals" from social and theological liberals.

It was not always the case, however, as Lindsell believed, that theological and social liberalism went together. Henry himself was somewhat of an exception to this rule. Though a supporter of inerrancy, Henry also supported some socially liberal views. He was, after all, one of the original signers of the Chicago declaration, with its statement on men's and women's mutual submission. In fact, Henry first became known in 1947 for *The Uneasy Conscience of Modern Fundamentalism.* This tract, attributed to helping usher in postwar evangelicalism, is a call to American evangelicals to reverse their lack of social activism. Throughout his career, Henry prodded evangelicals to be more open in considering social activism, ecumenism, and new intellectual ideas in order to see spiritual renewal in America. He believed that an evangelical faith true to its nineteenth-century inheritance would combine the best of both the liberal social gospel movement and fundamentalist orthodoxy, and because of this combination, it would be attractive to the secular world.

In his later work, *Evangelicals in Search of Identity*, Henry lamented that evangelicals were failing at this task because of their disunity. While he censured conservatives for threatening evangelical unity by their single emphasis on inerrancy, he chided progressive groups such as *The Other Side, Sojourners*, Evangelicals for Social Action, and the Evangelical Women's Caucus for their singular focus on social issues, which fragmented evangelicals into disparate interest groups. He entitled his review of a book on the more progressive evangelicals "Revolt on Evangelical Frontiers," thereby conveying the message that these younger scholars were evangelicals but that they were pushing the boundaries of the movement and drawing energies inward that were destructive to the coalition.[72] He chastised them for being too independent of the larger Christian community, for harboring exaggerated expectations of the sociopolitical arena, and for being committed "programmatically" to a cause rather than to a "comprehensive life-world view."[73] Henry believed that such divisions—between those who consider evangelism to be the church's only task (inerrantists) and those who argue against a personal conversion that ignores social justice (progressives)—divided evangelicalism and, rather than making the movement attractive to the modern world, reduced its effectiveness.

Were Evangelical Feminists Either One?

Two questions arise: just where did biblical feminism fit in the boundary divisions being debated in evangelicalism in the late 1970s and early 1980s, and where did they fit into the American feminist movement?

Were They Evangelical?

The final day of the second Evangelical Women's Caucus conference, held in Pasadena in 1978, was dedicated to a business meeting at which the group adopted its first official set of bylaws under the name Evangelical Women's Caucus, International. The bylaws stated that the caucus's purpose was "to honor and glorify the Lord Jesus Christ by engaging in religious, charitable, educational, and/or cultural activities in order to: a. Present God's teaching on male-female equality to the whole body of Christ's church. b. Call both women and men to mutual submission and active discipleship." They also included a statement of faith:

> We believe that God, the Creator and Ruler of all, has been self-revealed as the Trinity. We believe that God created humankind, female and male, in the divine image, for fellowship with God and one another. We further believe that because of human sinful disobedience, the right relationship with God was shattered, with a consequent disruption of all other relationships. We believe that God in love has made possible a new beginning through the Incarnation, in the life, death and resurrection of Jesus Christ, who was, and is, truly divine and truly human. We affirm a personal relationship with Jesus Christ as Savior and Lord. We believe that under Christ's headship and through the work of the Holy Spirit we are freed to exercise our gifts responsibly in our churches, home and society. We believe that the Bible which bears witness of Christ is the Word of God, inspired by the Holy Spirit, and is the infallible guide and final authority for Christian faith and life. We believe the church is the community of women and men who have been divinely called to fellowship with God and one another to seek and do God's will, looking forward to God's coming glorious kingdom.[74]

With this statement of faith, with which all EWC members were asked to agree, biblical feminists placed themselves into the progressive wing of the evangelical coalition. They adhered to a modified view of biblical inerrancy, infallibility, that many progressives held. They insisted on personal regeneration and supported the basic doctrines and creeds of the Christian church. In addition, many individual caucus members saw themselves as witnesses to secular feminists about the freedom that Christ brings to women. In this way, the Evangelical Women's Caucus shared the mission of evangelism that conservative evangelicals emphasized. Also, both the more conservative and the more liberal evangelical feminists strongly emphasized the Bible, its authority in the life of the believer, and its proper interpretation. Hardesty, for example, described the difference between feminism and biblical feminism in this way: "We believe in the Bible's authority and begin with what Scripture has to say about us and about God."[75] Someone like Carl Henry might have viewed biblical feminists in this way: they diverged on an issue on which there was a plurality of opinions. Since they started from the authority of scripture and then applied it to the contemporary situation, they should be "honored as evangelical." Henry might have wondered just how important this highly debated issue was, but he still could acknowledge their identity as evangelicals.

Still, evangelical feminism seemed to be helping fracture the evangelical coalition, as Carl F. H. Henry feared. Even within biblical feminism itself, two groups appeared to be forming. Those who were more liberal considered some of the apostle Paul's writing to be sexist and culturally conditioned. Others, who were more conservative, thought that historical criticism showed that all of Paul's writings were liberating for women. Within the broader evangelical coalition, the feminists' emphasis on a particular sociopolitical issue of much concern in contemporary American culture (women's roles), the widespread use of new hermeneutical methods, and the acceptance of limited definitions of biblical inerrancy were pushing the boundaries of evangelicalism beyond its previous limits.

Liberal evangelical feminists, specifically Virginia Mollenkott, further pushed the boundaries of evangelicalism because of what was, in reality, an awkward fit with the movement. For although she claimed a location within evangelicalism, she had as many—or more—ties, socially and theologically, to organizations outside the coalition. Certainly her background in the fundamentalist movement located her within the historical tradition of American revivalism shared by many evangelicals. Also, she asserted a belief in the traditional doctrines of the Christian community: the authority of scripture, the efficacy of Christ's atonement on the cross, the necessity of a personal salvation experience, and the importance of evangelism and a transformed life. Yet when her writing is analyzed, her lack of connection to the broader evangelical movement becomes evident. The authors she cites were either in the biblical feminist movement or nonevangelicals. For example, in addressing sex role stereotyping, she relies on feminist psychologist Phyllis Chesler and the poet and author Adrienne Rich. She also cites works from sociologist John and his wife Letha Scanzoni (who had specialized in writing sociology before she became well known for her writings on biblical feminism), who were also her friends in the biblical feminist movement. Mollenkott turns to Scanzoni and Hardesty, as well as another associate both in literature and biblical feminism, Margaret Hannay, in sorting through issues of gender in the godhead. She also cites Donald Dayton's work on Christian women in the earlier women's movement. Perhaps the key influence in Mollenkott's thinking on Pauline texts and biblical interpretation was Paul Jewett. In several articles, Mollenkott mentions her first meeting with him and the important role he played in her writing *Women, Men and the Bible*. It appears, then, that Mollenkott's influences were not primarily traditional evangelicals.

In fact, she had had little exposure to institutional evangelicalism. Her background was in fundamentalism, and when she moved out of that tradition, she entered the Episcopal Church, not generally considered an evangelical denomination. In a later essay that Mollenkott wrote for an edited collection on the struggles of women in the church, she indicates that much of her experience and concept of church came from the EWC and her biblical feminist friends, not from any evangelical denomination or tradition.[76] Mollenkott did write for *Christianity Today* in the early to mid-1970s and for several progressive evangelical journals, *Sojourners*, *The Other Side*, and *Daughters of Sarah*. However, she also wrote for the mainline journal *Christian Century* and did so more frequently as time passed.

In her article "An Evangelical Confronts the Goddess," Mollenkott states that her experience with goddess worship changed her mind about the use of language. This illustrates the difference between Mollenkott's ties to evangelicalism and those of other evangelical feminists. That realization was important to her because "for evangelical feminists . . . one of the surest signs of biblical inspiration is the fact that despite patriarchy, when the Bible is read contextually, a theme of male-female equality undeniably emerges."[77] One of the things she learned when she gave more thoughtful attention to this type of spirituality, Mollenkott writes, was the power of symbolic language and ritual. Thus she rejects the use of the term *goddess* as being idolatrous. That simply replaces worship of a male God with a female one. She does concede, though, that "we Christians can be convincing about our faith only if we are willing to refer to the God as 'she' just as often as 'he.'"[78]

Although other evangelical feminists also were concerned with issues of inclusive language, they handled the topic quite differently than Mollenkott did. For example, in 1979, Berkeley and Alvera Mickelsen wrote an article for *Christianity Today* in which they decried improper translations of the biblical text.[79] The difference between Mollenkott and the Mickelsens' handling of the issue would have been quite noticeable to most evangelicals. The origin of the Mickelsens' interest in inclusive language came from a comparative study of the original Greek text of the New Testament alongside several modern translations: the King James, Revised Standard, and New International Version. Through their examination, they found "traces of male chauvinism in Bible translations we use."[80] Plural pronouns were translated as masculine and the like. To most evangelicals, the Mickelsens' starting point from scripture would have been much more acceptable than Mollenkott's beginning from an analysis of what they would define as pagan culture. But then, most evangelicals probably did not see Mollenkott's article, since it was printed in a mainline journal, and the Mickelsens' was published in *Christianity Today*.

Mollenkott also had few ties to traditional evangelical organizations like Bible schools (such as the Moody Bible Institute), seminaries (Fuller Theological Seminary, Gordon Conwell, Trinity Evangelical Divinity School, Dallas Theological Seminary), or parachurch groups (InterVarsity, Youth for Christ). Professionally, Mollenkott was a member of the Modern Language Association of America, the Milton Society of America, and the Conference on Christianity and Literature (to which Margaret Hannay also belonged). Only one of these organizations, the Conference on Christianity and Literature, had ties to institutional evangelicalism. In her concern about inclusive language, Mollenkott worked with the National Council of Churches (an institution against which the National Association of Evangelicals was founded as a direct alternative) on an inclusive-language lectionary, which most evangelicals rejected. All in all, Mollenkott's primary connections to evangelicalism came as a Christian writer and through relationships with progressive evangelicals, specifically with those interested in the role of women, not through a broad network of evangelical institutions.

Early on, Mollenkott had her own doubts about whether she was a genuine evangelical. After the first conference on feminism and evangelicalism at Denver Seminary, at which Mollenkott gave the keynote address, a pastor's wife upset her with the accusation that she was not an evangelical. Mollenkott said that it was Paul Jewett and Letha Scanzoni who "loved me back into thinking of myself as something of an evangelical."[81] After that early struggle with her evangelical identity, Mollenkott did not waver. Thus, when the EWC began discussing in the early 1980s about whether to change their name to something more inclusive, like "ecumenical," Mollenkott insisted on retaining "evangelical." The term best expressed the heritage of the organization as well as their continued emphasis on the importance of the Bible as a central solution to the problems of inequality, oppression, and abuse that women faced.

Were They Feminists?

At its first national conference in 1967, the National Organization for Women adopted a women's "bill of rights" calling for an equal rights amendment to the U.S. Constitution, the enforcement of laws banning sex discrimination in employment, the right to maternity leave in the workplace and in Social Security benefits, tax deductions for home and child care expenses for working parents, the establishment of child care centers, equal and unsegregated education for women and men, equal job opportunities for women and men, and reproductive rights for women. At that time, NOW's practical definition of equality for women was one of equal opportunity.

With their emphasis on equality between men and women in both public and private spheres, up to this time biblical feminists fit into a liberal feminist model.[82] Because they reinterpreted biblical texts to show that both women and men were created equal in God's eyes and that both were fully capable of maintaining any role or function in the home, church, or society, feminist evangelicals were able to espouse equal opportunity for women. Like their secular counterparts, biblical feminists sought to mend the split between the public role of men and the private sphere of women. As Christian women, this meant urging men to become active in the home through egalitarian marriages and shared parenting, and women, to become active in the public life of the church through taking on leadership responsibilities, including ordained ministry. It also involved working actively toward the ratification of the equal rights amendment, often times alongside NOW.

An article by Mollenkott in the *Journal of Psychology and Theology* in the 1970s highlights the liberal emphasis of biblical feminism.[83] After identifying patriarchy as the problem women faced, Mollenkott addressed Sigmund Freud's famous question: "What does woman want?" Mollenkott responded that first of all, evangelical women wanted honest, respectful relationships between the sexes, not ones in which women were encouraged by their clergy to manipulate men under the guise of "submission." They needed the equalization of financial opportunities through education, employment, and tax, pension, and Social Security reform. Women also sought control over their lives and labor. Mollenkott thus suggested a change in the legal attitude that "the husband and wife are one, and that one is the husband," that women should have the right to combine family and career and to have a legal abortion, and that prostitutes and their customers should be given equal treatment. Even her suggestions as to how the church could maintain credibility with women in the 1970s focused on leveling the playing field. The church should adjust its biblical interpretation to emphasize male and female equality and the spiritual, nongendered, nature of God.[84]

But the secular feminist movement was moving beyond mere equality of opportunity. By the 1970s, the hegemony of middle-class, white, liberal feminism and NOW was being challenged by nonwhite, underprivileged, Marxist, and radical feminists. Radical feminists specifically questioned the role that sexuality, and its control, played in women's oppression, including compulsive heterosexuality.[85] Radical feminists believed that the source of women's oppression was due to more than simply socialized gender roles. It was based on the abuse and control of women's sexuality. These feminists sought to overthrow the patriarchal power structure that was maintained through institutions like the family, the church, and compulsory heterosexuality.

As a fledgling movement in the early 1970s, evangelical feminism was only beginning to address these issues. Hardesty and Mollenkott had discussed lesbianism in a seminar on "Woman to Woman Relationships" at the first national EWC conference in response to an audience member's question, and Hardesty had, as mentioned earlier, briefly touched on homosexuality in her chapter on singleness in *All We're Meant to Be*. Scanzoni had publicly addressed the issue of homosexuality more than any other evangelical feminist before the mid-1980s, in part due to her professional partnership with her husband John, a marriage and family sociologist. Together they wrote several books and articles on marriage, family, and sexuality. Alone, Letha also wrote several articles and books on the topic of sexuality, some that touch on homosexuality. It was on account of this expertise that when Mollenkott and Scanzoni teamed up to write a book on social concerns of interest to biblical feminists that Mollenkott asked Scanzoni to write the chapter on homosexuality. The book, still coauthored by Mollenkott, was eventually limited to the topic of homosexuality. *Is the Homosexual My Neighbor?* came out in 1978 and caused a stir in the evangelical community.[86] Mostly, though, evangelical feminists ignored or distanced themselves from lesbianism rather than questioning compulsory heterosexuality during the 1970s and early 1980s.

It may have been because of the attacks against biblical feminists from within the evangelical subculture that evangelical feminists tried to maintain a united front in spite of growing theological differences, as seen in the work of Virginia Mollenkott versus Patricia Gundry. But there were differences, particularly in their understanding of biblical authority. The more liberal evangelical feminists resorted more often to the argument that passages that appeared to subordinate women were concessions to the culture of their day and were not binding for all times. More conservative evangelical feminists, however, thought that such a solution to problem passages gave up too much of the authority of scripture by denying its authority whenever it contradicted contemporary mores. The theological work and social agenda of both more conservative and liberal evangelical feminists helped stretch the boundaries of coalition to make newer hermeneutical methods and limited definitions of inerrancy more acceptable.

4

Is the Homosexual
My Neighbor?
The Crisis in Biblical Feminism,
1984–1986

In 1978, Letha Scanzoni and Virginia Mollenkott teamed up to publish *Is the Homosexual My Neighbor?* They began by stating, "The question that makes up the title of this book shouldn't be necessary" because the Bible clearly indicates that every human being is our neighbor, including the homosexual.[1] Their goal was to counter Christian prejudice by presenting new biblical, sociological, and psychological data on homosexuality and to propose how the church could be more welcoming to homosexual persons. This book—one of the first by Christians (including Catholic, evangelical, and mainline Protestant denominations) on the topic of homosexuality—sparked a considerable amount of discussion in the evangelical community, so much so that *Christianity Today* named homosexuality the issue of the year. The topic, and the way it was raised in the EWC, eventually fractured the biblical feminist movement and led to the creation of an alternative organization, Christians for Biblical Equality (CBE).

At root, the disagreement among biblical feminists was over conflicting views of biblical authority. Scanzoni and Mollenkott argued that the practice of homosexuality was compatible with biblical Christianity. To prove this, they gave greater weight to the authority of reason and experience, but many biblical feminists thought that this was going too far toward denying the unique authority of scripture in determining doctrine. Homosexuality thus became a watershed issue, as it revealed the differences beneath the surface of feminist solidarity in the evangelical community, particularly in relation to the issue of biblical authority.

Is the Homosexual My Neighbor?

At the time of Scanzoni and Mollenkott's writing, little had been published on the topic of homosexuality from a Christian perspective. Father
John McNeill's *The Church and the Homosexual*, released in 1976, was
an exception and, thus, one of the few Christian sources to which Scanzoni and Mollenkott could refer when they wrote *Is the Homosexual My
Neighbor?* In *The Church and the Homosexual*, McNeill questions three
traditional Christian views of homosexuality. First, he rejects the belief
that God creates every human being to be heterosexual and that therefore
homosexuality is a sickness or a sin. Instead, he argues from a psychological basis that God creates people with a great variety of sexualities.
Second, using sociological studies, he proposes that gay people are not a
menace to society but make a positive contribution by helping the heterosexual community reach a fuller understanding of themselves by challenging dehumanizing sexual-identity images. Third, he tries to show
from a biblical standpoint that "constructive love" between two homosexuals is not sinful or outside God's plan.

Following McNeill's argument, Scanzoni and Mollenkott asserted that
scientific and biblical data show that some people have exclusively homosexual drives. Because this cannot be changed, the most Christian solution is a committed, permanent, homosexual relationship. Since their
targeted audience was evangelicals, the center of Scanzoni and Mollenkott's book focused on biblical exegesis. Few scriptural passages deal
directly with homosexuality. Genesis 19 and Leviticus 18:22 and 20:13
address the topic in the Hebrew scriptures, and Romans 1:26–27, 1
Corinthians 6:9–10, and 1 Timothy 1:9–10 discuss it in the New Testament. Of these, only Romans 1 can be interpreted as addressing the issue
of lesbianism.

Homosexuality according to Genesis

Scanzoni and Mollenkott begin by taking a fresh look at Genesis 19, the
account of the destruction of the city of Sodom. The story begins in chapter 18, verse 1, when "the Lord appeared to Abraham." In verse 2,
"Abraham looked up and saw three men," the implication being that God
and two angels appeared to Abraham in the form of men. After Abraham
showed the visitors hospitality, God told him that Sarah would bear a

child and that God intended to destroy Sodom and Gomorrah because "their sin is exceedingly grave" (v. 20). At this point, the other two "men" turned away and went toward Sodom," presumably to fulfill God's intention (v. 22). Abraham, however, bargained and convinced God to agree not to destroy Sodom if ten righteous men could be found in the city.

The opening lines of chapter 19 reveal what the reader has already assumed, that the two "men" who have just left Abraham and God are angels: "The two angels arrived at Sodom in the evening" (19:1). It is here that the reader is shown an illustration of Sodom's excessive sin. Lot, Abraham's nephew, is the first to meet the angels at the town gate, and he insists that they stay at his own home. But before the visitors can go to sleep, "all the men from every part of the city of Sodom—both young and old—surrounded the house," seeking to have sex with Lot's visitors (vv. 4–5). Lot refuses to give up his guests, instead offering his two virgin daughters, but the men of Sodom refuse. On the verge of breaking down the doors to Lot's home, all the men are blinded by the angels, who usher Lot and his family out of the city just before its destruction.

Most evangelicals, and most people vaguely familiar with this story, believe that the sin for which Sodom was destroyed was the sin of "sodomy." Scanzoni and Mollenkott, however, looked at Jesus' use of the story of Sodom's destruction to come to a different conclusion. In Luke 10, Jesus sends out his disciples to prepare the way in each town he was about to visit. When giving them instructions, Jesus tells them:

> But whatever city you enter and they do not receive you, go out into its streets and say, "Even the dust of your city which clings to our feet, we wipe off in protest against you; yet, be sure of this, that the kingdom of God has come near." I say to you, it will be more tolerable in that day for Sodom, than for that city. (10:10–12)

Scanzoni and Mollenkott deduce from this passage that the sin Jesus condemned was a lack of hospitality. Jesus' comparison of the judgments against unfriendly towns and against Sodom illustrated, they believe, that the grave sin of Sodom was one of inhospitality, not homosexuality or sodomy.

Many evangelicals, however, disagreed with their interpretation. One was Don Williams. Williams, a professor at Fuller Seminary, participated at the second EWC conference in Pasadena as session leader for a workshop on Christian responses to homosexuality. This was to complement one on the same topic led by Scanzoni and Mollenkott. In his session Williams emphasized that the Bible was opposed to homosexuality.[2] In a review of *Is the Homosexual My Neighbor?* Williams states that Scanzoni and Mollenkott's book contains "polemical apologetics carrying out biased exegesis, selective data and fallacious conclusions."[3] One illustration of this, he claims, is Scanzoni and Mollenkott's assertion that "some Bible scholars" did not believe that the intent of the men of Sodom in assaulting Lot's visitors was sexual.[4] These scholars, according to Scanzoni and Mollenkott, pointed out that the Hebrew word translated as "intercourse" could also be translated as "to know." Thus, they understood Genesis 19 to mean that the men of Sodom merely wanted to examine the strangers' credentials. According to Williams, only D. S. Bailey, writing in 1955, had ever held with that view,[5] and Scanzoni and Mollenkott did cite only Bailey in their footnote. Conversely, McNeill indicated in his book that the purpose of the men of Sodom was sexual. In the second edition of their book, Scanzoni and Mollenkott revised their views, adding that Lot had failed to get permission from the town elders to entertain visitors. This was a theory they found in the writings of the social historian John Boswell, whose work sought to uncover the long history of homosexuality in the church.[6] In this way, Scanzoni and Mollenkott implied that both Boswell and Bailey supported the interpretation that the men of Sodom merely sought to examine Lot's visitors.

Williams's complaint seems minor, considering that Scanzoni and Mollenkott agreed that the inhospitable treatment of the visitors to Sodom was the aggressive act of violent rape. Scanzoni and Mollenkott claim that the gang of men was not interested primarily in sex, however, for if they had been, Lot's daughters would have been an acceptable alternative. Instead, it was an issue of control. The men of Sodom tried to humiliate and exert power over Lot's guests through violent rape. Scanzoni and Mollenkott compare this with what happens in prison populations when new inmates are attacked. The aggressors do not see their actions as homosexual but as methods of control.

Levitical Laws on Homosexuality

Scanzoni and Mollenkott addressed the Levitical passages prohibiting homosexuality by locating them in their literary genre, the purity laws, and showing that these codes were culturally bound and no longer in force. In

Leviticus, the purity laws enjoin strict behavior concerning food, clothing, and relationships with paid laborers and neighbors. Both chapters 18 and 20 list appropriate sexual partners. They prohibit both various incestual relationships and some socially inappropriate ones. For example, they forbid sexual relations between a father and his daughter-in-law and between a man with both a mother and her daughter. Most of these injunctions are upheld socially, if not legally maintained, even in contemporary society.

But not all are. Verse 19 forbids sex with a menstruating woman. This and many of the nonsexual codes no longer carry the force of law. Christians are no longer prohibited from engaging in sexual relations with their spouse during menstruation. Nor must they refrain from wearing clothing made with two kinds of yarn (Leviticus 19:19), and probably few Christians refuse to eat the meat of animals considered to be unclean (at least not for reasons of ritual purity). For Christians, this last code was invalidated by a mandate from God through a vision given to Peter. In Acts 10:9–23, God three times showed Peter a host of unclean animals and told him to eat them. Each time Peter said, "Surely not, Lord! I have never eaten anything impure or unclean." God replied, "Do not call anything impure that God has made clean." According to Scanzoni and Mollenkott, this vision is a metaphor for how the church should deal with homosexuality. Since many other purity laws are no longer in force, the injunction against homosexuality should not be, either.

But should the ban against homosexuality be considered more like the laws against incest and adultery, which are still in effect? Scanzoni and Mollenkott contend that it should not because the purity laws were given for the purposes of ceremonial cleanliness and the avoidance of idolatry and also to distinguish Israel from its pagan neighbors, who practiced cultic rituals that used male prostitutes. Scanzoni and Mollenkott argue that the injunction not to "lie with a man as one lies with a woman" was really a prohibition on participating in those religious rituals that involved male prostitutes. They claim that "most scholars agree that in the fertility religions of Israel's neighbors, male-cult prostitutes were employed for homosexual acts."[7]

Critics of Scanzoni and Mollenkott's analysis pointed out that D. S. Bailey (one of Scanzoni and Mollenkott's sources) opposed this view because homosexual relations would be meaningless in a fertility ritual that had an exclusively heterosexual rationale.[8] Boswell also disagreed with this notion, the root of which could be found in the King James version of the Bible, which mistranslated the word *sodomite* in discussions of idolatrous practices (Deuteronomy 23:17, 1 Kings 14:24, etc.).[9] In a later edition of their book, published in 1994, Scanzoni and Mollenkott acknowledge Boswell's new evidence. They then cite another expert, George Edwards, who argued that "the possibility" of male cult prostitutes could not be ruled out entirely, since ritual sex was a symbolic union and because the point of the purity codes was to outlaw idolatrous practices in general, not just homosexual acts.[10]

Other evangelicals disagreed with Scanzoni and Mollenkott's argument that the purity laws were culturally limited. Several reviewers suggested that the prohibition on homosexuality was based on the order of creation.[11] If that were indeed the case, a strong argument could be made that the prohibition against homosexuality was still valid for modern times. Williams makes just this argument in his own book on the topic of homosexuality, *The Bond That Breaks*. Before determining how scripture judges homosexuality, Williams begins with a biblical perspective of human sexuality in general, which he finds in the opening chapters of Genesis. In the creation accounts, Williams claims that God's creation of humankind as male and female and not the blessing of marriage determines human beings' proper sexual relationship. Relying on Karl Barth, Williams argues that humans were created as male or female to relate to each other as male and female. He further contends that the purity code against homosexuality reflects this concern with proper sexual ordering and that the New Testament affirms it. Using this perspective, he then interprets the sin of Sodom not only as a violent, sexual attack but also as a challenge to God's order for human sexuality. Homosexuality, Williams concludes, is a sin because it is an abuse of human freedom, an attempt to live outside God's established order. A proper, pastoral approach to homosexuality calls for homosexual Christians' repentance, restoration, and renewed obedience.

Creation and a Theology of Human Sexuality

Williams's beginning with a theology of human sexuality differs from that of Scanzoni and Mollenkott, who did not discuss the creation accounts in their original edition. In 1994, their second, updated and revised, edition of *Is the Homosexual My Neighbor?* does address Genesis and several other criticisms. Overall, this strengthened their work, since by this time they had many other studies to support their arguments, such as Boswell's groundbreaking work *Christianity, Social Tolerance, and Homosexuality*, Scroggs's *The New Testament and Homosexuality*, William Countryman's *Dirt, Greed, and Sex*, and George Edwards's *Gay/Lesbian Liberation*.[12] Scanzoni and Mollenkott's response to Williams's criticism that they failed to develop a comprehensive theory of human sexuality is brief. In a two-page addition, they compare using Genesis to develop a theory of human sexuality with using it to develop a scientific theory of creation, and they argue that the creation accounts are not a scientific text and are intended to teach neither the mechanics of how the world was created nor proper sexual relations. Instead, their purpose is to teach how the world was created (by God) and how humanity came into existence. Scanzoni and Mollenkott argue that "in order to fulfill the second purpose, it was necessary for the first couple to be both heterosexual and fertile." Nothing more, they maintain, can be read into the text without violating its genre and literary style.

The Pauline Passages on Homosexuality

In addition to questioning Scanzoni and Mollenkott's theology of human sexuality, Tim Stafford and Don Williams also took issue with their hermeneutic to determine cultural relativity. Scanzoni and Mollenkott based their opinion that the purity laws were no longer in force in part on their view that the New Testament does not make these particular codes normative. It is silent on the issue of homosexuality. Before accepting that conclusion, however, one would have to agree with Scanzoni and Mollenkott that when the New Testament does mention homosexuality, it does not prohibit committed, monogamous, homosexual relationships.

Romans 1:26–28 states:

For this reason, God gave them over to degrading passions; for their women exchanged the natural function for that which is unnatural, and in the same way also the men abandoned the natural function of the woman and burned in their desire towards one another, men with men committing indecent acts and receiving in their own persons the due penalty of their error. And just as they did not see fit to acknowledge God any longer, God gave them over to a depraved mind, to do those things which are not proper. (NAS)

This passage comes in the midst of Paul's argument that human beings have turned from God and pursued their own evil desires: "For although they knew God, they neither glorified him as God nor gave thanks to him. . . . Therefore God gave them over in the sinful desires of their hearts" (vv. 21a, 24a). In addressing Paul's negative reference to homosexuality in this passage (the only one that explicitly refers to lesbianism), Scanzoni and Mollenkott first point out that Paul's line of reasoning concludes in chapter 2, verse 1: "You, therefore, have no excuse, you who pass judgment on someone else, for at whatever point you judge the other, you are condemning yourself, because you who pass judgment do the same things." Amid the sins that Paul disapprovingly catalogs are greed, envy, hate, gossip, arrogance, and disobeying one's parents. Thus, the full context of this passage indicates that Paul's main point is not to pass judgment on one category of people—homosexuals—but to show that all people are alienated from God. "All have sinned" (Romans 3:23) in one way or another.

In addition, Scanzoni and Mollenkott argue that Paul is not condemning love between two people who are homosexual by nature but is condemning homosexual activity performed by heterosexuals fulfilling their appetites for sexual adventure. They claim that Paul would not have had a concept of someone who was homosexual by nature. That is, in his culture everyone was considered heterosexual, although some people pursued their desires through pederasty and male prostitution. Scanzoni and Mollenkott claim that modern scientific evidence proves that some people are exclusively homosexual, that for them natural relations are with members of the same sex. They conclude therefore that Paul is condemning abusive sexual behaviors performed out of lust, not the expression of mature love between adults in a committed, permanent relationship. Verses 26 through 28 affirm their analysis, they assert, since its focus is on "unnaturalness" and a desire to avoid the acknowledgment of God, which do not fit the committed, sincere, homosexual Christian.

Although they agreed with Scanzoni and Mollenkott's interpretation of Paul's thinking in Romans 1, many evangelicals could not agree with their conclusion that Paul also was not condemning homosexual love.[13] In his exegesis of Romans 1, Richard Hays essentially agrees with Scanzoni and Mollenkott (and with John Boswell, from whom, he contends, they borrowed many of their arguments by way of John McNeill's work) that the text says nothing about the concept of "sexual orientation."[14] He draws an altogether different conclusion, however, arguing that it is anachronistic to apply such an idea to Paul. Rather, the concept of constitutional heterosexuality or homosexuality is a modern notion and did not exist in the ancient world. Thus to suggest that Paul is condemning homosexual acts only when performed by a constitutional heterosexual ("activity" versus "love") introduces a distinction completely foreign to the apostle. Hays quotes Bailey to support his position: "St. Paul's words can only be understood in the sense which he himself would have attached to them, without introducing distinctions which he did not intend, and which would have been unintelligible to him."[15]

Stafford, however, thought that Paul may have been aware of lasting, loving homosexual relationships, since homosexuality was commonly accepted in Roman society. Stafford suggests that the apostle would have mentioned any exceptions to a condemnation of homosexuality if he had thought there should be any. He agrees with Scanzoni and Mollenkott that the main point of Romans 1 was not to condemn homosexuality but disagrees by concluding that idolatry is censured, of which homosexuality is evidence.

A later author, Robin Scroggs, agreed with Scanzoni and Mollenkott that the New Testament was silent on homosexuality as it is known in modern America, but he used a different argument. In his 1983 book *The New Testament and Homosexuality*, Scroggs postulates that in Greek and Roman society, homosexuality was solely understood as pederasty. He contends, therefore, that the few passages restricting homosexuality do so in order to protect children from abusive adult practices. These passages do not refer to the practice of monogamous, consenting relationships between adults at all, and the Bible was silent on homosexuality as we know it. Scroggs nonetheless admits, "Much of my argument depends upon the judgment frequently stated above, that the only model of male homosexuality was pederasty. . . . Have I fairly presented all the evidence, or have I missed some that could call my conclusion into question?"[16]

Catherine Kroeger, a Patristic scholar and biblical feminist, and her husband Richard responded that indeed Scroggs had missed some significant evidence. In their research, the Kroegers claim to have found a wealth of information showing that pederasty was not the only prevailing model of homosexuality, that the model also included consenting adult, homosexual relationships. Hence, Paul's prohibition on homosexuality is not merely a matter of cultural limitations but is a normative principle, and the Bible restricts all homosexual practices.

Scientific Evidence in Support of Homosexuality

After concluding that the Bible does not discuss the issue of homosexuality between consenting adults, Scanzoni and Mollenkott turn to scientific evidence to prove their case: "Since the Bible is silent about the homosexual condition, those who want to understand it must rely on the findings of modern behavioral science research and on the testimony of those persons who are themselves homosexual."[17]

The heart of Scanzoni and Mollenkott's argument is that scientific research has proved that a homosexual orientation is involuntary and irreversible. They relied on research from the Kinsey Institute showing that people fall into a continuum of heterosexual to homosexual behavior. At each end of the spectrum are those with an exclusive sexual expression and orientation. Sociologists, Scanzoni and Mollenkott observe, have shown that those people with an exclusive sexual orientation are extremely resistant to change. This theory suggests that homosexuality is a variant, not a deviant, form of human sexuality. To understand this, Scanzoni and Mollenkott find helpful the comparison with being left-handed. Much like left-handedness, homosexuality is probably both innate and learned, they argue, and should be no more stigmatized than being left-handed is.

This was a turn in their argument with which many evangelicals could not agree. Most accepted the scientific evidence indicating that homosexuality was at least partly innate. But they did not agree that it therefore cleared homosexuals from all responsibility for their actions. Mary Stewart van Leeuwen, a professor of psychology and biblical feminist, arrived at the same conclusion that sexuality is partly learned and partly innate, but with different implications. In her book *Gender and Grace*, van Leeuwen states her view of human sexuality by quoting Lewis Smedes in *Sex for Christians*:

> Sexuality as part of God's image . . . "is the human drive toward intimate communion." More than a mere physical itch that needs scratching, it urges us "to experience the other, to trust the other, and to be trusted by [that other person], to enter the other's life by entering the vital embrace of his or her body."[18]

Van Leeuwen maintains that biological predisposition does not take away human responsibility. Research has shown that there are "certain critical periods when the mind is . . . primed for fixing certain sexual patterns," at which time gender orientation may go awry.[19] Instead of left-handedness, therefore, van Leeuwen compares the development of homosexuality with that of language acquisition: "Whatever its causal origins, homosexual orientation is often acquired . . . at a fairly young age. And, as with second language learning, the longer one waits to attempt redirection, the more difficult the process."[20] She does not accept that homosexuality cannot, therefore, be unlearned. Although it may be difficult to unlearn, but it is possible and desirable, given the Bible's commands.

Reviews of the book were mixed, especially concerning Scanzoni and Mollenkott's hermeneutical method. Kay Lindskoog, who reviewed the book for the *Wittenburg Door*, had only praise. She addressed the aspect of hermeneutics and biblical authority simply by stating that Scanzoni and Mollenkott "are loyal to the Bible" and did not "take Public Opinion as the voice of God."[21] Lindskoog meant that public opinion was against homosexuality, and so Scanzoni and Mollenkott were listening to God by affirming it. Tim Stafford, who reviewed the book in *Christianity Today*, thought that Scanzoni and Mollenkott did uphold evangelical hermeneutics despite his disagreement with their conclusions. But Don Williams, writing in *Eternity*, called their work "dangerous for the uninitiated" because of the authors' skewed hermeneutic. (These reviews seem almost the opposite of what one would have expected. *Christianity Today* was the more conservative journal, and *Eternity* had previously printed several articles by biblical feminists, including Scanzoni and Mollenkott.)

In his own book on homosexuality, *The Bond That Breaks*, Williams organizes his argument in much the same way as Scanzoni and Mollenkott had. After recounting his personal, pastoral experience in dealing with homosexual Christians, he analyzes four social/scientific views, three theological views (Barth, a traditionalist on the topic; Thielicke, a moderate; and McNeill, accepting), and the biblical record. He concludes that there is too much conflicting evidence provided by science and experience (many Christians recounted stories of their healing from homosexuality) to rely on those sources to settle the matter of how the church should view homosexuality. For his authority, Williams claims the biblical record, not behavioral science as he believed Scanzoni and Mollenkott had done. He explains: "We can never depend on observation leading us to divine order. Rather, we must let the revelation of God guide us in our observation of the world around us."[22]

Christian Ethics and Homosexuality

After evaluating the evidence—scientific, theological, anecdotal, and biblical—Scanzoni and Mollenkott conclude that the compassionate,
"neighborly" response by the church toward exclusively homosexual
persons is the acceptance of same-sex committed unions. They cite ethi-
cists Helmut Thielicke and Lewis Smedes, both respected by evangelicals,
to support their suggestion. Although neither gives quite the unconditional approval of homosexual unions that Scanzoni and Mollenkott do
(and they fail to mention this in Thielicke's case), both Thielicke and
Smedes nonetheless accept the argument for full acceptance by emphasizing compassionate pastoral counseling.

Along with Berkouwer, Thielicke is considered by some to be one of
Europe's most influential theologians among evangelicals. In *The Ethics
of Sex*, Thielicke understands sexuality as divinely intended to be heterosexual and so does not consider homosexuality to be merely a variant
form of human sexuality but a perverted form—although not a sin.[23] A
"sickness" would better describe the phenomenon. He also indicates that
the scriptures had enough interpretive problems to leave room for a re-
examination of the topic. For example, it could be considered significant
that Paul refers to homosexuality illustratively rather than substantively
in Romans 1. Thielicke's question then is how should a pastor counsel a
homosexual Christian about the practice, or outward expression, of his
or her sexuality? Thielicke concludes that as an aberration, homosexuality is not consciously chosen and therefore is ethically neutral. Pastoral
counsel should encourage homosexual Christians to seek healing first. If
that does not work, which Thielicke recognized was likely, they should
become celibate. But since celibacy is a special calling of God and is based
on an act of free will, the Christian community cannot demand celibacy
of a homosexual who remains unhealed. At that point, the pastor should
counsel the homosexual to seek a life partner as the "optimal ethical potential of sexual self-realization."[24]

Writing in *Sex for Christians*, Smedes comes to a similar conclusion.
He considers homosexuality to be a distortion of the channel in which
human sexuality is meant to be given full expression. This does not mean,
however, that Christians can come to any quick conclusions about how
best to minister to homosexuals. In an article in the *Reformed Journal*,
Smedes offers several ideas about homosexual behavior.[25] Among them
are his beliefs that (1) "the question of whether or not a homosexual per-

son is responsible for his or her sexual orientation is not pertinent to the question of the rightness of homosexual behavior," (2) "sufferings endured unfairly by homosexual people are not a reason for moral approval of homosexual activity," and (3) the fact "that personal relationships between people in homosexual union can be loving and enduring does not determine whether the sexual nature of the union is morally right." Smedes then suggests that homosexuals seek divine healing or modification of their behavior. However, if—and only if—those options prove impossible, homosexuals should seek to live an "optimum moral life within a deplorable situation" rather than live a life of chaos.[26]

Many other evangelicals, like van Leeuwen, Stafford, and Williams, disagree that homosexuality is irreversible. As mentioned earlier, van Leeuwen believed that while difficult to unlearn, sexual behavior is a trait that can be altered. Williams marshaled scientific evidence to show that it could be. He disparaged Scanzoni and Mollenkott's unwillingness to consider anything but a Freudian psychological model, which enabled them to ignore more recent theories that homosexuality arises in early puberty. He also cited a 1977 survey of 2,500 psychiatrists in which 69 percent responded that homosexuality was a pathological adaptation, not a normal variation.[27] Stafford argued that even if homosexuality were apparently irreversible, celibacy was the only other biblically condoned, morally acceptable option. He disputed Thielicke's premise that celibacy is truly an act of free will. He pointed out that many Christian singles remain celibate who, while they would gladly give up their calling, had used their status to further God's kingdom.

Biblical Authority and Homosexuality

There thus exists a range of evangelical views on dealing with the issue of homosexuality and with homosexuals in the church. Robert Johnston proposed a typology to describe the various positions being developed on this topic: rejecting-punitive, rejecting-nonpunitive, qualified acceptance, and full acceptance.[28] Anita Bryant and the Florida campaign, along with ministers who reviled homosexuals and denied them human dignity, typified the rejecting and punitive stance. Williams was used to illustrate the rejecting-nonpunitive group. Johnston considered Thielicke and Smedes among those who gave qualified acceptance and Scanzoni and Mollenkott, full acceptance. No evangelical feminists held the most extreme view that homosexuals should be excluded from the church and punished for their sexual orientation. Still, many feminist evangelicals disagreed with Scanzoni and Mollenkott's position of full acceptance, often because they felt that they were making culture, in the guise of science and liberation movements, more authoritative than the Bible.

Much of the difference between the more conservative and the more liberal evangelical scholars came down to hermeneutics. In his article responding to Boswell's interpretation of Romans 1, Richard B. Hays pinpointed this difference. He was convinced that Paul's judgment against homosexuality was definitive and not counterbalanced by any positive statements or accounts of homosexual relations elsewhere in scripture. Theological tradition also has opposed the acceptance of homosexuality. To Hays, then, the strongest arguments on behalf of same-sex relationships came—as opponents to them recognized—when experience and reason were given greater authority than scripture and tradition.

Hays chastised scholars like Scanzoni and Mollenkott who argued for acceptance of homosexual relationships by insisting on reinterpreting clearly antihomosexual texts. He felt they failed to address, or deflected attention from, the larger question of whether contemporary understandings of homosexuality might challenge the authority of scripture. Opponents of Scanzoni and Mollenkott recognized this challenge, as can be seen in their accusations that Scanzoni and Mollenkott gave greater authority to reason—in the form of scientific data on homosexuality and the experience of individual homosexual Christians—than to scripture. They skirted this issue, according to Hays, when they insisted on imposing modern categories (of homosexual orientation versus homosexual practice) on first-century texts in order to argue that biblical authority, too, was on the side of accepting homosexuality. Because Hays asserts that the Bible is definitively opposed to homosexual relationships and activity, only when the harder question of how to balance differing authorities is addressed can Christians make better ethical choices concerning homosexuality.

Biblical feminists who supported homosexual unions maintained that they had not given in to modern, secular feminist philosophy with its emphasis on women's experience, or even contemporary liberation theology with its similar emphasis on praxis and the experience of the downtrodden. Rather, they argued that there already existed a long theological tradition of using scripture, tradition, reason, and experience as sources of spiritual authority. The Methodist Church calls these four sources the Wesleyan quadrilateral. Nancy Hardesty said that the quadrilateral became a conscious part of her theology starting around 1976 when she taught courses on John Wesley's life and theology at Emory University. Even before that, while living in Chicago, working on *All We're Meant to Be* and participating in the *Daughters of Sarah* collective, Hardesty indicated that Donald Dayton and his emphasis on Wesleyan theology influenced her thinking. She stated that although the Bible was central and authoritative, tradition as passed down through the historical church, God-given reason, and her experience as a woman together gave her a sense of balance. The exaltation of biblical authority alone suggested "fundamentalist biblicism," a kind of faith in the Bible over faith in the God that revealed the Bible.[29] Some Methodists might have disagreed with her lack of emphasis on the primacy of scripture. Nonetheless, how to balance these four sources of authority was flexible and not unambiguous.

The Evangelical Women's Caucus Conference, Fresno 1986

Differences of opinion over the issue of homosexuality did not come to a head in evangelical feminism until many years after the publication of Scanzoni and Mollenkott's book. But tension over the topic eventually split the movement. At root, the difference was over conflicting views of biblical authority, with homosexuality serving as the social issue that revealed the differences beneath the surface of biblical feminist solidarity. Given the importance to Christians and feminists of the body, sex, and its control, it is not surprising that an intersection of questions about biblical authority, women's roles, and homosexuality would lead to so much strife.

Background to the Conference

The editor of *Daughters of Sarah*, Reta Finger, described the simmering conflict among feminist evangelicals over lesbianism when writing about her own struggle to determine what the Bible taught about homosexuality. While wanting to remain true to "the biblical message on human sexuality," she also was trying to figure out how to fit that message into the stories of homosexual Christians:

I know generally what side of the fence I'm on, but then I read something on the other side and start wavering. I agonize so much because I want to be true to the biblical message of human sexuality. At the same time, I want to understand how it fits with stories of earnest Christians whose sexual orientation differs in some ways from the norm. The Gospel tells us we are accepted as we are, but it also calls us to repent and change. How does it all come together?

On a more immediate and practical level, I want to avoid this topic because of its divisiveness among Christian feminists. I don't want lesbianism to be the main issue. We biblical feminists have a real message for the church that will not be heard otherwise. I don't want us to be dismissed out of hand by people who first need to find out what the Gospel says about women as a whole.[30]

It was at the EWC's conferences where the tension was most obvious. As early as the first conference in 1975, disagreements surfaced. One difference of opinion occurred over the issue of biblical authority. Sharon Gallagher has said that her view of scripture was more conservative than that of some of the other conference participants but indicated that there was no antagonism or public schism over the issue.[31]

Controversy did arise, however, over Nancy Hardesty and Virginia Mollenkott's seminar "Woman to Woman Relationships" at the 1975 conference. Hardesty was asked to lead the meeting, and she invited Mollenkott to join her. According to Hardesty, it was Mollenkott's idea to let the seminar participants turn in written questions for the coleaders to address. This allowed women more freedom, since they could raise their concerns anonymously. One question was, How do you handle the question of homosexuality? Hardesty described their response as "a bit of fancy footwork," but without explaining why.[32] From other accounts, however, it seemed that Hardesty and Mollenkott struggled neither to condemn nor to endorse homosexuality. Rumors of what was said at the session spread quickly. In April 1976, Hardesty addressed a letter to her sisters at the EWC, stating that the opinions she shared at the conference were her own and not those of the Evangelical Women's Caucus. She pointed out that the EWC deliberately did not take a stance on this issue so as not to be divisive.[33]

Perhaps this episode explains why the program book for the second EWC conference at Pasadena in 1978 pointedly stated that "no resolutions or declarations are anticipated." It may also have been a response to members' varied reactions to Virginia Mollenkott and Letha Scanzoni's recent collaboration on *Is the Homosexual My Neighbor?* In any case, alternative sessions were planned on the topic, one that was open on the question of homosexuality, led by Scanzoni and Mollenkott, and another that was against homosexuality, led by Don Williams.[34] Later conferences also addressed this issue. The 1980 conference at Saratoga Springs, New York, included a panel on the topic. In 1982, at the Seattle conference, a "lesbian and friends" caucus was held. This meeting was not an official part of the conference schedule but a time for women who felt ostracized in the evangelical church to come together for support. According to Hardesty, who attended the gathering, a political agenda was not discussed.[35]

It seems that the "lesbian and friends" caucus at a minimum emboldened the participants to push for social justice for themselves. In 1984, at the sixth EWC conference, held at Wellesley College in Massachusetts, the issue of lesbianism finally surfaced publicly when a resolution was proposed at the business meeting seeking recognition that homosexuals were children of God and therefore ought to be supported by the EWC.[36] This was not the only resolution proposed at the meeting. Additional propositions called for support of the equal rights amendment, peace, political activism, social and economic justice, and for action against pornography and violence against women.

It was not just the supportive stance toward homosexuality that caused conflict at the business meeting. The perceived shift in the direction of the EWC raised concern as well. In reporting on the meeting in *Update*, Dorothy Meyer (coordinator of the Wellesley conference) commented:

> Some believed the time had come for us to launch out and take stands on issues that go beyond the present scope and purpose of the organization. Others believed that the organization must continue to focus solely on its stated purpose of presenting "God's teaching on female-male equality to the whole body of Christ's church" and continue its endorsement of the Equal Rights Amendment in the United States.[37]

Disagreement was now out in the open as to the future of biblical feminism: was it to be narrowly focused on women's equality in the private and public spheres, or was it to be more broadly conceived as incorporating other issues of justice?

The conflict over the introduction of resolutions was not a surprise to the EWC leadership. In a letter addressed to workshop leaders at the 1984 conference, Kaye Cook, the program coordinator, asked:

Please respect our decision to take no stand as an organization on such issues as homosexuality and abortion. We are not unaware of the importance of these issues. We believe however that each one of us is responsible before God for the stand we take. In the past, when issues that were not the focus of the conference were raised, persons tended to polarize on topics and the focus and purpose of the conference became blurred.[38]

The caucus's executive council decided therefore to solicit in advance resolutions that would be brought up at the business meeting as a way to hear from members on issues of concern to them and to "make explicit some of the implications of a consistent biblical feminist position." The friction over the resolutions that ensued, however, led the council to table all the proposals, except support for the ERA. Instead, task forces were formed to study the issues for two years, until the next biennial meeting. Each task force was composed of two executive council members and three at-large EWC members, with those people representing all sides of the topics under consideration. One of the leaders for the task force on sexuality was Hardesty. In addition to the task forces, the executive council sent out a letter polling the membership on whether the EWC should consider any resolutions besides its historically traditional support of an equal rights amendment to the Constitution.

The poll only added to the confusion and conflict. As reported in the summer 1985 issue of *Update*, the results of the poll were 48 percent in favor of addressing other social justice issues, 46 percent opposed, 4 percent with no strong opinion either way, and 2 percent with unclear responses.[39] A paper entitled "Results of the EWCI [Evangelical Women's Caucus International] Membership Poll (1984)," showed the vote to be fifty-nine votes in favor of other resolutions, fifty-nine votes against other resolutions, two votes with both these responses marked off, seven votes for the "no strong opinion" option, and seven ballots with nothing checked off.[40] In part, the discrepancy can be resolved by noting that additional late returns may have come in after the initial ballots were tabulated. Still, as Virginia Hearn wrote in a letter to the EWC council, those additional returns did not significantly change the conclusion.[41] Either result indicated a dramatically split membership on the issue of resolutions.

On her returned ballot, one member, Gretchen Gaebelein Hull, explained why she voted against considering resolutions.

> [I regard] whether or not to pass extra resolutions as a water-shed choice for EWCI. If we remain a single-purpose organization (striving for equality of women and men) I feel we will remain unified. If we begin to endorse specific areas of social, political, environmental, etc. concern we risk grave disunity.
>
> Oswald Chambers pointed out somewhere: "Never say, 'What's the harm in it?' Push it to its logical conclusion and ask 'Where will it end?'" I feel that endorsing resolutions will end in a never-ending stream of resolutions. How could EWCI possibly be fair and "cut off" resolutions and say "no more"? Each entire conference would have to be given over to resolutions—lobbying for them and discussing them like a political convention.[42]

Other members indicated that taking a position on issues beyond women's equality was natural and part of the biblical imperative to strive for justice: "We are not the people of God if we do not strongly support issues of peace and justice"; "If we remain politically inactive we will fail to take the prophetic stance that the Scriptures call us toward."[43]

Underlying the rhetoric about unity, divisiveness, and justice were the issues themselves. *Update* reported that one of the most divisive topics was homosexuality. Some women thought that any resolution on homosexuality would indicate support for sexual acts prohibited in scripture. Among these members, some questioned the EWC's purpose and identity: was its purpose to teach about male-female equality before God, and was it still evangelical? Others were afraid that the resolution, while itself not an endorsement of homosexuality, would be viewed as such by more conservative churches and therefore would harm the Evangelical Women's Caucus's ability to reach them. Still others, especially lesbians, felt they would be unwelcome in the EWC if the resolution on homosexuality could not be passed.

Given the close vote in the poll and the emotions generated, the executive council decided by consensus at their 1985 meeting to let the resolutions die and not propose any more. Since the first EWC gathering in Washington, D.C., at which several resolutions were passed, the EWC had limited itself to taking an active stance on only one political issue, passage of the equal rights amendment. By letting the resolutions die, the council was tacitly maintaining the status quo. Council members published a statement about their decision in *Update* and selected Hardesty to write it.[44] In her report, Hardesty indicated that the proposals did not promote the desired result—dialogue—but, rather, discord and polarization. "In short, they turned out to be counterproductive for our organization . . . we concluded that resolutions are not the way to proceed. Even some people who supported the stance of all of the resolutions realized that the resolution process is not appropriate to our group." She concluded: "Thus we will continue to explore these issues and others as they arise, although we will not formulate an 'official stance.' Nonetheless, from the beginning, EWCI [Evangelical Women's Caucus International] has been convinced that biblical feminism is a global vision, a unifying perspective for an integrated Christian faith."[45]

Fresno

Despite this apparent ban on resolutions at future Evangelical Women's Caucus business meetings, the issue of lesbianism finally split the biblical feminist movement after its biennial conference in 1986 in Fresno, California.[46] Several events at this conference seemed to signal an approach to lesbian issues that was different from that at earlier ones. There was the presentation from the task force on sexuality that Hardesty helped lead. Hardesty also moderated a session in which lesbians were able to share their struggles in the evangelical church. Also, in the final address of the conference, in which Mollenkott was asked to present a vision for the future of the EWC, she called for the rejection of heterosexism. The by-now usual gathering of "lesbians and friends" drafted resolutions calling for justice and equality for racial minorities, deploring violence against women and children, and asking the EWC to recognize the presence of a lesbian minority in the organization and to advocate for their civil rights. According to Anne Eggebroten, no one came to the informal gathering with an agenda to force the EWC to consider resolutions. But when "someone new" asked whether something like that could be done, a discussion ensued as to whether the executive council had the power "to muzzle the assembled membership."[47]

In the conference business meeting on July 8, the proposals were brought forward for a vote. As a member of the executive council, Hardesty had volunteered to chair the new business portion of the meeting.[48] The council accepted her offer but asked her to read the official statement against resolutions that Hardesty herself had written. According to some members present, she did not do this. At the beginning of the open-mike session, Michelle Borba, of the Bay Area EWC, made a motion on the first resolution, calling for racial justice. Immediately a debate about the appropriateness of introducing resolutions began. At this point, Hardesty expressed the opinion that the council's statement was not binding but advisatory and pointed out that the ballot had been in favor of resolutions, albeit narrowly. Catherine Kroeger immediately moved to amend the motion already proposed to forbid further resolutions. Borba, as the author of the initial motion, did not accept Kroeger's amendment. The first resolution passed.

After the first vote, two different women sought recognition from the chair. Hardesty chose to recognize Jeanne Baly, from the "lesbian and friends" gathering, who had been selected to present the second resolution, against domestic violence. When it passed with little debate, Eggebroten proposed the third motion, urging civil rights for homosexuals:

> I move that, whereas homosexual people are children of God, and because of the biblical mandate of Jesus Christ that we are all created equal in God's sight, and in recognition of the presence of the lesbian minority in EWCI take a firm stand in favor of civil-rights protection for homosexual persons.[49]

There was a lengthy debate on many aspects of the resolution, but when all was done, the final vote was eighty in favor, sixteen opposed, and twenty-three abstentions out of six hundred registrants. Because of the strong feelings on the issue, both a voice and a hand vote were too confusing to determine an outcome. Thus, everyone voting had to stand in order to be counted, even the abstentions.

Several issues had intertwined to make the third proposed resolution so controversial. First was the topic: many members felt that despite the resolution's moderate wording, its purpose was not merely to seek recognition for a lesbian minority within the EWC but also to seek approval of a lesbian lifestyle as being congruent with scripture. In addition, these members felt that even if approval were not the intention of the proposal, it would be interpreted as such by the press and conservative evangelical churches and thus would hurt the EWC's witness to the community they wanted to reach. Second, the presentation of the resolution appeared to transgress the council's decision to drop resolutions.

Those supporting the resolution believed that the EWC had always been political, and so to address the civil rights of another oppressed group in society was only natural. According to the EWC's national co-ordinator, Britt Vanden Eykel, the resolution was "not any kind of en-dorsement of the gay lifestyle or comment on biblical interpretation."[50] Some proponents believed that such a resolution was necessary to move the EWC forward by addressing more current issues. According to Nancy Hardesty: "A number of us have been saying for years that the organiza-tion has to move forward or die. This is a step of maturity within the or-ganization to say we're willing to tackle harder issues."[51] Hardesty be-lieved that the EWC had always been a political organization because it had taken stands and lobbied for issues like the ERA and support for the ordination of women. She pointed to the telegram of solidarity sent from the first EWC gathering to the Catholic women meeting in Detroit in 1975 to discuss ordination as evidence of the group's political nature.[52] Mollenkott's plenary address in Fresno had emphasized similar ideas, calling for the EWC to oppose the politics of patriarchy across the board and listed several controversial stances she would like to see it take (among them, support of homosexual rights).[53]

Letters to *Update* following the conference indicated that a number of people agreed with Scanzoni and Mollenkott's position in *All We're Meant to Be*. As one writer declared,

> I am glad to be able to tell my friends and co-volunteers that EWCI is a viable organization in spite of the fact that they [the friends] shy away from the word evangelical because of abuses of that word. Being able to tell these friends that the leadership is not only biblical in the best sense, but are "with it" in today's world, and are not afraid of risk as they pro-ceed, is a great help.[54]

Another reader stated that he did not have a problem with the resolutions or the Evangelical Women's Caucus's taking a stand on issues other than women's equality but that the meeting and resolutions "put off" the evan-gelical friends he brought to the conference. He suggested that the EWC take such stances but keep them in low profile so as not to scare away people in evangelical churches.[55]

Those opposed to the resolution did see it as an endorsement of ho-mosexuality, although no one admitted to being against civil rights for homosexuals. Hearn voted for the resolutions for that reason, despite her personal belief that the Bible did not condone homosexuality. Still, these women felt that the intention of introducing this resolution was to imply that scripture approved of homosexuality and that it would ruin the EWC's outreach to evangelical women and men. Alvera Mickelsen, who along with Kroeger spoke out against the measure, wrote:

> To pretend that this was a "civil rights" issue is ridiculous. Most of us believe in civil rights for everyone—even criminals. The crucial phrase was not "civil rights" but rather, "in recognition of the presence of the lesbian minority in EWCI." That's what the battle was about—official recognition of lesbianism as being congruent with EWCI.[56]

Others felt that the EWC was weakening the organization by broadening its focus too much. These members believed that the organization's goal was to speak to the church about male and female equality. Among others, Kroeger felt that many women and men in conservative churches needed the EWC and that this resolution would hinder its influence among those churches.[57] Reminiscent of Carl Henry's concern about the broader evangelical movement, a member from Canada expressed the widespread concern that the EWC would lose its cohesiveness and therefore its effectiveness by taking on ever more diverse issues: "Where does a group united around a particular and distinct concern begin to lose its cohesiveness as other concerns (about which there may be divergent views) are added to the original emphasis and focus?"[58] This writer suggested that individual members align themselves with particular organizations effecting change on those and other specific issues but that as an organization, the caucus should not weaken its thrust by becoming too broad. Instead it should focus on reaching evangelicals in conservative churches with the message of biblical gender equality. Co-coordinator Britt Vanden Eykel agreed. Although she maintained a public stance that downplayed the potential impact of the Fresno vote, in a letter to the EWC's membership she warned against losing its call to hold the evangelical community accountable on women's issues. She also suggested that some members of the EWC, such as Mollenkott, ought to work through other organizations to achieve their social aims, concluding that "EWC cannot take theological positions such as these without consensus and the guidance of the Holy Spirit and the Word of God. In addition, our membership is committed to reconciliation between the sexes, not separatism."[59]

In a report of the conference for *Green Leaf*, Virginia Hearn stated that for her the business meeting was the low point of the conference. "I personally had the sense of a juggernaut being rolled over the assembly, even though the issues involved . . . [which she listed] are not ones that I would oppose." She continued:

I doubt if any one present was opposed in principle to any of the issues. But the question remains: what is the purpose of EWC and whom are we trying to reach? Does it make sense to take what will appear to be an official position on issues (specifically, the third one) that obfuscate biblical feminist concerns: to reach women and men in conservative churches with the good news that in Christ there is neither Jew nor Greek, slave nor free, male nor female? I personally agree with an emphasis I heard throughout this conference—that each of us must discern our own calling, and work for whichever causes our God has directed us toward in our individual lives. I cannot see the wisdom in forcing an entire organization to make declarations on controversial theological/social issues that will surely serve to undermine that organization's unique calling.[60]

Letters to the editor in the following edition of *Green Leaf* expressed a range of opinions on Hearn's analysis within the Bay Area Evangelical Women's Caucus, although the published letters ran three to one in agreement with her. One founding member of the BAEWC, Christiane Carlson-Thies, wrote:

I am against resolutions on issues not intrinsic to the biblical message of male/female equality because I don't want EWCI to decide my politics. . . . I joined EWCI in order to become part of an association of biblical feminists who wanted to concentrate on the task of developing and spreading the message that women are "free indeed" to anyone who will listen. Doing the specific job is going to be much more difficult now. . . . EWCI is narrowing the door by which people can enter the organization. EWCI has begun to suggest that authentic biblical feminism must of necessity be hitched to a specific stance on other questions as well.[61]

From all accounts of the 1986 business meeting, it was an emotional and confusing event. Most women attending the conference had no idea that any resolutions would be introduced, believing from the council's decision—as reported in *Update*—that they would not be allowed. Hence, some attendees claimed that they themselves, or others they knew, skipped the business meeting to have lunch or take a break from the rigorous schedule. Others indicated that they came in late and were bewildered by the controversy. One participant at the business meeting reported that after the proposed resolution on homosexuality was read and the divisive discussion ensued, several women left the room in tears.

Accusations of backroom politics were raised by each side on the issue. There were allegations that Hardesty had either violated rules of order or abused her power as chair of the meeting, first by allowing the resolutions and then by recognizing the women whom she knew would introduce them.[62] Other charges were that nonmembers voted for the proposed resolutions, in violation of the organization's bylaws. Correspondence in the *Update* files indicates that someone checked the membership of Borba, who had introduced the first resolution, and found it to have lapsed. This appeared to be a temporary situation, which Borba soon corrected, but checking the records for discrepancies created bad feelings among members and leaders in the organization.[63] Yet another participant alleged that it appeared some people knew very well what was coming and arrived in Fresno specifically and only for the business meeting.

A few women, both for and against resolutions, admitted knowing that they would be introduced. There were those women who attended the "lesbian and friends" gathering, including Borba, Baly, Eggebroten, and Hardesty. Hardesty also stated that when Virginia Mollenkott arrived at the conference, the two women discussed working on resolutions to introduce at the business meeting. According to Hardesty, the council knew that their statement against resolutions was unclear; thus there was no reason not to draft something.[64] Still, this gave the business meeting the feel of a planned surprise attack to those who assumed that resolutions could not be introduced. Pat Ward, a founding member of the Evangelical Women's Caucus and participant in the Thanksgiving Day conference of the Evangelicals for Social Action, said that both she and Margaret Hannay heard rumors that Hardesty and some of her friends would introduce a social justice plank. They accordingly were prepared and spoke out against resolutions at the meeting. According to Ward, lesbianism was not their primary concern in the beginning; it was the divisiveness of introducing politics to the EWC.[65] In fact, Ward saw the EWC as a very mutually accepting group. She, nevertheless, opposed the resolution on lesbianism as not being about ending the condemnation of one group of people but about condoning homosexual behavior.

The controversy at the Fresno business meeting only grew over time. As the months passed, the two sides of the debate charged each other with planning clandestine meetings to plot strategy. Mollenkott, Hardesty, and some of their supporters believed that Hannay, Ward, and others who opposed the resolutions had met prior to the 1984 Wellesley conference to torpedo the initial resolutions that the executive council had wanted. In a letter to the editor of *Update*, later made into a lengthy article for *The Other Side*, Anne Eggebroten argued that those who were opposed to the EWC's voting on resolutions were playing a type of "female manipulative politics." Along the lines of Carol Gilligan's popular thesis, Eggebroten suggested that this group of women was overly concerned with avoiding divisiveness and conflict, to the point that they undermined the basic democratic process. Eggebroten admitted that she and the others who proposed the resolutions also were practicing a kind of power politics, but she felt they had been democratic, settling their disagreements by ballot and being honest about what they had done.[66]

Ward, Hannay, and several others, as revealed in letters to the editor of *Update*, were convinced that Hardesty and Mollenkott had acted improperly to overthrow the council's decision that the EWC would refrain from making further resolutions, other than supporting equal rights for women. Others attending the business meeting were convinced that "ringers"—lesbians who were not members and had not been present for the rest of the conference—were brought in to the business meeting specifically to tell their stories and stack the voting in favor of the proposed resolutions.

It was not long before both Ward and Hannay submitted their resignations from the EWC. As the president of the Conference on Christianity and Literature, Hannay wrote that she felt forced to resign to maintain her credibility in the evangelical community.[67] Others who resigned included Kroeger, Mickelsen, Carlson-Thies, and Gretchen Gaebelein-Hull. In addition, the entire Minnesota and Portland chapters renounced their memberships. The Minnesota chapter also withdrew its invitation to host the 1988 convention. Thirty-seven women urged Kroeger to organize another group that could continue with the more moderate goals of influencing people in evangelical churches. Some of these women ultimately decided to remain in the EWC, but the meeting shook them up enough that they reconsidered their membership. Others, such as Virginia Hearn, remained in the EWC but became inactive after a few years.

Initially, Kroeger and the former Minnesota chapter of the EWC contacted a group recently formed in Britain (known as Men, Women and God), associated with John Stott's London Institute for Contemporary Christianity, about forming a branch of their organization in the United States. She and several others visited London, but because of U.S. restrictions they were not able to form a subsidiary here. Still, they found its statement of faith helpful in putting together one of their own, and they began to call themselves Men, Women, and God/Christians for Biblical Equality (MWG/CBE). They also began to publish a newsletter, *Priscilla Papers*, containing articles on equality and information about the progress of the new organization. In February 1987, less than a year after the Fresno convention, Kroeger and approximately two hundred other women met in Minnesota to discuss forming a new organization. By August of that year, at another meeting in Cape Cod, Christians for Biblical Equality (CBE) was voted into existence.

A Comparison with Secular Feminism

As one member of the EWC noted about her withdrawal from the organization after the Fresno meeting, she felt that it was following a similar historical path as the National Organization of Women, which itself suffered conflict over the issue of lesbianism. Up to this point evangelical feminism had much in common with the liberal feminism of the 1960s. An early student of biblical feminism noted, "These feminists espouse a fairly straightforward practical sort of feminism that would be at home in the National Organization of Women."[68]

In 1970, owing to similar disagreements, the secular feminist movement split into two. Unlike the liberal feminists, who wanted to reform the economic and political system to make it more equal for men and women, the radical feminists believed that patriarchy had to be overthrown, not reformed. They thought that male control of sex and women's bodies was the issue; thus they focused on personal issues as political, and many of these feminists experimented with lesbianism or revealed their lesbian orientation. Alice Echols recorded that on May 1, 1970, at the opening night of the second Congress to Unite Women, in which radical and reformist feminist organizations participated, forty lesbians staged an action to take over the scheduled proceedings:

> About 300 women were quietly sitting in the auditorium of intermediate
> school 70 waiting for the Congress to Unite Women to come to order.
> The lights went out, people heard running, laughter, a rebel yell here and
> there, and when those lights were turned back on, those same 300
> women found themselves in the hands of the LAVENDER MENACE.[69]

While the events at the EWC were not quite so theatrical, they felt just as
dramatic to many of the women at that Fresno business meeting. The split
in biblical feminism shows similarities beyond the dramatic to the split
that occurred in secular feminism. As in the 1970s when it became common to excoriate the secular feminist movement as heterosexist, so too it
became routine for some members of the EWC to revile the heterosexism
in evangelicalism.

Similarly, much like Kate Millet's "coming out" as bisexual, Virginia
Mollenkott and Nancy Hardesty openly admitted their own lesbianism.
By at least 1987, Mollenkott was referring to her "life-long, unchosen homosexual orientation."[70] In 1992, she revealed even more about her lifelong homosexual orientation: "I speak and always have spoken in a lesbian voice; the feminism came much later than the lesbianism, signs of
which were apparent in me by age four." She explained her heterosexual
marriage as "the attempt of a brainwashed fundamentalist to fit herself
into the heteropatriarchal mold."[71] In 1988, in an oral history project of
the Claremont Graduate University, Hardesty mentioned that it was as
early as 1975 that she first began discussing her sexual orientation with
Mollenkott.[72] Much later, in 1995, in a collection of essays that told the
stories of several biblical feminists, Hardesty also felt comfortable
enough to refer to her lesbian orientation.[73] Even before coming out of
the closet publicly, Mollenkott and Hardesty had associated themselves
with the cause of homosexual justice. Both met with the EWC's "lesbian
and friends" group, and Mollenkott openly expressed her biblical support of homosexual relationships as a member of Evangelicals Concerned
and in one of her early books, *Speech, Silence, Action!*

In their earlier writings, Hardesty and Scanzoni also indicated that it
was possible for a Christian to affirm some homosexual relationships. Before *All We're Meant to Be*, Scanzoni wrote a sex education book for
Christian families entitled *Sex Is a Parent Affair*. Among the perspectives
on homosexuality she includes was one that mildly approved of committed, lifelong homosexual unions, although she indicates that this Christian view also held that such unions were less than God's ideal.[74] As al-

ready mentioned, in the first edition of *All We're Meant to Be*, Hardesty wrote a chapter, "The Single Woman," in which she discusses the morality of lesbian relationships for Christians. In a section labeled "Sexual Needs," Hardesty points out that although the scripture prohibited homosexual acts, "neither Paul nor any other biblical writer speaks of a 'homosexual orientation' or of an attraction for members of one's own sex."[75] She concludes that compassion, not condemnation, should be the Christian response to homosexual persons because "many times even overt homosexual behavior is only a manifestation of a deeper psychological problem and a cry for help."[76]

Hardesty quickly came to regret these words. In the 1986 second edition, she states in a personal foreword that she had been "mean-spirited" and "wrong" about lesbianism in the first edition. Thus, in the section on sexual needs of the single person, Hardesty addresses both heterosexual and homosexual women. She deletes any discussion of Paul, the biblical text, or its silence on homosexual orientation. Rather, she declares that

> We are sexual persons—single or married, young or old, gay or straight. We are all embodied, incredible, delightful, integrated organisms, created by God who said, "It is good." One of the most devastating dualities the church has fostered is the duality of body and spirit. This division has caused and continues to cause the world untold grief. Added to the duality of male and female, it has brought pernicious dimensions to sexism. Defining ourselves, human beings, as spiritual beings with a heavenly home has led to the rape of the physical earth, our embodied environment. Always identifying ourselves with mind and spirit while projecting sexuality and physicality onto others has multiplied the horrors of slavery, racism, homophobia, nationalism, and militarism.[77]

In the third edition, published in 1992, Hardesty added a section, "Lesbians and Gay Men," in which she pleads with the church to support Christians with a homosexual orientation.[78] She argues that "the church remains one of the institutions most oppressive to gay people, sometimes even opposing their basic civil rights." To convince her readers that the church should allow lesbians and gays to express who God made them to be, she utilized the broader research available by that time, citing Scanzoni and Mollenkott, Scroggs, and William Countryman to contend once again that the Bible was silent on homosexual orientation and committed relationships.

Alice Echols wrote that the slogan "the personal is political" had a huge impact on radical feminism, by making "questions of lifestyle absolutely central" to feminism.[79] Members of radical feminism complained that "'women who weren't gay were treated as second-class citizens." Echols claimed that many heterosexual women left the movement "as lesbianism became coterminous with radical feminism."[80] Many evangelicals wondered whether this was what was happening to the EWC. Perhaps biblical feminism was slowly but surely following in the footsteps of secular feminism by splitting into a more liberal, practical wing and a more radical wing preoccupied with questions of lifestyle.

By the end of the EWC's 1986 conference in Fresno, it looked as though radical feminist ideas indeed had spread to the biblical feminist movement. Scanzoni, Mollenkott, and Hardesty all were advocating support for committed homosexual partnerships. Mollenkott and Hardesty helped advance this agenda in the EWC, and they also opened up about their own lesbian orientation. Lesbianism, however, was the issue that brought to the surface the underlying theological differences in biblical feminism. In short, the decisive role of homosexuality in biblical feminism can be traced back to conflicting views of the authority of scripture. Those opposed to accepting lesbianism as congruent with scripture regarded the Bible as the ultimate authority of right and wrong. Those who advocated lesbianism as consistent with the biblical witness considered other sources of authority to determine proper guidelines for living in contemporary society.

Scripture, Authority, and the Body

But why was lesbianism the location of a conflict over biblical authority? Because of the role that the body, sex, procreation, marriage, and family have played in maintaining a civil society. In particular, the family is considered a primary bulwark against rampant individualism, unbridled male aggression, and unchecked competition. It also is seen as promoting discipline and connecting individuals to a community. The family thus has been a fundamental building block for the civil order of society, and many people believe that homosexuality threatens to disrupt this foundation.

Since the time of the early church, restraint of bodily urges—whether for food, sex, or sleep—was used as a means to instill individual discipline and community order. For Augustine, lust was one of two main effects that resulted from the fall. Controlling sexual desire, therefore, helped Christians tame their will, leading them to become better citizens generally. In the Middle Ages, priestly celibacy and Christian monogamy were primary ways in which both church and state consolidated and increased their power, economically, socially, and politically.[81] After the Reformation, Protestants came to see marriage as a positive good because the family unit, which was strengthened through sexual fidelity, bolstered civic order. Many current arguments against heterosexual divorce and promiscuity, and against homosexual unions, often stress the role that unrestrained sexuality would play in the downfall of civilized society.[82]

Thus, until the mid- to late-twentieth century, homosexuality was considered criminal behavior throughout the United States. A turning point occurred in June 1969 when New York City police raided a gay bar, the Stonewall Inn. Against expectations, the patrons resisted, and a riot began that lasted for three nights. Occurring against the backdrop of other civil rights movements—for African Americans, women, and other minorities—the Stonewall riots launched the modern gay rights movement. By the 1980s, some states were beginning to outlaw discrimination based on sexual orientation and decriminalize sodomy laws. But the 1980s also saw a backlash from the new religious right and the onslaught of AIDS. Finally, in 2000, thirty-one years after the Stonewall riots, Vermont became the first state to legalize civil unions between gay or lesbian partners.

Thus the question of the body and its control have been important to both the church and the contemporary civil rights movements.

The question of authority—who has the authority to settle questions of morality and how individuals can live together in harmony—also has been an enduring one. Before the Reformation, authority for how one lived was vested in the Catholic Church and what it said the scripture taught. The wars of religion and Enlightenment philosophy that followed the Reformation redefined the traditional meaning of authority. Autonomy and individual consent to reason challenged the magisterial authority of the church and the powers of divine right. In Protestantism, authority was vested in the scripture, unfiltered through the interpretation of an official guarantor of its accuracy.[83] The authority of the church was subordinated to the authority of the Bible, and every person had the right to interpret the Bible for himself or herself. This did not mean, however, that the reformers believed every Christian had an equal ability to understand the text of scripture unaided. The reformers also believed that to understand the Bible correctly, one had to go back to the original sources and read them in the original language. Thus, the slogan *sola scriptura*, "scripture alone," did not preclude other modes of authority, including preachers and catechisms to teach the proper doctrine, whose status derived from their faithfulness to the Word of God.[84]

In America, with its unique historical "point of departure," scripture has become isolated from these other modes of authority. Religious freedom and the opportunity to begin anew in the new world removed ecclesiastical restrictions and allowed for the rejection of tradition and an emphasis on scripture alone. Add to these religious factors the influence of Enlightenment reason and individualism in American culture, and the result has been a unique organizational form of free churches (independent of the state) based on the voluntary association of individuals united by a common purpose, primarily the propagation of its own view. Characteristics of the American church have included its tendency to divide into factions, its voluntary nature, its mission enterprise, revivalism, competition, and individualism.[85]

The contemporary evangelical movement, lacking authoritative church bodies to assert ecclesiastical control, relies on inerrancy to serve as a theological, almost creedal, guideline to help evangelicals determine their membership and guide their behavior. Inerrancy focuses on the issue of biblical authority, which is central to debates between fundamentalists and liberals. A "looser" view of biblical authority is associated with postwar liberalism, which also advocates "looser" social mores. Thus, by maintaining a high definition of scriptural authority, evangelicals have been able to distinguish between their fellows and those who are progressive in other social issues as well. It also has enabled them to urge their constituency to live according to strict standards of moral behavior. Younger, more progressive evangelicals who have accepted modern methods of interpretation and have made evangelicalism more relevant to its contemporary situation thus are challenging the movement's identity and boundaries. Biblical feminists who advocate the evangelical acceptance of homosexuality and use the authority of reason and experience are thereby violating both the theological and the social norms of postwar evangelicalism.

It is no surprise, then, that the issue of homosexuality came to be the dividing issue in a movement of evangelical feminists. The convergence of historical movements (the gay and women's civil rights movements and the progressive evangelical movement) combined with issues of authority (inerrancy and the control of the body and sexuality) to make it an explosive issue in the late 1980s.

5

Empowered by the Word, I
*Theological Changes in
Biblical Feminism, 1986–*

"Now Sophia, dream the vision, share the wisdom dwelling deep within."[1] With these words of invocation, the "Re-Imagining Conference," an event sponsored by the World Council of Churches with the goal of revisioning religious traditions and women's places in them, began. For the opening session in 1993, 1,743 women and 83 men met, among them several members of the Evangelical Women's Caucus. Shortly after the closing ceremonies, a firestorm erupted among more traditional Protestants, including many of those in Christians for Biblical Equality. The reason for the uproar was that many Christians who heard about the gathering thought that it had gone beyond the bounds of traditional theology to "reimagine" a new church and a new God(dess). They based this conclusion on reports of what had occurred at the conference.

The first thing most people heard about the Re-Imagining Conference was that its participants worshiped the goddess Sophia, including in a "celebration of milk and honey" reminiscent of communion. Throughout the event, the participants sang to and praised Sophia. In addition, one plenary speaker, Chung Hyun-Kyung, who was from South Korea and trained at Union Theological Seminary in New York, announced that her "new Trinity" was Kali, the Hindu goddess of justice; Kwan-In, the Buddhist goddess of compassion; and Ina, a Philippine goddess whose name means both "mother" and "earth."[2] Other speakers questioned the salvific value of Christ's death on the cross. Delores Williams, a black feminist theologian from Union, argued that the cross presented salvation as the suffering of the innocent and thus condoned violence and taught African American women to suffer passively. Williams uttered perhaps

110

the most frequently quoted phrase of the conference: "We don't need folks hanging on crosses and blood dripping and all that weird stuff."[3] Virginia Mollenkott seemed to concur, stating in her presentation that she could "no longer worship in a theological context that depicts God as an abusive parent and Jesus as the obedient trusting child."[4]

As this illustration suggests, biblical feminist interpretation went in distinct directions after the split into two organizations following the Fresno EWC conference in 1986. Neither the more traditionalist evangelical feminists nor the more progressive ones attempted to develop a systematic theology. Although each addressed several key doctrines, the focus of their attention remained on the reinterpretation of scripture. Traditionalist biblical feminists, represented by Christians for Biblical Equality, were concerned with equal opportunity for women and thus reconsidered biblical passages traditionally used to argue that the Bible taught women's subordination to men. Progressive biblical feminists, those in the EWC, focused on justice and inclusivity, reinterpreting scripture to show that it liberated all oppressed women from the domination of patriarchy.

Even though they did not treat Christian doctrine systematically, the feminists' interpretative efforts reflected their views on several important theological issues. Owing to their commitment to biblical authority, traditionalist biblical feminists remained within the boundaries of contemporary evangelicalism in doctrine, hermeneutical method, and most behavioral norms. Progressive biblical feminist doctrine, methodology, and moral values, however, had changed so radically that they were no longer considered evangelical by most evangelicals and even by some women in the EWC.

Theology Proper: The Trinity and the Gender of God

Many feminists, evangelical and secular, charged that androcentrism in the church begins with the concept of a male God, who rules in a patriarchal, authoritarian manner over his creation. The Trinity was often accused of perpetuating that image, and many feminists wanted to do away with it. Some tried to reform it. Others, biblical feminists among them, attempted to show that the Trinity was not a patriarchal symbol or one that harmed women.

Reta Finger used the doxology to illustrate the problem many feminists had with the concept of the Trinity. "Doxology" refers to the offering of worship to God. In the Christian tradition, one particular song of praise has come to be known simply as the "Doxology." Its lyrics are from Psalm 100:

> Praise God from whom all blessings flow;
> Praise Him, all creatures here below;
>   Praise Him above, ye heavenly host:
> Praise Father, Son, and Holy Ghost.

Finger made this observation:

> How many of us wince when we sing the doxology in church on Sunday mornings? We're hit in the stomach by the "Hims." The last line, a grand finale meant to call forth praise from human, bird, or blade of grass, ends up sounding like an all-male team that women can only cheer on from the sidelines. For many people, the image of an old man, a younger man, and a hybrid dove/disembodied phantom does not do much for their worship.[5]

Finger suggested four problems with the all-male, trinitarian conception of God. First, the traditional formulation of "Father, Son, and Holy Spirit" is totally male. Second, the trinitarian relationship is hierarchical and patriarchal. Third, the trinitarian formula confuses the language describing God with God's very being. Fourth, some feminists view any concept of God as transcendent as being harmful to women.

In response to these objections, evangelical feminists began to develop a theology concerning the gender of God. As we have seen, they argued based on the Genesis accounts that both men and women were created in God's image. If that is so, then God cannot be male; rather, God transcends all human limitations, including sexuality.[6] Virginia Mollenkott believed that the feminine images for God found in the Bible were further evidence of this. Thus, in *The Divine Feminine* she features fifteen feminine metaphors for God. In her book *Beyond the Curse*, traditionalist biblical feminist Aida Besançon Spencer argues similarly, maintaining that God had to use metaphors, similes, and other images to help humans understand what God was like. If males were the sole reflection of God's image, then feminine images of God would not exist. Yet they did. For example, both Mollenkott and Spencer point out that the scripture uses illustrations of God as a human mother. In Isaiah 46:3–4, God speaks of the house of Israel as "those carried in my womb." Other mother images include those of God as a nursing mother and comforter (Isaiah 42:14–16, 66:13; Psalm 131:2). Biblical feminists find the inclusion of feminine images for God, even in writings from a highly patriarchal culture, to be significant. They indicate that God does not want humans to fixate on sexuality or gender as a spiritual marker.

Women still acknowledged that the Trinity appeared overwhelmingly male: Father and Son are worshiped along with a "neuter" Holy Spirit. It is not enough, then, simply to recover the few feminine similes and metaphors used for God in the face of the many male ones in the scripture. Women need a positive, feminine representation of God. Some progressive biblical feminists found such an image in the Holy Spirit, arguing that the Spirit symbolizes the feminine aspect of God in the Trinity.

As early as 1983, Mollenkott considered this possibility in her book *The Divine Feminine*, noting that most scholars recognized the depiction of wisdom as "an expression of the divine personality" in the Hebrew Bible. Going further, other scholars made a connection between wisdom's deification and its personification as a woman.[7] For example, the book of Proverbs portrays wisdom as a woman crying out in the streets for people to follow her (8:1–36). Mollenkott does just this when she traces some of the parallels between wisdom and God in scripture. She points out that both God and wisdom are said to reside in a pillar of cloud and that both are said to have been rejected by the Israelites.

In addition, Mollenkott argues that wisdom can be equated directly with the third person of the Trinity in several ways. Wisdom is referred to as "the holy spirit of instruction" in Wisdom 1:5, much as the Holy Spirit is in John 16:13. In another passage, the terms *wisdom*, *God*, and the *Spirit of Yahweh* appear to be interchangeable:

> Wisdom is a spirit friendly to humanity, though she will not let a blasphemer's words go unpunished; since God observes the very soul and accurately surveys the heart, listening to every word. For the spirit of the Lord fills the world, and that which holds everything together knows every word said. (Wisdom 1:6–7; New Jerusalem Bible)

Mollenkott goes on to point out that wisdom can also be associated with the second person of the Trinity. In Wisdom 8:1–8, wisdom is described as having shared in the knowledge of and work of creation. Similarly, in Colossians 1:16 Christ is accorded the status of creator of everything. It is this aspect of wisdom that progressive biblical feminists later developed to reimagine new ways to worship God that were more empowering for women.

After some early efforts to show that God is not male—by recovering feminine images in the Bible—many traditionalist biblical feminists abandoned this strategy as being ill conceived. Rebecca Merrill Groothuis, a former staff member of InterVarsity, was one traditionalist feminist who felt that focusing on any gender only caused people to believe erroneously that God was one or the other sex. In a sense, Groothuis agreed with Mary Daly's famous syllogism that "if God is male, then the male is God" and also with its inverse: if God is female, then the female is God. Thus, feminists ended up worshiping a goddess, and traditionalists worshiped a male deity. Instead, Groothuis reminded her audience that God is spirit (John 4:24). "Categories of sexuality are rightly deemed irrelevant to God's spiritual nature," and the divine image resides in essential humanness and not essential sexuality.[8]

A progressive evangelical feminist and the chair of the women's studies program at the Claremont Graduate University, Karen Torjesen, and her husband Leif agreed with Groothuis. In an article entitled, "Inclusive Orthodoxy," the Torjesens state that an orthodox theology of the Trinity would have to affirm the traditional doctrine of full unity of the personhood of God amid a diversity of characteristics: three persons ("particular existences" of God) and one nature, with no subordination of any particular existence allowed.[9] Thus, they argue, the doctrine of the Trinity has been, from its earliest formulation, inclusive. Those descriptions of God that incorporate both feminine and masculine images, then, most accurately convey God's nature:

> All the characteristics in God which connote rule, supremacy, direction—and all the characteristics in God which suggest obedience, fulfillment, service—all belong to one and the same triune personhood. They are complex dimensions of one triune personality.
>
> Gender traits which we in our human culture generally associate with the male in opposition to the female—and traits which we generally associate with the female in opposition to the male—are found together in the Trinitarian doctrine of personality in God. They are not only found

together. They are accompanied by a radical claim of absolute equality and unity within the person of God, who is Trinity.[10]

Viewed through a trinitarian lens, the question of whether women should be subordinate to the spiritual authority of men is ultimately a theological issue, not simply a women's issue. It is about worshiping God correctly, as neither male nor female: "Far more important than giving women the equal rights that are due them is our obligation to give God the glory that is due him."[11] Groothuis chastised as unorthodox those evangelicals who taught women's subordination by basing it on "functional subordination" in the Trinity.

Functional subordination, Groothuis explains, is a theological concept, debated since the time of the early church, which posits that the second person of the Trinity chose to subordinate himself to the Father for a limited time and purpose, in being incarnate as Jesus of Nazareth. Although functional subordination does not imply inferiority in essence or being, some opponents of evangelical feminism argue that women, though equal in being to men, are subordinate to men in their roles at home and in the church. In essence, they are arguing for women's functional subordination to men based on the functional subordination found in the Trinity: women are to men as Jesus is to the Father. Groothuis points out, however, that subordination is functional only when the subordinated person's abilities has the potential to outgrow the limitations of her role or when the job is finished. Groothuis cites as an example a coworker who serves on a committee under someone who, outside the committee, is otherwise her equal. In this illustration, when the committee finishes its task, both workers again are equals. It is in this way that functional subordination applies to the Trinity; the incarnation necessarily entailed Jesus submitting himself to the Father, and his subordination to the Father ended when he ascended back to heaven.

Female subordination, however, is not based on an office or task. It is based solely on who the person is—a woman—and lasts throughout her entire life. According to Groothuis, those arguing for hierarchy are suggesting not women's functional subordination but their ontological subordination. Recognizing this, hierarchalists began to argue that ontological subordination, too, is inherent in the Trinity, claiming that the Son is eternally subordinate to the Father. Wayne Grudem, who helped found Council on Biblical Manhood and Womanhood to oppose biblical feminism, claimed that "the doctrine of an eternally hierarchical structure of the godhead is a 'truth' that is 'clearly' an 'essential' element of orthodox trinitarian theology."[12] Such a strategy is questionable, according to Groothuis. First, conservative scholars disagree on the concept of an eternal structure of rule and authority in the godhead. Second, the submission of the Son to the Father during his time on earth was not intended to illustrate the subordination of one entire group of people to another. Third, to argue for Christ's ontological subordination as supporting women's subordination is letting the less important issue determine doctrine. Groothuis quotes biblical scholar Royce Gruenler, commenting on the hierarchalist theory of eternal submission in the godhead, that "it would not be good exegesis to reintroduce such subordinationism into the Trinity in order to sanction unequal roles of authority and obedience within the believing community."[13]

Other evangelical feminists sought to emphasize the ways in which the Trinity acts as a positive symbol of God for women. In an appendix to their *Study Bible for Women*, Catherine Kroeger, Mary Evans, and Elaine Storkey use the early church fathers to argue that the doctrine of the Trinity emphasizes "being-in-relationship" and unity in love amid diversity.[14] Reta Finger came to a similar conclusion, based on the teachings of a modern, not ancient, theologian. Finger credits Jürgen Moltmann's writings with radically changing her view of the Trinity. Before reading Moltmann's works, Finger writes that her view of the godhead was somewhat modalist. Modalists believe in one God to the point of blurring distinctions among the Father, Son, and Spirit. God is one but with three separate aspects or titles. Moltmann's description of a "trinitarian love story," based on the relationship between three distinct persons, convinced Finger that a truly biblical model of the Trinity is of mutuality, self-giving, and reciprocity, as exemplified by the how intimately the Father and Spirit related to Jesus' life.

Christology: The Person and Works of Christ

If some feminists found it difficult to envision how God as the Father could empower women, many more found a male savior even harder to accept: can a male savior save women? Traditionalist biblical feminists and some progressives answer this question affirmatively because it is not Jesus' maleness that saves. In an orthodox understanding of the Trinity, what belongs to the nature of God must also belong to the nature of the Messiah. The Trinity thus becomes "a first commentary on the divine nature of Christ."[15] So if God cannot be exclusively male, then neither can Christ be seen as an exclusively male savior. Jesus' "nominal maleness" is evident in his cultural characteristics: "Jesus is a first-century Jewish carpenter's son from Galilee. Thus he is temporally, geographically, ethnically, occupationally, educationally and sexually different from generations of sympathizers and followers. Gender is one and only one of many differences."[16]

Jesus' sex says no more about his divine nature than did his Galilean accent or occupation. Cornelius Plantinga Jr., a professor of systematic theology at Calvin College, commented that "one might as well argue that because God incarnate was Jewish, single, and an inhabitant of a pastoral setting, that Jewishness, bachelorhood, and thorough knowledge of sheep are all basic to Jesus' saving us."[17] Biblical feminists contend that the emphasis of the incarnation is not on Jesus' maleness but on Jesus' common humanity with human beings. Thus whenever referring to the incarnation, the Greek text always uses *anthropos*, meaning human. It never uses *aner*, the word for male. The term *aner* is used to refer to other men, such as Joseph in Luke 1:27, but not to Jesus.

Jesus and Sophia

As mentioned earlier, Mollenkott traced parallels between wisdom and God the Father and the Holy Spirit. Later, progressive biblical feminists tried to deemphasize Jesus' maleness by connecting him to Sophia, "wisdom." A Methodist minister, Susan Cady, and a Methodist teacher, Hal Taussig, explained more fully in *Daughters of Sarah* how Jesus and Wisdom were related.[18] "Wisdom," *sophia* in Greek, often is personified in the Old Testament. Because it is a feminine noun, *sophia* is referred to as a woman. Proverbs 8:1–5 states:

> Does not wisdom call out? Does not understanding raise her voice? On the heights along the way, where the paths meet, she takes her stand; beside the gates leading into the city, at the entrances, she cries aloud: To you, O men, I call out; I raise my voice to all mankind. You who are simple gain prudence; you who are foolish, gain understanding. (NIV)

Further on in this passage, verses 35 and 36 describe Sophia's role in salvation: "Whoever finds me finds life and receives favor from the Lord. But whoever fails to find me harms himself; all who hate me love death." Even several of the church fathers interpreted this passage christologically, seeing in it the foreshadowing of the revelation of Christ as God's Word and Wisdom. Theophilus of Antioch wrote about the Trinity as "God, His Word, and His Wisdom."

Cady and Taussig explain that it is Sophia to whom Jesus is referring when he says, "Wisdom is proved right by all her children" (Luke 7:35), and "That is why God in his wisdom [or the wisdom of God] said, 'I will send them prophets'" (Luke 11:49). This suggested to many progressive biblical feminists that Jesus was the "Son of Sophia," a title for the second person of the Trinity, like "the Son of God" or "the Word." With this in mind, Cady and Taussig argue that platonic influences led the writer of the Gospel of John to change the title used in John 1:1–3 from Sophia to Logos. ("In the beginning was the Word, and the Word was with God, and the Word was God. He was with God in the beginning. Through him all things were made; without him nothing was made that has been made.") Their reasoning is that the Word had never been described this way in the Old Testament but that Sophia had. This evidence led Cady and Taussig to conclude that Sophia was the preincarnate Christ.

Traditionalist biblical feminists, however, refuted the use of Sophia as an orthodox alternative by which to worship the second person of the Trinity. In response to the furor over the Re-Imagining Conference, *Priscilla Papers* published several studies of Sophia. In one article, Tina Ostrander, a student of Catherine Kroeger's at Gordon-Conwell, explains that *sophia* is a transliteration of the Greek word for "wisdom."[19] She acknowledges that Proverbs and several Apocryphal texts personify wisdom as a woman. She also notes that interest in Sophia is not new. Gnosticism, an early church heresy, sometimes taught that Sophia was a superior God. Shakers, Ostrander said, understood Sophia as the fourth person of the "Trinity," and in the Orthodox Church, one priest taught that Sophia was the glue that bound the Trinity together.

Ostrander maintains that Sophia should not be understood as a divine person but as an abstract aspect of God's character. First, Ostrander disagrees, however, with progressive biblical feminists' heavy reliance on Apocryphal and even Gnostic sources. If one looks only at texts in the Hebrew Bible, Sophia is nowhere used as a name for God. In Proverbs the personification of one aspect of God's character, wisdom, is not to show personhood but was a common literary device in wisdom literature. Folly, too, is often personified, but no feminists read this literally. In another article, Aida Besançon Spencer points out that God is often called by descriptive adjectives, such as when Paul refers to Christ as "the wisdom of God." This does not make it proper, though, to call wisdom God. God could be wisdom without wisdom's being God.

The Atonement

In *Daughters of Sarah*, over which she probably had more influence than anyone else after editing it for almost twenty years, Finger provided an overview of feminist theories of atonement.[20] She begins by outlining the three primary models of atonement: substitutionary, moral influence, and Christus Victor. She then offers a feminist analysis of each one, indicating their strengths and weaknesses. The substitutionary model emphasizes the death of Jesus to pay the penalty of God's wrath brought about by sin. Most evangelicals—Reformed, Wesleyan, and nondenominational— hold this view of the atonement. It is, in fact, one of the fundamentals of the faith unquestioned by evangelicals in their boundary debates. Finger, however, found this the least helpful theory for biblical feminists. Like Williams, Finger saw it often used as a club to encourage women to suffer for their husbands and families. Finger also believes that it has discouraged believers from actively working out their salvation. That is, women holding a substitutionary view of the atonement are less likely to seek leadership roles or to be socially active in society. In addition, the stress on individual sin and salvation ignores the presence of systemic evil, and last, by focusing on Jesus' death, it downplays his life and revolutionary treatment of women.

The moral influence theory of atonement puts more emphasis on Jesus' life than on his death, according to Finger. Through his example, human beings are made aware of God and of their need for moral development. This is the theory into which Williams's view of the cross, discussed at the beginning of this chapter, best fits. In fact, Williams questioned the need for an atonement at all. How can God be reconciled to humans through a death? Instead, Williams thinks that Christians should see the cross for what it is: "a symbol of evil."[21] Finger objects to this view, despite the possibilities for women to find love, grace, and inclusion in the model of Jesus' life. She thinks that it does not adequately account for the presence of real evil in the world, including patriarchy, since it seems to deny the reality of sin.

The final theory of atonement is the Christus Victor model. Finger calls this "the dominant one in the church for the first thousand years after Christ."[22] It is like substitutionary atonement in that it views humans as needing divine salvation that only Jesus can offer. Deliverance is not from God's wrath but from the bondage of evil forces. Jesus' resurrection, rather than his death, achieved victory over his enemies by vindicating his life and defeating death. It is this model that, Finger asserts, holds the most hope for Christian feminists. By identifying with the victorious Christ, women can achieve individual salvation as well as help overcome systems of evil with the hope that in God's new creation, all will be resurrected and all evil will be overcome. In addition, according to Finger, the vindication of Jesus' life has allowed women to recover Jesus as a person who powerfully opposed the patriarchal system of his day: "Power reversals and liberation of the oppressed were the content of his 'inauguration speech' (Luke 4). . . . In his revolutionary attitude toward women, in treating them as full human beings, he directly confronted the evil of sexism." Finger concludes:

> Can we as feminists trust in Christ to deliver us from evil? Can we believe that this man Jesus stripped himself of whatever male rights and privileges a sexist society gave him and engaged in mortal combat with the power of patriarchy? Can we trust that his resurrection in the power of God's Spirit is the beginning of the end of patriarchal oppression? I believe we can.[23]

Mollenkott's Universalist Christology

Other progressive biblical feminists, such as Virginia Mollenkott, speaking at the Re-Imagining Conference, seemed to deny the efficacy of a male savior. Mollenkott preferred to meditate on Sophia who, feminists claim, is never identified with suffering and death. Mollenkott argues that Sophia's lack of suffering and dying gives women an image of God and atonement that is both feminine and strong. Sophia thereby discourages women from suffering passively in silence, as Jesus dying on the cross does. Instead, Sophia instills in women a "deep quiet," "never affected by our ego-nature's thrashings and sufferings and feelings of abandonment."

Even Jesus experienced this characteristic of Sophia, Mollenkott stated, after the feeling of abandonment he felt on the cross, when he "committed his spirit (Self/Sophia) into the hands of God."[24]

Even before the Re-Imagining Conference, Mollenkott admitted to adjusting her view on Christ's work of salvation. In a discussion in the *Journal of Feminist Studies in Religion*, spurred by a criticism from the lesbian theologian Carter Heyward that her Christology was too exclusive, Mollenkott states that she believes that salvation is universal and is not accomplished through Jesus' death on the cross. By speaking of Jesus as the Messiah, she writes, she did not intend to exclude "Muslim, Jewish, and post-Christian and post-Judaic feminist women." She does not think that only Jesus Christ can save. Rather, Mollenkott uses the "symbol systems" of her own religious tradition to speak of the one, inclusive "divine Source of all being and becoming" and the one experience of faith.[25] In other words, Mollenkott invokes the name of Jesus to refer to one, universal God, to which all religions pray and worship. She goes on to say that she thus understands the apostle Paul to be speaking of the "New Humanity" when he uses the phrase "in Christ." This new humanity includes all people oriented toward justice, of any faith, who work to "cocreate with God." It is not limited to those who have personally accepted Jesus' atoning work on the cross, as evangelicals believe. Mollenkott's Christology thus focuses on the vision of Jesus to create a just society, not on his person (divine) or his work (salvation and the redemption of sin).

Mollenkott came to her Christology through a hermeneutic of liberation. Liberation theology began in the early 1970s out of the experience of Catholic priests who worked in the poorest barrios of Latin America. They argued that the church ought to serve the oppressed by working toward social justice—liberation—on earth, not just by preaching a heavenly kingdom yet to come, and they believed that theology had to begin with the experience of the oppressed. This method gave credence to experience as a legitimate beginning point for theological reflection. The feminist scholar Letty Russell described liberation theologies as "genitive theologies" of women, blacks, Latinos, and the like.[26] Such theologies had to be formulated by those who had concrete experience of social oppression.

Rosemary Radford Ruether was a feminist theologian who became interested in the possibilities that liberation theology held for women. While studying the early church, she came to believe that the Christian Bible was corrupted by dualism and, therefore, was oppressive to women.

Dualism describes a split in reality between "transcendent Spirit (mind, ego) and inferior and dependent physical nature." It is evidenced by a series of polarities: mind-body, individual-collective, grace-nature, spirit-matter, man-woman, God-creation. Each of these fit into a hierarchy of good and evil that associate man with "the male transcendent ego or God" and woman with the lower, material world. This assigns to her a negative identity in relation to the divine.[27] Gender, therefore, is the primary symbol of dualism and can be seen clearly in the subordinate way in which women are viewed in scripture. Thus, Ruether concludes that feminist theology cannot be based on the Christian Bible.

Probably the most detailed feminist theology to arise out of liberation theology came from Elisabeth Schüssler Fiorenza. A Catholic, like Ruether, Schüssler Fiorenza did not believe in normative authority located in the biblical texts. She argues that the biblical writers' intention was to serve particular communities, not to reveal timeless truths or relate historically accurate information, and so the biblical texts are not revelatory.[28] Authority comes from a community appropriating and interacting with the texts, not from the texts themselves. This stance allows Schüssler Fiorenza to locate revelation in the current community of faith, not in past texts. With the community as the locus of authority, Schüssler Fiorenza bases her feminist method of biblical interpretation on the experience of women, and since women have been suppressed through scripture, "biblical revelation and truth are given only in those texts and interpretive models that transcend critically their patriarchal frameworks."[29] Therefore, feminists must begin their biblical study with a hermeneutics of suspicion, in which all biblical texts are assumed to be androcentric and to serve the patriarchal structure.[30] She argues that texts found to be sexist should not be kept: "the litmus test for invoking scripture as the Word of God must be whether or not biblical texts and traditions seek to end relations of domination and exploitation."[31]

Mollenkott's book *Godding: Human Responsibility and the Bible* offers a good study of the progression of her theology from a historical-critical methodology to liberation theology. Mollenkott uses the principle of justice as a key theme of the Bible to argue that humans are responsible for bringing about righteousness on earth. "Godding," she explains, refers to the "embodiment or incarnation of God's love in human flesh, with the goal of cocreating with God a just and loving human society."[32] In other words, *godding* is the term she uses to describe humans embodying justice.[33] Mollenkott suggests that many aspects of American society would be changed if Christians (a term she uses inclusively) embodied justice, because a just and loving society would be characterized by mutual interdependence rather than by hierarchical relationships: "But in accepting our union with the Christ-nature, that is, in affirming our willingness to do God's will, we become the New Humanity in which are dissolved all the barriers of racism, classism, sexism, heterosexism, and the militarism that grows out of them."[34]

In her last book, *Omnigender*, Mollenkott again uses justice as her primary interpretive principle. This time, though, she argues that a binary gender construct is outmoded. Mollenkott offers as an alternative a paradigm of "omnigender" in which people of every gender, including homosexual, bisexual, and transgendered, should be fully embraced by society. She bases her new paradigm on the biblical mandate for human fulfillment and wholeness and Jesus' model of inclusivity. Mollenkott then turns to Muslim, Jewish, and other religious sources to find alternative, more inclusive, concepts of gender.

Such inclusiveness produces a universalist conception of salvation. Like most liberation theologians, Mollenkott believes that those who do justice and mercy are followers of God (cf. Micah 6:8). Since it is the struggle against exploitation and injustice that shows saving faith, people of every religion, ethnicity, and lifestyle can be "in Christ." Mollenkott acknowledges that Jesus is the exemplary model of godding, to whom people from all religious traditions should look, hence the focus on him in Christianity. She contends, however, that traditional Christianity has focused too exclusively on Jesus, to the detriment of accomplishing the goal of a just society:

> The traditional interpretation of the righteous servant tends to spotlight Jesus of Nazareth as a one-time-only phenomenon, someone out of the past at whose feet we may happily and lazily grovel, someone who will rescue us single-handedly and who thus relieves us of our contemporary responsibility to struggle to bring forth justice in our world.[35]

In this light, Mollenkott does not interpret the suffering servant of Isaiah 42 ("I have put my Spirit upon my servant who will bring forth justice to the nations," v. 1) traditionally as a reference to a single savior, Jesus, who will come to rescue the world, but as all persons who love their neighbors as themselves. This is what the Bible means by salvation.

Traditionalist Biblical Feminists' Christology

For traditionalist biblical feminists the question of whether a male savior can save women is unquestioningly yes. Their conception of women's need for redemption and Jesus' ability to provide it have continued to conform to traditional evangelical doctrine. Instead, traditionalist feminists concentrate on proving to their fellow evangelicals that Jesus' treatment of women is empowering and thus models how his followers should act.

Traditionalist biblical feminists do not have a problem separating Jesus' ontological maleness with an essentially ungendered divine nature. In fact, they use cultural-historical criticism to argue that Jesus' maleness helped him liberate women in the culture of his day. During Jesus' lifetime, they observe, a woman would have made little impact on societal norms because of her low status. Josephus, they maintain, summed up the view of women at that time when he said: "The woman . . . is in all things inferior to the man."[36] In Jewish society, women were confined to the domestic sphere. They were expected to keep out of the public eye, and especially in Jerusalem, women were to be veiled in public. Men were to speak to women as little as possible. Much of the reason for this caution was because men might be tempted by women's sensuality, "whose heart is snares and nets and whose hands are fetters."[37] This perception originated, at least partially, from the view of Eve as being a temptress who led Adam into sin. Also, deuteronomic law states that men were to avoid women at times when their sexuality was explicitly manifest—during menstruation and after childbirth (there was a longer period of ceremonial uncleanness after the birth of a female child than after a male). The result, according to biblical feminists, was that women were viewed as second-class citizens, whom men blamed when they were tempted into sexual sin.

According to evangelical feminists, several stories in the gospels illustrate the way that Jesus liberated women from such cultural constraints based on gender. Biblical feminists, for example, maintain that Jesus treated women as subjects rather than sex objects, as illustrated by the Sermon on the Mount (Matthew 5:27–28), in which Jesus says that a man who looks on a woman with lust already has committed the sin of adultery. And in both Luke 7:36–50 and Mark 5:25–34, against social norms and Levitical law, Jesus allows a "sinful woman" and a woman who is menstruating (respectively) to touch him and even praises their faith for doing so.

Perhaps the most radical display of Jesus' breaking the traditional so-cial constraints on women is in John 8:1–11, in which the Pharisees bring to Jesus a woman caught in the act of adultery. Mary Evans argues that they were trying to trap him, since they knew that stoning was against Roman law, even though it was required by Jewish law in such a situa-tion. In their attempt at entrapment, the Pharisees show their misogynist attitude toward women. First, Jewish law stated that both the man and the woman caught in the act of adultery were to be stoned, but they de-livered only the woman. Second, they were willing to use this woman merely as an object in a trap to achieve their goal. Jesus' response to the dilemma is to turn the tables on them: "Let anyone of you who is with-out sin be the first to throw a stone at her" (v. 7). With these words, he indicates that the woman indeed may have sinned, but so too had her ac-cusers. Her sin was no worse in the eyes of God than theirs. When each accuser finally leaves, Jesus deals with her sin: "Neither do I condemn you; go now and leave your life of sin" (v. 11). Traditionalist biblical fem-inists believed it was significant that Jesus confronts her sin compassion-ately in order to treat her as a fully responsible adult, capable of being held accountable for her actions. To be sure, the Pharisees also want to hold her accountable. The difference is that the Pharisees are willing to ignore the man's sins, but not the woman's. Jesus' behavior in this situa-tion shows that he was willing to go outside his patriarchal surroundings by treating women as responsible human beings, not as sex objects or the possessions of men.

In contrast to the first-century rabbi Eliezer, who wrote, "Rather should the words of the Torah be burned than entrusted to a woman . . . whoever teaches his daughter the Torah is like one who teaches her las-civiousness," Jesus taught women (Luke 8:1–3 and 10:38–41).[38] Ac-cording to traditionalist biblical feminists, this elevated women's status in that culture, as did the fact that Jesus chose to reveal to women some of the most significant theological insights of the gospels. In John 11:1–27, when Jesus came to heal the sick brother of Mary and Martha, Jesus re-vealed to Martha that he was the resurrection and the life. Biblical femi-nists point out that this is the only place in the gospels where Jesus reveals this fact, and he chose to disclose it to a woman.

Jesus disclosed another important theological idea to the woman at the well (John 4:1–42). His conversation with the woman, a Samaritan, begins when he requests a drink of water. Jesus and the samaritan woman quickly turn to spiritual topics, including the nature of God and worship: "God is spirit, and those who worship him must worship in spirit and truth" (v. 24). Finally, Jesus reveals to her that he is the Messiah, and the woman responds, "I know that Messiah (called Christ) is coming. When he comes, he will explain everything to us." Jesus replies, "I who speak to you am he" (vv. 25–26). The expression Jesus uses, "I am," was the name God had given himself when speaking to Moses from the burning bush (Exodus 3:14). Jesus thus proclaims his divinity. This conversation—full of significant truths about the nature of God, worship, eternity, and salvation—and the conversation with Martha illustrates to evangelical feminists that Jesus believed that women were worthy and capable of receiving his teaching.

Anthropology: Male and Female Relationships, Human Sexuality, Sin, and Grace

In Christian theology, the word *anthropology* refers to the doctrine of the nature of humankind, and its study begins with the creation accounts in Genesis. Many feminists find these texts among the most offensive in the Bible, as it was on Genesis that patriarchal, Western society justified and perpetuated women's subjection to men. In the fourth century, Augustine argued that according to Genesis, a woman could possess the image of God only when joined with a man, whereas a man alone fully reflected God's image (although Augustine did concede that women could be redeemed). In the Middle Ages, Aquinas taught that women existed only because of their ability to procreate. During the Reformation, both Luther and Calvin affirmed the equality of male and female in their original creation but taught that women were subordinate to men, either as punishment for Eve's sin (Luther) or as part of a divinely instituted social order (Calvin). For these reasons, many feminists, including many from the Christian tradition, concluded that Christianity, or at least the Bible, was hopelessly lost to patriarchy. Mary Daly, who began her career as a Catholic theologian, came to reject Christianity entirely because it was hopelessly patriarchal, in large part due to the negative view of women it taught in the opening pages of the Bible.[39]

Evangelical feminists, though, believed that Genesis had made many contributions to the construction of a positive view of women and their role in the world. As we have already seen, Scanzoni and Hardesty argue in *All We're Meant to Be* that Genesis does not teach a divine relational order. Rather, it teaches the essential unity of men and women in nature and in the stewardship of the earth. Mollenkott, Jewett, Scanzoni, Hardesty, Gundry, Kroeger, and others have long since dealt exegetically with the basic questions raised about the creation accounts: Were men and women created equally in God's image? Was woman made to be a subordinate helper to man? What was the meaning of *ezer k'nego* (translated as "helpmeet" in the King James Version of the Bible)? Did God give both Adam and Eve the authority to be stewards of the earth? And was God's intention with the curse to subjugate women to men? For every solution biblical feminists offered, however, traditional scholars found other criticisms of the text.

Male and Female Relationships in the Creation Accounts

Both traditionalists and feminists complain that Genesis 2 teaches women's inferiority to man through the order of creation. Traditionalists believe that Eve was created almost as an afterthought, merely as a companion for Adam. But biblical feminists believe that the purpose of the second creation account is to teach man and woman's relatedness rather than their difference. Both man and woman were created by God: the rib, in Eve's case, or dust, in Adam's, were simply the raw materials.[40] This intention can be seen in verse 23 with man's soliloquy that woman is "bone of my bones, and flesh of my flesh." The focus of Adam's words is on the complementarity of woman, not on her uniqueness.

Others see in Genesis 2 a problem with the naming of woman. In the Hebrew scriptures, the act of naming sometimes indicates power over the object named. Examples of this occur in Genesis 2:19–20 (when God brings the animals to Adam to be named), Genesis 4:17 (when Cain builds and names a city), and Genesis 16:11 (where Abram is told to name his son Ishmael). Some critics argue that Adam's act of naming "woman" ("she shall be called 'woman' for she was taken out of man," 2:23) indicates his sovereignty over her and, by extension, men's continued supremacy over women.

Biblical feminists disagreed and applied feminist theologian Phyllis Trible's exegesis of the Hebrew to explain why. In *God and the Rhetoric of Sexuality*, Trible explains that throughout the Hebrew Bible the "verb 'to call' only connoted an establishment of power over something when it was linked with the noun 'name.'"[41] This is not the case in Genesis 2:23, however, in which Adam states, "She shall be called 'woman.'" In this passage, the noun *name* does not appear. Trible concludes that this verse shows Adam's recognition of woman's (*issa*) sexuality in the context of man and woman's common humanity; it was not a naming. Thus it does not indicate man's power over woman.

Evangelical feminists also have used Trible's interpretation of Genesis 1:27 to help clarify further what it means for men and women to be created in the image of God.[42] As Paul Jewett did, Trible contends that "clearly, 'male and female' correspond structurally to 'the image of God' and this formal parallelism indicates a semantic correspondence."[43] In her opinion, the phrase ("in the image of God he created them, male and female") is a metaphor using "male and female" as the better-known element to illuminate the lesser-known element, "in the image of God." Once she has established this, she looks for places where biblical language further illuminates what it means for God's image to be male and female. One such place is in the consistent use of the word *compassion* or *mercy* to describe God. The Hebrew word for "compassion" is *rahum*, a form of the noun *rehem*, meaning "womb." Trible traces the use of *rahum* and finds that it is used throughout the Hebrew scriptures only in reference to the creator, never of God's creation, humanity. She concludes that the use of this feminine, formulaic language throughout the "law, prophets, and writings" is one instance in which a new and feminine dimension of God is revealed.

Traditionalist evangelical feminists also continued to fight claims for women's subordination to man based on the curse pronounced in Genesis 3. Similar to Mollenkott's early interpretive model, Gilbert Bilezekian defines his basic interpretive method as following the creation, fall, and redemption.[44] God's original purpose, mutuality, is reflected in creation. Sin distorted God's created order and introduced discord in relationships. The new covenant in Christ restored God's original intention of mutuality. Since Genesis 1 and 2 describe life as God intended it to be, Bilezekian finds it meaningful that any suggestion of man's authority over woman is "conspicuously absent" from these passages. The only references to authority in these two chapters involve God's sovereignty over humans and humans' dominion over the earth and its creatures.

According to Bilezekian, man's rule over woman enters the picture only in the context of the fall in chapter 3. Bilezekian thinks it important that Eve was not present with Adam when God told him not to eat the fruit from the tree of life (having given Adam this command in 2:16–17 before Eve was created, vv. 21–22). Bilezekian postulates from this that Eve possessed only "theoretical knowledge" and so was less well prepared to deal with the lies of the serpent. It does not indicate that Eve was less intelligent or able to handle knowledge. It simply shows that Eve did not have the same access to the teachings and command that Adam had. Thus, "lacking adequate teaching and experience, she listened to the wrong teacher and was duped."[45]

Bilezekian also addresses later traditionalist claims that God's summoning Adam to account for his actions first (vv. 8–9) indicates that Adam exercised a "priestly role" over Eve. Bilezekian disagrees, pointing out that God asked Adam no questions pertaining to Eve, nor did Adam act as a pastor or supervisor for Eve. Instead, Adam acted as her accuser. Eve's turn before God would come, and Bilezekian notes that she had to account for her own actions. He determines that rather than implying that man held a priestly role over woman, this section of the text (vv. 8–13) actually reveals the "frightful degree of deterioration" in human relationships so soon after the entrance of sin into the world.

The level of deterioration in relationships after the fall extended to Adam and Eve's relationship with God as well. The consequences that God pronounced on Adam and Eve—toil in the field and pain in childbirth—were only the visible marks of the new distance between God and them. Now humans would experience death, separation from God, and suffering as a preliminary form death. Bilezekian further proposed that the statement that woman's desire would be for her husband meant that as the one who bore children, she would yearn for the mutuality that had defined the family before the fall. The husband, however, would not reciprocate that desire. Instead of providing love and support, he would rule over her. Bilezekian determined that suffering, death, and male dominance are not part of God's original intention in creation. All are the result of sin.

Another traditionalist biblical feminist, Mary Stewart van Leeuwen, used the research of feminist Carol Gilligan in combination with that by evangelicals like Bilezekian to establish her theory of the fall. Gilligan was a professor at Harvard who studied the moral development of children. Basing her work on earlier research conducted only on boys, Gilligan followed both boys and girls and found that boys' and girls' ideas of morality are different, based on two separate ways of relating to others. Boys relate to others through competition, and thus early on they acquire a sense of justice and fair play. Girls relate to others by connectedness and so focus on minimizing pain and harm to all involved. Applied to the creation accounts, Gilligan's theory suggested to van Leeuwen that the consequences of Adam's and Eve's sins corresponded to their gender. In "The Christian Mind and the Challenge of Gender Relations," van Leeuwen claims that the primary consequence for Adam's sin is separation and dominance:

> a propensity in man to let the dominion run wild—to impose it in cavalier and illegitimate ways not only upon the earth and upon other men . . . but also upon the person who is "bone of (his) bones and flesh of (his) flesh—the helper corresponding to (his very) self."[46]

The consequence of woman's sin, in contrast, coincides with her desire to be connected to man. Van Leeuwen suggests that woman now has an unreciprocated desire for intimacy and for the preservation of relationships at the expense of exercising accountable dominion herself.

Male and Female Relationships in the Pauline Corpus

The consequences of the fall did not affect only individual relationships. Van Leeuwen believes that they also have distorted societal institutions, such as the family. Thus God's grace through Christ's redemption should, in turn, affect not only individuals but also institutions. This belief comes from van Leeuwen's commitment to Dutch Reformed theology. Reformed theology generally is better known for its "other-worldly" perspective on individual sin and future transformation. Dutch Calvinism, however, stresses engaging every aspect of society from a distinctly Christian point of view, since both individuals and institutions have been infected by sin and require transformation. Christians, therefore, ought to work for systemic change through agencies that mediate God's grace to the world at large by restraining sin and promoting God's kingdom. Van Leeuwen thinks that this includes the societal problem of gender inequity within the institutions of marriage, family, and the church.

Biblical feminists turned to the Pauline epistles to reinterpret the passages in which Paul addresses these institutions. We have seen how Jewett and Mollenkott argued that Paul's most androcentric writings are evidence of his struggle with the patriarchal culture of his day versus the freedom that Christ had brought. Traditionalist biblical feminists concluded instead that all the Pauline passages can be read as overthrowing patriarchy in light of Paul's overarching theme of Galatians 3:28, that there is "neither Jew nor Greek, there is neither slave nor free man, there is neither male nor female; for you are all one in Christ."

Craig Keener on Ephesians 5

Craig Keener, an ordained minister in the National Baptist Convention (a traditionally black denomination) and a professor of New Testament at Hood Seminary, agreed with the biblical feminist understanding of the Pauline epistles but admitted that he had not always held egalitarian views of women in the church and home. As an undergraduate, Keener "thought that it was safer" to hold to more traditional views of women's roles until he could determine with certainty what the Bible said. As he began to research the biblical texts, he found he needed to understand the culture and history of the world in which the New Testament was written, since most of the texts on women appeared in letters to specific audiences in specific locations. Upon doing so, he determined that much of what Paul wrote about women addressed specific congregational situations and was not transcultural.

Keener's treatment of Ephesians 5:22–33 illustrates his conclusions about the cultural relativity of many of Paul's teachings on women. Keener's general argument is that Paul wanted the gospel to gain a strong hearing in Greco-Roman society, and so he tempered the liberating radicalism of the gospel with sensitivity to his culture. This means that Paul couched his message of mutuality between husbands and wives in the language of submission to which his audience was accustomed. Aristotle introduced the concept of "household codes." These guidelines for family relationships stressed the submission of the wife to the husband and encouraged the husband to rule over his household.[47] Keener argues that in the world of the New Testament, societal changes threatened this traditional marital structure as women gained more freedoms. Christianity and Judaism, along with other new mystery cults, were suspected of having a subversive role in these changes. Accordingly, in Ephesians 5:21–33, Paul phrased his own instructions to husbands and wives in a way that would demonstrate that Christians were upstanding members of society.

At the same time, however, Keener argues that Paul opposed Greco-Roman societal values where they fell short of the gospel. So Paul preached not only wifely submission but the submission of all believers to one another. In Ephesians 5:21–24 Paul urges:

> Submit to one another out of reverence for Christ. Wives, submit to your husbands as to the Lord. For the husband is the head of the wife as Christ is the head of the church, his body, of which he is the Saviour. Now as the church submits to Christ, so also wives should submit to their husbands in everything.

According to Keener, in the passage preceding this (vv. 15–21), Paul is describing what it looks like for believers to be filled the Holy Spirit. They corporately worship God, confessing faith in God's sovereignty, and they have different relationships within their family. They submit to each other in love. Verse 21 is the hinge between the two passages. In fact, Keener points out that verse 22, "wives submit to your husbands," depends on verse 21 for the verb *submit*. Thus, verse 22 could be translated "for example, wives to your husbands."[48] In other words, Christian wives' submission to their husbands is a model of what all Christians' submission to one another should look like. More radical still is Paul's admonition to Christian husbands that describes husbandly "submission" in a Christian marriage (vv. 25–33). Unlike secular society, which emphasized the husband's rule, Paul focuses on the husband's sacrificial love for his wife. Keener concludes that Paul "subordinates wives so weakly, and emphasizes mutuality so strongly, that it is difficult to believe that he is arguing for their transcultural subordination."[49]

Human Sexuality in the Scriptures

Just as the fall distorted mutual submission between husbands and wives, evangelical feminists believed that God's creative act of sexual union, too, was warped by separation and dominance. According to traditionalist biblical feminists, God intended sexual intercourse as a means of physically uniting a man and woman, who already were joined spiritually in the act of marriage. It was an important part of God's original intention for "oneness" between a man and a woman. Sin, however, affected human sexuality by splitting mind and body, making sex a wholly physical act. Van Leeuwen commented: "As sex becomes more available and casual, it becomes something I do with my body, but it has less and less power to touch the deep well-springs of my full sexuality."[50] American society, therefore, exhibits the effects of such a division by its preoccupation with sex as an undeniable physical urge, resulting in casual, deviant, and commercial sex and its consequences.

The social implication of this view led many traditionalist feminists to disapprove of casual sex, prostitution, pornography, abortion, and homosexuality. A survey of the members of Christians for Biblical Equality by Kaye Cook, a member of both the CBE and the EWC, found that only 3 percent supported homosexual rights.[51] It is possible that even fewer believed that the Bible condones homosexuality. For example, Virginia Hearn stated that she had voted for the EWC's resolution on homosexuality in 1986 because it concerned civil rights for homosexuals, with which she agreed, although she did not believe that the Bible could be interpreted to condone homosexuality. In addition, the survey showed that only 13 percent of the CBE's members (versus 100% for EWC members) supported legislation that gave women the right to safe abortions. This 13 percent also may have included women who still believed that abortion on demand should be restricted, and it is possible as well that some traditionalist biblical feminists did not approve of abortion but still thought that making it illegal was an incorrect way to deal with the problem of unwanted pregnancies. (Virginia Hearn, for example, noted that she fit into this latter category.)

Progressive biblical feminists agreed with traditionalist feminists that American society needs to adjust its view of human sexuality to look at sexual relationships with a view toward intimacy and wholeness. They did not, however, confine this kind of mutuality to heterosexual marriage. In a survey similar to the one taken of CBE members, Cook found that 83 percent of the EWC members supported a homosexual rights agenda.[52]

Mollenkott, who often played a prophetic role in the EWC by pushing the organization to pursue justice in new arenas, continued to push it in this area. As in other areas of her theology, Mollenkott began to reinterpret the Bible in accordance with her own experience, in this case as a lesbian. She described that as a child, she was taught that homosexuality was a sin, and thus she concluded that God was not loving but judgmental, angry, and capricious if he would condemn someone for the way that he had made him or her. Even so, she still believed the Bible taught that God was loving and just. She reflected on Jesus' words in Matthew 22:37–40 in which Jesus states that to love God and to love one's neighbor are the two greatest commandments and that "all the Law and the Prophets hang on these." Mollenkott interpreted this to mean that love defined what was normative in scripture. If an act is truly loving and not abusive or exploitive, it is good in the sight of God. In consequence, Mollenkott argues, the Bible could not advocate a position that oppressed any group by not accepting its created identity, including that of homosexual, for it would not be loving. Any texts that seem to do so either were cultural concessions or were not referring to homosexual orientation. As we have seen, this led Mollenkott to argue in her book *Omni-Gender* that in fact, the scripture teaches a gender-fluid view of human sexuality, not a binary, male-female sexuality.

Scanzoni also reexamined her stance on homosexuality and her biblical hermeneutic based on Mollenkott's experiences as a Christian lesbian. In the preface to the 1994 edition of *Is the Homosexual My Neighbor?* Scanzoni and Mollenkott shared some of the correspondence between them when Mollenkott revealed her sexual orientation to Scanzoni. In the final letter, Scanzoni wrote that she had a "Peter vision" in which God showed her that compassion and love should be her guide regarding how to deal with those of a homosexual orientation. In Acts 10, God showed Peter that he should follow the inner voice of God rather than the letter of the law in regard to dietary laws. Scanzoni and Mollenkott argued that in the same way, God can use an inner voice to lead people to reject societal rules and biblical guidelines. They admitted that this carried a risk of mistaking one's subjective desires for God's inner voice but decided that the risk was equally great to stick with outdated rules of the past. They concluded that even apparently clear biblical injunctions did not relieve Christians from having to deal with the complexities concerning social issues.[53]

In addition to advocating for equal rights for homosexual people, progressive evangelical feminists expressed unconditional love and promoted justice by maintaining a nonjudgmental position on the issue of abortion. According to Cook, 100 percent of EWC members supported legalizing abortion.[54] Reta Finger suggested one reason for progressive biblical feminists' view:

> We live in a fallen world where mutual caring is often unknown and contraceptives frequently unavailable, where abortions occur and children are born, neglected, and ruined. . . . If she has a relationship with a man willing to share as equally as possible with child care and support,

that man's desires must be equally considered. Where a woman has a community or extended family willing to share love and responsibility, that community or family should have input. But to the degree that a woman is alone, or knows others will not come through . . . to that degree a woman must make her own decision.[55]

For progressive feminists, abortion is a larger, societal problem. It is not simply the result of individual sin; it results from the lack of mutual caring and justice in American society. Accordingly, they support women's right to abortion, perhaps as a necessary evil, in order to free women from an oppressive, patriarchal system while encouraging women who found themselves burdened by an unwanted pregnancy to consider every other option.[56]

Virginia Mollenkott's View of Sin

Traditionalist biblical feminists' views of sin and grace remained largely within orthodox theological conceptions. Many progressive biblical feminists changed their conceptions of sin and grace, however. For example, Virginia Mollenkott's switch to a theology of liberation also affected her conception of sin. Traditionally, evangelicals have believed in original sin. This means that sin entered the world through Adam and Eve's rebellion and was imparted to every human being as a tendency to rebel against God. As such, many evangelicals believe that the first sin is that of pride. Mollenkott, however, used liberation theology to argue that the definition of sin as selfish pride was fine when it came to dominant groups but that

> what any oppressed person needs to repent of is not pride, but lack of it! Girls and women in our culture need to turn away from self-denigration and learn to respect and develop their own gifts. Many peasants in Latin America have discovered a need to let go of passivity in the face of poverty, recognizing God's love for them and their entitlement to the good basics of life. To preach Christlike servanthood to people who have never been in touch with their power and autonomy, is to commit an obscenity. First, people must be empowered. . . . The gospel speaks empowerment to our oppressed aspects, and repentance and responsibility to our powerfulness.[57]

Later, in *Sensuous Spirituality*, Mollenkott incorporated a variety of sources and methodologies, several non-Christian, to argue that people are not originally sinful.[58] Rather, humans are essentially innocent, spiritual beings "who [are] temporarily having human experiences." Mollenkott describes this change in her theology as moving away from a "sin-centered" to a "blessing-centered" theology, in which sin is defined as the egotistic human tendency to imagine itself "separate from God and separate from all other creatures."[59] Christians bring grace to the world by accepting their union with God (to whom Mollenkott also refers as "the Source," "Energizer," "Essence of our deepest nature," "the Cosmic Lover," and "the Christ-nature") and embodying unconditional love to all.[60] Mollenkott readily admitted that this view of God as a part of creation is panentheistic. (Panentheism teaches that although God has an identity larger than creation; creation is part of God, but it is not the same as God. This differs from pantheism, in which God and the universe are one and the same.) But she felt that panentheism more accurately describes what the Bible teaches about God's transcendent and immanent nature and that she was being more faithful to scripture than her fundamentalist forebears had been.

Ecclesiology: Women's Roles in the Church

By believing in universal salvation (salvation that is not limited to those who personally accept Christ's death on the cross in payment for their sins but that is open to all), the nature of progressive biblical feminist ecclesiology is clear. It is pluralistic. In contrast, traditionalist feminists rarely address the nature of the church, assuming, as do most evangelicals, that the church is made up of the community of believers, the body of Christ. For evangelicals, this body is exclusive. Anyone is welcome to attend, but only true believers, those who trust in Christ's death on the cross to redeem their sins and who submit to God's authority, are true members of God's kingdom. As in other areas of doctrine, the focus of biblical feminists' interest in ecclesiology resides in its practical outworkings: who can serve as an ordained minister of Christ, whether women can be leaders in the church, and whether the body of Christ should use gender-neutral language.

Traditionalist Biblical Feminists on Women in Church Leadership

Biblical feminists strongly support women in every aspect of church leadership. According to Cook, 94 percent of the people she surveyed in the CBE and 98 percent of those in the EWC supported the ordination of women.[61] It is no surprise, then, that the passages of scripture most often reinterpreted by biblical feminists are the Pauline epistles so frequently used to bar women from leadership roles.[62] After the early years, progressive biblical feminists did little to address those passages, but traditionalist biblical feminists continued to apply historical and cultural criticism to the Pauline texts. This was because traditionalist feminists remained, for the most part, in mainstream evangelical churches.[63] They thus sought to convince their fellow evangelicals to change their opinions through the Bible, the only infallible source of authority for faith and practice.

1 Timothy 2

One of the passages cited most often as the basis for excluding women from leadership in the church is 1 Timothy 2:11–14:

> A woman should learn in quietness and full submission. I do not permit a woman to teach or to have authority over a man; she must be silent. For Adam was formed first, then Eve. And Adam was not the one deceived; it was the woman who was deceived and became a sinner.

Most evangelicals accept that Paul wrote this epistle and understand that it was written to Timothy, the young pastor and former companion of Paul, at Ephesus in Asia Minor. In addition, most believe that it clearly proscribes a transcultural rule that women should not be in authoritative or teaching positions in the church, based on woman's culpability in the fall. Traditionalist biblical feminists, however, argue that studying the historical and literary context of this passage reveals that it does not teach a timeless principle at all. Rather, Paul's main concern was with combating the heresy being promoted by false teachers and maintaining the reputation of the church in Greco-Roman society.

David Scholer begins his interpretation of 1 Timothy by pointing out the textual indicators of the cultural situation at Ephesus.[64] Several times

Paul mentions heretical teachers (1:3–7, 18–20; 4:1–8; 5:16, and 6:3–10). In his first mention of heresy, Paul indicates that it spread through "meaningless talk." In another passage (4:1–8), Paul specifically addresses a false teaching that forbids people to marry and that was spread through gossip, "old wives' tales." In another section of this first letter to Timothy, Paul is particularly concerned about the behavior of the women in the church. He suggests that widows under sixty remarry, that women avoid "malicious talk" and idle conversation, and that women be temperate and trustworthy. The apostle also expresses a concern for propriety in the behavior of members of the congregation at Ephesus: "I am writing you these instructions so that, if I am delayed, you will know how people ought to conduct themselves in God's household" (3:14–15).

These textual hints suggested to Scholer that Paul was battling a heresy at the church in Ephesus that was leading idle women to indecorous behavior, which reflected poorly on the young church. This would have been of particular importance in a city like Ephesus, where the Christian church may have been seen as just one more cultic religion in a city known for its many religions and teachers. In order for the church to remain above reproach in Greco-Roman society and maintain its witness, Paul instructed the Ephesians to observe a higher standard of cultural decency, including in women's roles.

Scholer argues that this call is found in the surrounding text. For example, just before his statement that women should learn in quietness, Paul wrote: "I also want women to dress modestly, with decency and propriety, not with braided hair or gold or pearls or expensive clothes, but with good deeds, appropriate for women who profess to worship God" (2:9–10). Most conservative interpreters do not claim that these earlier verses indicate normative action for all time but instead outline a standard of decency based on the cultural situation of Greco-Roman society. It would be incongruous, then, to consider verses 11 and 12 to be normative. In other words, since the motive behind verses 9–10 was to maintain a good reputation in secular society and since there was nothing to indicate that verses 11–12 were different from their surrounding context, they too should be seen as appropriate to a specific setting in order to maintain the church's good reputation.

Part of maintaining a good reputation is correctly imparting the teachings of the church. Scholer contends that much of the false teaching in Ephesus involved women as followers and possibly teachers. Scholer believes that women were engaged in "meaningless talk" with false teachers (1:6) and "desired to be teachers of the law" but that they were not yet familiar with the true doctrine of the church (1:7). Hence Paul enjoined the women to remain silent until they could be properly educated, rather than spread false teaching that would hinder the gospel. Because this problem applied only to Ephesus at that time, Scholer maintains that the injunction for women to keep silent should not be made normative in the modern church. Instead, the timeless principle from this passage is that no one should be put in a position of authority before learning the essentials of the faith.

In bolstering his argument for cultural limitedness, Scholer points out that throughout the book of Acts and Paul's letters, women minister alongside men; therefore, Paul could not have been stating a normative principle in 1 Timothy. Many interpreters claim, though, that Paul's use of Genesis was meant to make 2:10–11 normative. Scholer responds that this would be the case only if the creation accounts were intended to teach women's subordination to man. As we have already seen, biblical feminists denied that this was the case. Scholer believes, instead, that Paul cited the Genesis story only as an illustration. Women in Ephesus were falling prey to false teachers just as Eve fell prey to a false teacher. This does not mean that only Eve was to blame for sin any more than it means that women are to keep silent forever. Scholer concludes, therefore, that Paul did not intend to set up patriarchy as the norm in the church. Instead, Paul gave instructions to a specific church for a specific time in order to maintain the church's reputation to the glory of God and the building up of the church body (much as Paul stated in another passage: "I have made myself a slave to all, that I might win the more," 1 Corinthians 9:19).[65]

1 Corinthians 11

Another passage that is often used to limit women's roles in the church is 1 Corinthians 11:2–10.[66] It is a long and convoluted argument, and earlier attempts to interpret this passage failed to convince opponents of gender equality in the churches. Thus, later evangelical feminists tried to finally untangle this text.

Mary Hayter, a chaplain at Cambridge University, was one biblical feminist who addressed this difficult passage. Although she is not an American biblical feminist, many evangelicals in the United States have cited her work in their own discussions of 1 Corinthians. Hayter first studied the cultural situation at the time of Paul's writing. Not unlike earlier interpretations of this passage by biblical feminists, she suggests that Hellenistic and Gnostic philosophies influenced the interpretation of Paul's texts relating to women, primarily by promoting a negative view of sexuality and the feminine. As already noted, one of Gnosticism's basic beliefs was that matter is evil. Because the body is matter, it is seen as evil, which leads to a denigration of sex and an elevation of pure spirituality and androgyny. The result was that Gnostic philosophy subjugated women to men because women are more closely associated with matter and the body, and men are associated with rationality and the mind. Hayter argues that these views not only permeated society at that time but that the influence of Hellenistic philosophy on Western culture also has been so great that, as H. E. Brunner stated, this idea has "more or less unconsciously and secretly . . . determined the thought of Christendom down to the present day."[67] The premise that Hellenistic culture influenced early church theologians and later interpretations of Genesis became the background for Hayter's reinterpretation of 1 Corinthians.

Hayter next points out that the immediate context in which 1 Corinthians 11 appeared dealt with instructions on community worship. Hayter believes that Paul's main concern was for the right order of worship, toward the end that the gospel would be promoted. She also argues that in this passage, Paul was referring to the arrangement of women's hair, not a head covering. In Hellenistic culture, Hayter observed, pagan worship was marked by frenetic movement with loose, flowing hair. So Paul was indicating that "women should not worship as cultically unclean persons by letting their hair down" because intelligible missionary proclamation, not frenzy, was the true sign of the Christian community and the indwelling of Christ.[68]

There are other problems with the complicated passage in 1 Corinthians 11, including its grammatical context. For example, conservative theologians believe about 1 Corinthians 11, as they do for Ephesians 5, that the word *head* and the reference to Genesis prove that this text teaches woman's subordination to man. Hayter, however, once more points out that the term *kephale* (head) can mean "source" as well as "superior rank."[69] She cites a study by Bilezekian in which he states that in no instances is *kephale* used to mean "ruler or person of superior authority or rank."[70] Hayter concludes that the signification of "head" as "source" makes more sense in light of the fact that in Greco-Roman society, the heart was seen as the source of logic and the head as the source of life and emotions.

Another grammatical difficulty is the proper translation of the word *exousia*. Traditional theologians translate it "as a symbol of authority." The text would then imply that Paul thought women ought to wear a symbol of man's authority over her during worship. This is why, for example, many Plymouth Brethren congregations insist that women wear head coverings. Hayter argues that the other instances in which Paul used *exousia*, it is translated as "control over one's own will" (1 Corinthians 7:37), "freedom" (1 Corinthians 8:9), or "right" (1 Corinthians 9:4, 5, 12, 18; Romans 9:21; 2 Thessalonians 3:9). By applying principles of grammar and literary context, Hayter determines, it is more appropriate to assume that Paul meant no more than what he said: "authority," not "a symbol of man's authority." Thus, *exousia* refers to the woman's "own authority to pray and prophesy in the new order of the Christian community. . . . There is no plausible reason why it should be presupposed that in 1 Corinthians 11:10 Paul used the word in an abnormal sense."[71]

Hayter concludes that I Corinthians 11 does not teach that because woman was created after man that she needs a symbol of man's authority covering her (a head covering or veil) while praying or prophesying. Indeed, it was radical of Paul to assume that women should pray and prophesy. Hayter believes that for cultural reasons (tradition, honor, seemly conduct, and custom), Paul merely wanted women not to transgress societal norms for the sake of the gospel. In other words, in seeking to create a distinctive missionary community, Paul admonished women to use their newfound freedom in an orderly way so as not to allow outsiders to confuse the church with cultic worship. His main argument was for order in worship to promote the proclamation of the gospel.

This conclusion does not mean that the text has no practical application for the present. The principle behind Paul's argument remains the same even if the practice does not. Thus, Hayter does not think that women today should be forced to wear their hair bound up when in church. Rather, the church today should encourage women to participate in worship in a way that does not offend the broader cultural norms. In the modern world, women being silent in church would be more likely to repulse people than to attract them. As a good analogy, Hayter cited Paul's teaching on the question of meat sacrificed to idols. In 1 Corinthians 8 Paul said that there was nothing intrinsically wrong with eating meat sacrificed to idols, since the idols were not really gods. Nonetheless, he warned his audience to be careful about such a practice because of how it might look to others, that it could appear to be a recognition of pagan gods and thus could harm Christians' witness. What Hayter thought the church could learn from 1 Corinthians 11 was that freedom should not be abused in such a way that it detracted from the gospel. Paul was not sanctioning patriarchy; he was using a particular teaching for a specific and limited time.

In accordance with these interpretations, biblical feminists believe that strict gender roles within the church are an accommodation to social forces. Those forces began with Hellenistic dualism and continued into modern times, resulting in misinterpretations of the Bible which, rather than reflecting the radical call to mutuality that God intended, Christians used to mirror and even strengthen the power imbalance in society that was a consequence of the fall. Because female subordination was not biblically but culturally conditioned, traditionalist feminists have called for an end to restrictions on women's roles in the church.

Inclusive Language in the Church

Scholars from a variety of disciplines long have recognized the power of language to shape society as well as to mirror it. Postmodernism, poststructuralism, and deconstruction all are theories that hinge on the inherent power of words, which in turn both create and direct reality. Anthropologist Clifford Geertz argued that the language of religion has a particular power to affect human beings and culture.[72] It is the public nature of language as a symbol of deeply held beliefs that has made religion particularly effective in shaping the consciousness of a people or culture. Consequently, whoever controls the language used in society holds the power to shape culture.

It was for this reason that the feminist Carol Christ called for a unique women's spirituality. By determining the symbols of religion, feminists could shape a culture empowering to women.[73] Christ explained that patriarchal religious symbols legitimize male power. A system of female symbols, therefore, is needed to legitimize women's power. Likewise, Mary Daly deconstructed the male language and reconstructed a feminist one, calling this the "castration of language."[74] What these feminists advocated was nothing less than a change in ideology. They did not merely want to change structure and legislation; they wanted to overthrow patriarchal American culture through the control of religious symbols. The Re-Imagining Conference was just this kind of attempt to determine the language and symbols of religion.

It is no surprise then that biblical feminists wanted to see the language of the church reflect the equality between genders that they were convinced the Bible advocated. As we have seen, biblical feminists argued before 1986 that inclusive language was a theological issue. When Christians insist on using only male images to convey God, biblical feminists claim that the church idolizes the masculine. The first and second of the Ten Commandments state: "You shall have no other gods before Me. You shall not make for yourself an idol, or any likeness of what is in heaven above or on the earth beneath or in the water under the earth" (Exodus 20:3–4). Thus, envisioning God with both feminine and masculine imagery, they believe, could keep the church from this sin.

Inclusive language is also a biblical issue, however, because how a scholar translates the original language of the Bible may make it appear more sexist than it really is. For example, Mollenkott pointed out that "the new Revised Standard Version translation committee reports literally hundreds of places where English translations have been more sexist than the original usage. They've given to us a man instead of a person, he instead of one, and brothers instead of siblings or relatives."[75] An example of this is 1 Timothy 3:1–11, in which male translators chose to translate the word *diakonoi* as "servant" or "wives" when referring to women but as "deacon" when referring to men.

Deciding what pronoun to use for God creates another translation problem. Hardesty complained that using the masculine pronoun, which, most translators believe, should not imply sexual identity, helps tie the male to God's very being.[76] She suggested instead that clergy and lay people alike refrain from capitalizing pronouns used in place of "God" or refrain from using pronouns entirely. One way to do so is to refer to God according to the topic being discussed. If the topic is creation, use Creator; if it is salvation, use Savior, and so on. If pronouns must be used, Hardesty encouraged the writer or speaker to balance masculine and feminine pronouns. A final possibility is to use the plural pronoun *they* in place of the singular pronoun *he*. Hardesty observed that Shakespeare used pronouns in this way and that the grammatical rule establishing *he* as a generic pronoun for the English language was instituted only in 1850.

Hardesty also proposed that titles for God—Son, Father, Lord—be altered so as to express gender inclusivity. She suggested that "Son of God" could be changed to "Child of God" and still express relatedness. For this same reason of relatedness, however, she recommended that "Father" not be dropped but be used in conjunction with, or interchangeably with, "Mother" or "Parent." Nor did she have a problem with "Lord," as it connoted sovereignty, not the rule of a British lord. Still, she conceded that if "Lord" was offensive, it could be replaced with "Sovereign."[77]

Not all biblical feminists agreed with these suggestions or to the extent to which inclusive language, not just imagery, should be used in the church. Cook found that traditionalist biblical feminists supported the use of inclusive language regarding people but not God. They wanted gender-accurate Bible translations to be used in evangelical churches, but they less frequently supported the use of *mother* in place of *father* for God. The CBE's own survey of its members found that inclusive language did not rank among their highest concerns. Many stated that it simply was not a big issue for them.

Nonetheless, when attempts were made to make biblical language more inclusive, a storm of controversy ensued. The Re-Imagining Conference is one example. The appearance of the Inclusive Language Lectionary, daily Bible readings for the church that use gender-inclusive language, prepared by the National Council of Churches, is another. *Christianity Today* published articles with titles like "God Our Father and Mother? A Bisexual Nightmare from the National Council of Churches." *Time* magazine printed a similarly captioned story, which elicited a number of outraged letters to the editor.[78] As Nancy Hardesty put it: "If the issue is so trivial, why all the fuss?"[79]

The NIVI Debate

That the use of inclusive language was not considered trivial by most evangelicals can be seen in the response by some segments of the evangelical community to an announcement in 1997 that the International Bible Society (IBS) was going to release an inclusive-language edition of the New International Version Bible (NIV).[80] The NIV was a completely new translation of the Bible (not a revision of an existing translation). Beginning in 1965, hundreds of scholars worked from the best Hebrew, Aramaic, and Greek scriptural texts available. Upon its release in 1973, the NIV soon became the best-selling English-language version of the Bible and was particularly popular among evangelicals. By some estimates, the NIV captured 45 percent of that market.[81]

When the first report came out that the International Bible Society was working on a gender-neutral edition (referred to as the NIVI), it was heralded as "the Feminist Seduction of the Evangelical Church."[82] Susan Olasky, the author of this piece, was an assistant editor for *World*, a conservative Christian news journal based in Asheville, North Carolina. Using inflammatory language, Olasky claimed that the society intended to eventually substitute the NIVI for the NIV, so that evangelicals would be able to buy only the NIVI. She called the NIVI the "stealth Bible" and claimed that the International Bible Society was "quietly going 'gender neutral'" and described it as "unisex."

This announcement in a small-circulation journal caused an uproar in the evangelical community. Such influential evangelicals as J. I. Packer, Wayne Grudem, Jerry Falwell, Paige Patterson, and James Dobson (president of Focus on the Family) all opposed the publication of the NIVI. When Focus on the Family, a conservative, evangelical organization that promoted traditional family values, discovered that its own children's Bible already contained gender-inclusive language, they pulled it from the market. Similarly, Cook Communications, a distributor of Sunday-school curricula, stopped using the NIrV (New International Reader's Version) for quotations in its material because the NIrV contained gender-neutral language. The Southern Baptist Convention considered replacing the NIrV in its Sunday-school curriculum as well.

Opposition to the prospect of an inclusive-language evangelical Bible coalesced into a gathering arranged by James Dobson at his headquarters in Colorado Springs. Just days before the meeting, the International Bible Society announced that it had abandoned all plans to make the NIV gender inclusive. This did not stop Dobson's event from taking place, however, which resulted in the affirmation of a series of guidelines on the use of gender-related language in Bible translations.

Not all biblical scholars agreed with the furor that some evangelical organizations were fomenting, though. Those who worked on the Committee on Bible Translation felt that they were doing nothing more than updating obsolete language. They certainly were not pushing a feminist political agenda. D. A. Carson and Mark Strauss, two New Testament scholars who described themselves as traditionalists on women's roles in the church, both pointed out that gender-inclusive language was not even an accurate description of the new translation. In their opinions, the new translation would have been more appropriately called "gender neutral"; the translators were merely attempting to make neutral those words that had, for years, been translated with male language. For example, the Greek word for a generic human being had long been translated as "man" rather than "human" or "person." Carson and Strauss argued that in modern American culture, people no longer understood "man" to be a gender-inclusive term for "humanity." Larry Walker, a professor of Old Testament at the Mid-America Baptist Theological and a member of the Committee on Bible Translation, also felt that he was merely helping update archaic language in the NIV. Thus, when asked to resign from the committee over the NIVI, he refused at the cost of his job at Mid-America.[83]

Many New Testament scholars, including Strauss and Carson (who had been invited to Dobson's Colorado meeting but declined to attend) opposed the translation guidelines issued by Dobson's "Conference on Gender-Related Language in Scripture" because they were of poor scholarly quality. Most of the contributors to the guidelines were not biblical scholars. The majority were simply invited as opponents of inclusive language, including the publisher of *World* and the president of Council on Biblical Manhood and Womanhood (CBMW), an organization that advocated male authority in the church and home. Carson even resigned from the board of CBMW, not because he disagreed with the hierarchicalism it advocated, but because he disagreed "(1) with its tightly linking the issue of complementarianism [the word Christians for Biblical Manhood and Womanhood use to describe its traditionalist theology] to that of gender-inclusive translations and (2) with at least some of the principles the critics [of inclusive language] had advanced in Colorado Springs and which CBMW subsequently endorsed."[84] Carson added that

> I cannot help but conclude that what drew many of them to sign this document [the translation guidelines] is their concern to maintain complementarianism, and this out of strong biblical convictions, and their belief that the question of gender-inclusive translations is a necessary component of this conviction. Quite a number of them, I think, would make no pretense of having much grasp of Hebrew, Aramaic, Greek, translation theory, and linguistics.[85]

Other Bible translations had used gender-inclusive language before: the New Jerusalem, the New Revised Standard Version, the Good News

Bible, and the Message, for example. Some of these—notably the Good News and the Message, which is a paraphrase by evangelical author Eugene Peterson—are popular among evangelicals. In addition, the NIVI was already being published in Great Britain. So, why was there so much controversy over the NIVI? The debate over the NIVI demonstrated that inclusive language was more than a biblical or even theological issue; it was an issue of power.[86] The NIVI had become a part of the cultural debate over women's roles in the church. Hardesty suggested that the insistence on exclusively male language was about the dominance of one group over another.[87] If Carson was right in his analysis of the motives for the opposition to the NIVI, then Hardesty was correct. By controlling the language of the Bible, traditionalists (at least those opposing the NIVI) hoped to govern the symbols by which evangelicals understood and shaped their world and that influenced American culture. The language of religion had become a primary battleground for those who desired to reverse, maintain, or change American cultural values.

Summary of Biblical Feminist Theology

The divergent directions in which biblical feminist theology went after the split over the issue of homosexuality brought to the surface its conflicting views of biblical and, therefore, moral authority. Progressive evangelical feminists began to turn to other sources of authority, such as science, reason, and experience, in addition to the biblical witness. They also began to use nonevangelical methods of interpretation, such as liberation theology.[88] As their view of the Bible and how to read it evolved, so too did their positions on doctrinal and moral issues. Doctrinally, progressive biblical feminists became more pluralistic.[89] God the Father also became God the Mother, and in Mollenkott's theology, theism was rejected for panentheism. Some progressive feminists accepted a universal view of salvation that was not dependent on Jesus' substitutionary atonement for sin. Instead, they viewed Christ's death as an exemplary model of selfless love or, as in Mollenkott's case, as a regrettable model for women that should not be dwelt on overly much. Sin also was redefined as that which kept women from seeing their human value and connection to God and others. It was what kept human beings from pursuing justice for all other persons. In pursuit of justice, feminists in the EWC became more tolerant of divorce, homosexuality and homosexual rights, and abortion and abortion rights. Kaye Cook's survey supports these conclusions. She found that the EWC became less bibliocentric over time and, consequently, more accepting of secular feminist social and political agendas.[90] Cook concluded that its members "are solidly in the feminist camp and less clearly evangelical."[91]

Traditionalist biblical feminists, like those in Christians for Biblical Equality, however, remained committed to the external, definable, and transcendent authority of the biblical witness. As a result of their adherence to inerrancy and evangelical methods of biblical interpretation, traditionalist biblical feminist doctrine and social practice have remained, for the most part, solidly evangelical. They maintain a traditional conception of the Trinity. They also are orthodox in their doctrine concerning the person and work of Christ and in their definitions of sin and grace. The biggest potential area of difference between these feminist evangelicals and their larger community is in their interpretation of passages relating to women's roles. Yet even here a large number of evangelicals agree with them. They are strong supporters of heterosexual marriage, although not as traditionally conceived, and celibate singleness. They support inclusive language related to people, but not God, and they oppose abortion and same-sex relationships. This has resulted in a social agenda that fits well into the broader evangelical coalition. Cook concluded from her survey that traditionalist evangelical feminists believe in the inerrancy of scripture and are "clearly within the evangelical camp."[92]

6

Empowered by the Word, II

Organizational Changes
in Biblical Feminism, 1986–

In the latter months of 1975, Deborah Jang was touring the United States, exploring new horizons. On Thanksgiving weekend, she arrived at the Greyhound bus station in Washington, D.C., to begin another step on her journey, this one spiritual.[1] Jang had become a "born-again" Christian as a youth, through the influence of neighbors and friends. During high school, she attended an evangelical church, but in 1975, Jang found herself struggling with questions about her faith, particularly its exclusivity and gender inequities. When she read a flyer about the EWC's first conference, Jang decided to attend. One of her strongest memories of that first conference was Virginia Mollenkott's address, which gave her a "flicker of hope as I struggled within the cultural and doctrinal confines of evangelical Christianity."[2]

Although Jang initially did not stay connected with the EWC, in 1982 she returned to one of its conferences. Afterward she attended most of the caucus's biennial meetings until 1994 and served as the editor of *Update* between the summer of 1989 and the fall of 1994. When she left *Update*, Jang commented that she was "a little darker than most [EWC members], and a little less scholarly than others. . . . I was also a little less rooted in evangelical Christian convictions and cultures."[3] Nonetheless, she still felt a connection to the "gutsy," "life-giving," "justice-loving" bunch of women in the Evangelical Women's Caucus.

Much as Anne Eggebroten's spiritual pilgrimage serves as an illustration of the EWC prior to the 1986 Fresno conference, Jang's spiritual journey serves as a portrait of the EWC after 1986. Like Jang, the EWC struggled against the doctrinal and cultural constraints of evangelicalism.

And also like Jang, the eventual identity of the EWC no longer allowed it to remain in that community.

Following biblical feminism's split into two organizations after the 1986 Fresno conference, the Evangelical Women's Caucus struggled financially, numerically, and organizationally. But by 1990, it had found a new purpose: providing an inclusive, diverse home for biblical feminists who were not as conservative theologically or socially as the typical evangelical was. The caucus's biblical feminist theology began to take a less stringent position on biblical authority and turned to liberation theology for a methodology that gave authority to the experience of women's oppression. As a result, the EWC became more of a prophetic voice from outside evangelicalism.

Christians for Biblical Equality, the younger of the two groups, grew financially, numerically, and organizationally and quickly took over as the voice of evangelical feminism within conservative American Christianity. The CBE maintained its strong stance on biblical authority and used evangelical methods of biblical interpretation to argue for women's equality. As such, the feminists in this organization played a significant role in the continuing boundary debates of the postwar evangelical coalition. The disagreement over the conception of biblical authority had lingering effects on the movement of biblical feminism long after it had split over the issue of homosexuality.

Christians for Biblical Equality

Catherine Kroeger, the first president of Christians for Biblical Equality (a post she held until 1995), maintained, "We just wanted to be a prophetic voice. We never expected to have more than 100 members."[4] In several ways, the group exceeded her expectation. Even before the CBE officially existed, interest in a new organization for evangelical feminists had grown. According to Kroeger, the idea for such a group was conceived at the EWC's 1984 conference, where it had become clear that the EWC was now less welcoming to more conservative Christians. But this idea did not materialize until after the events at the Fresno conference.[5] By 1988, when the CBE was officially incorporated, local chapters were already meeting in Minnesota, Denver, and Boston. Local conferences were held in Minnesota, Pittsburgh, and Denver, and there were discussions about having a national conference.

Christians for Biblical Equality organized itself similar to that of the Evangelical Women's Caucus. It instituted chapter and individual memberships (which included a subscription to a new publication, *Priscilla Papers*) and planned biennial conferences for the summers that the EWC was not meeting. By 2000, it had 2,300 individual members, representing every state in the United States, and a mailing list of 16,000. The number of chapters stabilized at about thirty, including some in Canada, Norway, South Africa, Germany, Austria, Ireland, and Australia, and it established church memberships as well. In the 1990s, the CBE launched a second publication, *Mutuality*, for organizational news, including announcements of honors for its members.[6] This freed *Priscilla Papers* to focus on scholarly articles conveying the message of biblical equality. Also, through *Mutuality* and later its Web site, the CBE made available books and articles on the topic of biblical equality. By 2003 it offered more than 160 titles and was turning away authors who wanted it to list their books.

The CBE's conferences grew as well, in both attendance and frequency. Its first meeting, held at Bethel College in St. Paul, attracted an audience of almost 300. The attendance at later conferences ranged from about 175 to more than 350, depending on their location.[7] The conference in Dallas in 2001, which was held after the Southern Baptist Convention released a regressive statement on the role of women in that denomination, was their largest.[8] Beginning in 2000, the CBE began to host topical conferences in addition to the biennial events promoting the biblical message of egalitarianism. In 2000 and 2002, topical seminars taught how to practice gender equality within marriage, and in 2004, organizers began planning for a "relationship seminar" in 2006 to address singleness, divorce, remarriage, and parenting issues.[9] It also staged several international gatherings, in Austria in 1993, Norway in 1996, and Great Britain in 2004.

The Women of Christians for Biblical Equality

Who were the women and men joining Christians for Biblical Equality? In 1991 and 1995, the CBE surveyed its membership.[10] Both surveys showed that most members were well-educated, middle-class, married women with children, who worked outside the home, although 25 percent were men.[11] The CBE's members did not appear to be aging in the same way that the readers of *Daughters of Sarah* were, which was more closely associated with the EWC.[12] Overall, the surveys showed that the CBE was attracting a somewhat broader range of women, not just those who had "come of age" in the early years of the "second wave" of secular feminism in the 1960s.

In addition to questions of basic identity—age, marital status, income—Kaye Cook added several new questions to help analyze the members' theological and biblical positions.[13] Using questions developed by James Davison Hunter for his book on college-age evangelicals, Cook asked respondents to agree to one of the following statements: (1) The Bible is the inspired Word of God, not mistaken in its statements and teachings, and is to be taken literally, word for word. (2) The Bible is the inspired Word of God, not mistaken in its teachings but is not always to be taken literally in its statements concerning matters of science, history, and so on. (3) The Bible becomes the Word of God for a person when he or she reads it in faith. (4) The Bible is an ancient book of legend/history/moral precepts recorded by men.[14] The first two definitions corresponded to two versions of inerrancy. The first described a position of strict inerrancy, and the second described those who were "inerrantists but not literalists," that is, those who subscribed to limited inerrancy or infallibility.[15] Eighty-six percent of the Christians for Biblical Equality agreed with one of the first two statements. Thirty-one percent held the strict inerrantist position, and 65 percent believed in limited inerrancy. Cook also learned that the majority of members believed that the Bible supports egalitarian marriages and the ordination of women but did not endorse homosexuality or abortion. She concluded: "Despite what appear to be the fears of the larger evangelical community, biblical feminists are, ideologically and theologically, biblical centrists."[16]

These survey results resonated well with the beliefs that the CBE espoused in its statement of faith. The statement begins with the basic tenets of Christian faith—the inspiration of scripture, the Trinity, incarnation, sin, salvation, and the Holy Spirit—before addressing male and female equality in the last three propositions. The issue of equality is covered at the end because it is seen as a direct outgrowth of the gospel. As Alvera Mickelsen explained, "You don't find that language in anybody else's statement of faith, with the emphasis on relationships. You know, that's the very basis of the Christian faith. It's all about relationships, relationships with God and relationships with each other."[17]

The CBE's affirmations state:

- We believe the Bible is the inspired Word of God, is reliable, and is the final authority for faith and practice.
- We believe in the unity and trinity of God, equally existing as three equal persons.
- We believe in the full deity and full humanity of Jesus Christ.
- We believe in the sinfulness of all persons. One result of sin is shattered relationship with God, others, and self.
- We believe that eternal salvation and restored relationships are possible through faith in Jesus Christ who died for us, rose from the dead, and is coming again. This salvation is offered to all people.
- We believe in the work of the Holy Spirit in salvation, and in the power and presence of the Holy Spirit in the life of believers.
- We believe in the essential dignity of men and women of all races, ages, classes. We recognize that all persons are made in the image of God and are to reflect that image in the community of believers, in the home, and in society.
- We believe that men and women are to diligently develop and use their God-given gifts for the good of the home, church, and society.
- We believe in the family, celibate singleness, and heterosexual marriage as the patterns God designed for us.

Mickelsen indicated that there was some discussion over the last statement. Some of those who helped draft the affirmations felt that this clause was unwarranted, as it was not related to the topic of gender equality. Others, though, believed it was necessary to ensure that homosexual issues never took over Christians for Biblical Equality. The organization's statement of faith has remained the same over the years, except for the addition of one word, *faithful*, in this last affirmation, a change that also was related to the issue of homosexuality. In this case, though, the adjustment was meant to emphasize that it was not enough simply to have a heterosexual marriage. Rather, the marriage had to be one in which both partners were faithful to each other. The last proposal now reads: "We believe in the family, celibate singleness, and faithful heterosexual marriage as the patterns God designed for us."

Christians for Biblical Equality and the Evangelical Establishment

These affirmations were well within the bounds acceptable to many evangelicals by the late 1980s when the Christians for Biblical Equality officially incorporated. In fact, several leading evangelicals participated in the formation of Christians for Biblical Equality and sat on the board of directors, including James Beck, who was a professor at Denver Conservative Baptist Seminary, Gretchen Gaebelein Hull, and Berkeley and Alvera Mickelsen. Others signed a declaration published by the CBE as a two-page advertisement in the April 9, 1990, issue of *Christianity Today*. Among the signers of the statement, entitled "Men, Women and Biblical Equality," were David Hubbard, president of Fuller Theological Seminary; Bill Hybels, founding pastor of Willow Creek Community Church; Cornelius Plantinga, a professor at Calvin College (and later its president); Ronald J. Sider, a founder of Evangelicals for Social Action; Lewis Smedes, a faculty member of Fuller; and Kenneth Kantzer, a former editor of *Christianity Today* and director of the doctoral program and chancellor of Trinity College. In all, more than two hundred evangelicals signed this initial statement. In 1991, Kenneth Kanzter further endorsed the CBE by addressing its second biennial conference, at which time he reiterated his belief that scripture teaches the equality of men and women. This advocacy, coming from a staunch defender of inerrancy and a member of the International Conference on Biblical Inerrancy (ICBI), gave legitimacy to the CBE's claim to be within evangelical boundaries. Later endorsements also came from Craig Keener, an author and professor at Eastern Seminary, and author John Kohlenberger.

In addition to these associations, the CBE's national conferences were held in the early years at several evangelical colleges, including Bethel, Gordon, and Wheaton. Although hosting these conferences did not signify complete agreement with their views, it did imbue some legitimacy to the CBE's evangelical claims. Each of these undergraduate institutions is a leading evangelical college, and each also had faculty with ties to the CBE. Kaye Cook taught at Gordon, and Catherine Kroeger and Aida Besançon Spencer taught at Gordon-Conwell Seminary. Gilbert Bilezekian, a frequent lecturer for the Christians for Biblical Equality and a member of its board of reference, taught biblical studies at Wheaton. Alvera and Berkeley Mickelsen taught at Bethel College and Seminary. And David Scholer taught at Gordon-Conwell before moving to Northern Baptist Seminary and then to Fuller Theological Seminary.

By the end of its first year, the CBE's leaders had participated in several international evangelical events. They hosted a meeting at the Lausanne International Congress, an international event attended by evangelical leaders from around the world to discuss evangelization. Gretchen Gaebelein Hull gave a paper at the third meeting of the International Conference on Biblical Inerrancy (ICBI), the only woman to do so. The ICBI was a coalition of Christian scholars who met to discuss and defend the doctrine of biblical inerrancy from 1978 to the mid-1980s. These scholars produced two collections of papers given at the first and second conferences. Together their books expounded what might be called "traditional" evangelical hermeneutics for those who adhered to inerrancy. In accordance with their beliefs and their pedigree, the CBE was in the mainstream of post–World War II evangelicalism.

More specifically, the CBE fit best among the younger generation who were poised to become the direction setters for American evangelicalism. So although the organization gained legitimacy and encouragement from leaders like Kantzer and John Stott, most of their support came from evangelicals like Ron Sider, David Scholer, Cornelius Plantinga, Craig Keener, Bill Hybels, and Gilbert Bilezekian. Bilezekian was an early supporter of the CBE who helped draw up the statement "Men, Women, and Biblical Equality," which was published in *Christianity Today*. As a professor at Wheaton College, he mentored Bill Hybels as Hybels was establishing the Willow Creek Community Church.[18]

Hybels was a youth pastor when he started the Willow Creek Community Church in 1975 in the Chicago suburbs.[19] Within three years it had a weekly attendance of almost three thousand. By 2000, an estimated fifteen thousand people attended its services each week. Given this success, the church established the Willow Creek Association (WCA) to provide training and resources for other congregations who wanted to emulate Willow Creek. By 2000, approximately five thousand churches had joined the association, with Baptists and Presbyterians as two of the three most highly represented denominations.[20]

Bilezekian and Hybels, along with the rest of Willow Creek's resources, supported the CBE's moderate biblical feminism from its beginning. In one sermon, Hybels preached:

> God knew that some people would become self-centered and controlling and authoritative. Some men would even say, "I'm the man of this house and the Bible says that I'm the head of this place, so you do my

bidding." That's not what the scripture talks about when it talks about headship. It doesn't mean power and authority and the rule of the roost. It means being a life-giver. It means being a fountainhead of love and nurture to those in the family.[21]

In another example of support, two Willow Creek staff members, including Jim Mellado, president of the Willow Creek Association, were plenary speakers for a marriage conference that the CBE sponsored in October 2000. Mellado also sent out a letter of endorsement for the event.

Even so, women's equality in evangelical churches and homes was not so easily accepted by all members of the evangelical coalition. Much like the backlash against secular feminism in the broader American society, some segments of evangelicalism opposed biblical feminism.[22] In her book *Backlash*, Susan Faludi contends that this counterassault on feminist advances began on the evangelical right and found its way into popular culture during the years of the Reagan administration. Certainly, many evangelical churches, in addition to the political right, did deplore the cultural influence of feminism on the church. Concern for the survival of the family, "the most rudimentary context in which religious faith is expressed in day-to-day living," prompted much of the negative reaction. Sociologist James Davison Hunter argued that the family had become more than just a community in which people lived their lives; it had gained symbolic proportions as a bulwark of social stability and traditional moral virtue.[23]

In these people's view, biblical feminists threatened to introduce instability and moral decline in America through their suggestions for coparenting and women in the workplace, whether in the church, seminary, or the secular world. Opponents of evangelical feminism did not question their own assumptions about "traditional" family life, despite evidence that called into question their model of "traditional." For example, James Hunter and his coauthor Helen Stehlin pointed out that historical facts about the traditional Christian family revealed an altogether different model from that of a loving, emotionally nurturing, two-parent family, with only the father working outside the home and most of the parents' attention focused on rearing their children. By contrast, "from the late Middle Ages to the eighteenth century" the most important function of the family was survival.[24] Thus, the family was defined more as an economic enterprise than an emotional one. Hunter and Stehlin therefore were puzzled at the evangelical ideology regarding the family, since as much as it claimed to be traditional, it was in reality novel in its emphasis on the nuclear family (instead of on the larger community), the quality of relationships (nurturing versus economic), and the family's function in the modern world (as retreat).

A backlash within American evangelicalism to both secular and biblical feminism (the two were intertwined in the minds of opponents) could be seen in a number of places. On an individual level, some supporters of evangelical feminism suffered in their jobs. For example, Alvin Schmidt, a professor at Concordia Seminary in St. Louis, a Missouri-Synod Lutheran institution, was fired over a disagreement with his denomination's view of male dominance. (Schmidt later wrote *Veiled and Silenced: How Culture Shaped Sexist Theology*, in which he argues that throughout church history theologians have been shaped primarily by secular culture and not by the Bible in their sexist views of women.) George and Emily Walther, cofounders of the Christian Marriage Enhancement seminars, lost financial support after they declared that marriage should be based on mutuality.

On an institutional level, several organizations were formed to defend "the traditional family." After seventeen years in child development, James Dobson was convinced that American families faced massive internal and external pressures, leading to unprecedented disintegration, so in 1977 he founded Focus on the Family. By 2000, his syndicated radio program was airing on almost three thousand stations in the United States. In addition, the organization produces books and films for use in churches, classrooms, and homes, and Dobson serves on several governmental task forces to lobby for protection of the American family.

Others who disagreed with the evangelical feminists did so on the basis of biblical interpretation. They insisted that equality, in the sense of equal opportunity, could not be deduced from a literal reading of scripture. These opponents of egalitarianism accused biblical feminists of denying the inspiration of scripture and accommodating contemporary cultural norms (meaning secular feminism). They often did not bother to address biblical feminist interpretations, preferring instead to accuse biblical feminists of denying biblical inerrancy. Thus Craig Keener, a professor of New Testament at Eastern Baptist Theological Seminary and an ordained minister in the National Baptist Convention, made this appeal in his book on Paul's view of women's roles:

I do hope that those who disagree will honestly address the issues raised in this book and not repeat the sort of accusations a few writers have leveled against equally evangelical colleagues. I hope that those who disagree will challenge my interpretations, rather than question my commitment to the authority of scripture.[25]

Keener's evangelical credentials were not questioned in the reviews of his other books. In fact, his commentary on the historical and cultural background of the New Testament placed seventh on *Christianity Today*'s 1995 books-of-the-year list, making it the highest-ranked biblical study that year.

A backlash that combined both the accusation that supporters of women's rights denied inerrancy and that egalitarianism threatened the family occurred in the Southern Baptist Convention. A sociologist and Southern Baptist, Nancy Ammerman recounts in *Baptist Battles* the struggle that took place in her denomination when fundamentalists (her term) sought to take over the leadership. The fundamentalists held theologically to biblical inerrancy and ideologically to pastoral authority, "traditional family values," and social and political conservatism. They thus opposed the ordination of women. The moderates, who were in power for much of the 1960s and 1970s, were more concerned with maintaining the Baptist traditions of soul competency (individual accountability before God) and the priesthood of all believers. These traditions led the moderates to value greater theological diversity within certain parameters. For example, while the moderates held power, the convention's statement of faith followed Baptist doctrines but did not define those doctrines precisely, so as to allow individual pastors and congregations some room for interpretation. As a result, during this time many women held leadership positions, including as ordained ministers. Then the fundamentalists, led by Paige Patterson, then president of the Criswell Center for Biblical Studies in Dallas, staged a step-by-step takeover of the denomination, starting with the local offices and boards in 1979. The conservatives wrested final control from the moderates in a bitter convention in 1985.

On June 14, 2000, the conservatives added the following article to the doctrinal statement:

The husband and wife are of equal worth before God, since both are created in God's image. The marriage relationship models the way God relates to His people. A husband is to love his wife as Christ loved the church. He has the God-given responsibility to provide for, to protect, and to lead his family. A wife is to submit herself graciously to the servant leadership of her husband even as the church willingly submits to the headship of Christ. She, being in the image of God as is her husband and thus equal to him, has the God-given responsibility to respect her husband and to serve as his helper in managing the household and nurturing the next generation.[26]

This statement was covered widely in the press and, ironically, led to significant press coverage of the CBE and its October 2000 marriage conference and 2001 biennial conference. A number of Southern Baptist congregants and ministers (male and female) both attended and spoke at these events. Later, several of these Southern Baptists were awarded Christians for Biblical Equality's "Priscilla and Aquila Award"—given to persons who have taken risks or expended great effort on behalf of biblical equality—as a result of their personal suffering from taking a public stance against their denomination's amended statement on the family. For example, Dan Gentry Kent chose early retirement from his teaching post at Southwestern Seminary; Alan Brehm was forced to resign from his teaching post at Southwestern Seminary when he refused to sign the amended Faith and Message Statement; and seventeen others left the denomination over the statement.

In December 1973, the Presbyterian Church in America (PCA) was formed when it broke with the Presbyterian Church in the United States (PCUS), over the creeping liberalism in the assembly's theology. In their "Message to all Churches of Jesus Christ throughout the World," the PCA's founders stated that the PCUS's theology had become "diluted" with "an unbiblical view of marriage and divorce, the ordination of women, financing of abortion . . . and numerous other non-Biblical positions . . . all traceable to a different view of Scripture from that we hold."[27] As recently as 1997, the PCA voted to sever its fraternal ties with the Christian Reformed Church (CRC) for similar reasons. A leader in the PCA church explained, "They are no longer being guided by scripture in the ordination of women. . . . Our concern, quite honestly, is that the Christian Reformed Church has begun to move away from its historic position on the authority of Scripture." Another PCA leader commented that the CRC was "on a slippery slope" that would lead to the acceptance of homosexuality and support for evolution.[28]

One of the strongest responses to biblical feminism came not from a denomination but from a group formed specifically to combat its successes. In 1987 John Piper, an author and the senior pastor of Bethlehem Baptist Church in Minneapolis (Minneapolis is also the home of CBE's headquarters), and Wayne Grudem, an associate professor of biblical and systematic theology at Trinity Evangelical Divinity School, founded the Council on Biblical Manhood and Womanhood (CBMW) as a result of their deep concern about the promotion of feminist egalitarianism. According to a statement that the council published in 1988, biblical feminism distorted or neglected "the glad harmony portrayed in Scripture between the loving, humble leadership of redeemed husbands and the intelligent, willing support of that leadership by redeemed wives."[29] In addition, feminists like those in the CBE used "hermeneutical oddities devised to reinterpret apparently plain meanings of Biblical texts," and subsequently they threatened biblical authority by jeopardizing the clarity of scripture and limiting its access to "the restricted realm of technical ingenuity."[30]

In the preface of their work on how Christians could recover a true sense of masculinity and femininity, Piper and Grudem complained, by name, about Letha Scanzoni, Nancy Hardesty, Paul Jewett, Patricia Gundry, Berkeley and Alvera Mickelsen, Gilbert Bilezekian, Aida Besançon Spencer, and Gretchen Gaebelein Hull because they defended the view that the Bible opposed unique leadership roles for men in the family and the church.[31] These feminists particularly bothered the CBMW because they were evangelicals. They did not reject the truthfulness of the Bible; they maintained a personal commitment to Jesus Christ; and they gave detailed, earnest, and persuasive arguments that women were equal to men in the church and home. Consequently, the council believed that biblical feminists were having some success in evangelical churches and that they were confusing many individual Christians and harming both the family and the church. The CBMW's response to biblical feminist arguments came in a large volume entitled *Recovering Biblical Manhood and Womanhood: A Response to Biblical Feminism*, which expounded their view of biblical "complementarianism," the idea that men and women were created differently to fulfill different, but complementary, roles.

All the opposition to what were seen as feminist inroads into the church indicated that biblical feminism was already having an impact on the evangelical community. As mentioned earlier, the purpose of the Council on Biblical Manhood and Womanhood was directly influenced by the success of biblical feminists like those in Christians for Biblical Equality. The council opposed both the social positions and interpretive methods of evangelical feminists, and the CBE was the CBMW's primary sparring partner, as the two organizations traded arguments for and against particular interpretations of scripture. So after the Southern Baptist Convention released its statement on the family, the CBMW and the CBE traded position statements that were released in evangelicalism's flagship journal, *Christianity Today*. What is significant is that the CBMW continued its dialogue with the CBE, thereby acknowledging in practice the latter's location within the boundaries of American evangelicalism.

Such controversy also meant that biblical feminist ideas were diffused throughout the evangelical community, as their views were addressed in books, journals, and churches and at conferences. It is not surprising, then, that recent studies have found that traditionalist biblical feminist ideas are filtering into the evangelical culture, including the home and institutions of higher learning. One researcher, Sally Gallagher, found that although most evangelical couples gave lip service to the male as head of the family, few marriages actually operated in this way. Gallagher also discovered that evangelical wives were just as likely to be employed outside the home as were American women generally and that there was little difference on gender issues between evangelicals subscribing to a strict definition of inerrancy and those with a more moderate definition. She concluded from these facts that gender issues do indeed define evangelical boundaries.[32]

James Davison Hunter's study of college-age evangelicals showed that in the early 1980s they already were moving away from a traditional conception of the family. Only about one-tenth of the students endorsed the traditional model, while another 10 percent vigorously supported a family structure based on the equal status and authority of both men and women, with no essential role distinctions between the sexes. Hunter suggested that since women were in the majority in American evangelicalism and since more of them were receiving professional training, his findings could portend a wider acceptance of the egalitarian model of relationships in the family.[33] He concluded that according to his poll, the professors at evangelical colleges, who were even less traditional than the students, played a large role in these changes.[34]

Given the number of evangelical feminists who teach at Christian colleges, it appears that Hunter's prediction has come true, for more recent studies support his prediction that egalitarian views would increase among Christian college students. In one study, James Penning and Corwin Smidt, both professors of political science at Calvin College, found that between 1984 and 1996, the views of evangelical college students did become more egalitarian.[35] Naomi Schaefer, a journalism student at the Phillips Foundation, used personal interviews and a collection of more recent surveys to show that women at traditional religious colleges had become more egalitarian in their views of gender roles.[36] In fact, one of Christians for Biblical Equality's newer chapters has begun to recruit at Urbana, InterVarsity's collegiate mission convention.

Several of the colleges—Seattle Pacific University, Messiah College, North Park University, Eastern College, and Calvin College—that Hunter studied in the early 1980s have even begun to offer a minor in women's or gender studies. Eastern College also opened the Hestenes Center for Christian Women in Leadership (named after its founder, Roberta Hestenes). In addition, several other evangelical colleges, for example, Gordon, began to offer courses in women's studies through other departments such as sociology, anthropology, history, and religion. The Oregon Extension of Houghton College offers a May term women's studies course. According to Joyce Erickson, a former coordinator of the Evangelical Women's Caucus and a former dean of the College of Arts and Sciences at Seattle Pacific University, it is no coincidence that egalitarian ideas and women's studies programs have proliferated at campuses where women evangelical feminists teach: "If biblical feminism had not provided the rationale from a scriptural perspective for the valuing of women and their experience, I doubt if a traditional Christian institution or its faculty would have supported such a program."[37]

Evangelicalism in the 1990s: From Inerrancy to Hermeneutics as Symbolic Boundary

It is ironic that those churches in denominations opposing egalitarianism—like the Southern Baptist Convention, Presbyterian Church in America, and conservative nondenominational churches—were three of the most highly represented groups in the Willow Creek Association, given its ties to evangelical feminism.[38] This paradox—between the association's phenomenal success and the growing conservatism in some evangelical denominations and organizations—can be attributed largely to the decentralized, fragmented, populist nature of contemporary American evangelicalism. Evangelicals have tended not to be loyal to any one denomination but instead to shop for the church that best meets their particular needs and desires, regardless of its denominational affiliation or lack thereof.

The Willow Creek Association itself is an illustration of the decentralized, populist nature of American evangelicalism. The number of churches that have joined it has been the result of Willow Creek's success in bringing large numbers of worshipers to its services, which, in turn, has been based on the charisma of its leaders and preachers. In addition, the association does not have a centralized, denominational structure. Instead it was formed as an affiliation of churches, some bound to particular denominations, that desired to pattern themselves as closely or loosely as they chose to a successful model. This helps explain why Willow Creek failed to sway many of its affiliates to accept an egalitarian stance on women. According to one researcher, 60 percent of the seeker churches had a woman on their pastoral staff, but none was in a senior position, nor were any of them preaching or teaching pastors. Most often they were directors of programming or of adult or children's ministries.[39]

In addition to the decentralized, populist nature of American evangelicalism, both the support for and the backlash against evangelical feminism can be accounted for in another way, specific to the historical moment in evangelicalism. This is the shift in emphasis from inerrancy to hermeneutics as the symbolic boundary for determining evangelical identity. There were two changes in American evangelicalism in the 1970s and early 1980s that led many well-respected evangelical leaders to support a biblical feminist position that used modern methods of interpretation and a limited definition of inerrancy. The first, discussed earlier in reference to Bill Hybels, was that the younger, more progressive evangelicals were assuming positions of authority and respect, and so their social opinions and views on the use of new hermeneutical methods were becoming more accepted. These methods are outlined next in a discussion of evangelical hermeneutics.

The second change was that many evangelicals were growing tired of the inerrancy battles that threatened to splinter the postwar evangelical coalition and had already hindered its outreach. Some of these evangelicals were willing to accept the moderate social agenda and mostly traditional hermeneutics of an organization like the CBE. The definition of scriptural authority, however, continued to be debated throughout the 1980s.

Toward the goal of settling an acceptable definition of inerrancy by which evangelical boundaries could be established, Carl Henry and Kenneth Kantzer convened a gathering of distinguished evangelical leaders in 1989. The event resulted in nine doctrinal affirmations that together served as—according to Henry and D. A. Carson, coeditors of the conference papers—"a confession of what it means to be an evangelical."[40] The conference papers revealed, however, that serious disagreement continued in regard to the role of biblical authority and what it meant to be an evangelical.[41] In the keynote address, Carl Henry expounded on the question that had gathered these leaders of evangelicalism together, reiterating his hope for a coalition united in faith and action. In a response to Henry's paper, Nathan Hatch, an eminent historian of American religious history, rejoined that "there is no such thing as evangelicalism." Instead of Henry's ideal, he said, there existed only a fragmented, competitive, and decentralized structure. Hatch's vision of evangelicalism sprang from his historical studies. He believed that the marks of evangelicalism were "its entrepreneurial quality, its populist and decentralized structure, and its penchant for splitting, forming, and reforming."[42] For these reasons—its populist, entrepreneurial, and decentralized nature—Hatch predicted that setting theological boundaries to determine who was an evangelical would be unsuccessful, that there would constantly be new leaders and movements arising from a populist agenda.

Indeed, this seemed to be the case (as the Willow Creek Association, Bill Hybels, James Dobson and Focus on the Family, and John Piper of the Council for Biblical Manhood and Womanhood illustrate), and the affirmations approved at the conference failed to gain widespread acceptance. In part this was because of the ongoing disagreement over the definition of biblical authority. The affirmation on Holy Scripture included the following:

> Attempts to limit the truthfulness of inspired scripture to "faith and practice," viewed as less than the whole of scripture, or worse, to assert that it errs in such matters as history or the world of nature, depart not only from the Bible's representation of its own veracity, but also from the central tradition of the Christian churches.[43]

This obviously was directed at the more progressive evangelicals. In his introduction to the affirmations, Henry referred again to the second generation in refuting the claim "by some" that certain evangelical doctrines (i.e., inerrancy) were theologically innovative and did not represent the central traditions of the church.[44] Those enmeshed in the inerrancy debates would understand his comment to be referring to the progressives, who argued that inerrancy was invented by fundamentalists in their defense of the trustworthiness of the Bible. Yet that difference of opinion would not have resulted in lack of interest in the affirmations if the postwar evangelical coalition had not already been fragmented beyond repair. As Hatch suggested, a new generation of evangelical leaders was coming to the fore, and their opinions on a range of issues that included social and theological agendas differed from those of their elders.

They did not, however, differ from the older generation in their commitment to biblical authority. They may have defined it differently, used different terminology, or interpreted the Bible differently, but evangelicals still defined themselves by their adherence to the binding nature of the words of scripture. The debate over evangelical boundaries—how to tell who was in and who was out—shifted from the issue of inerrancy (is the Bible true in what it says?) to that of hermeneutics (how do we know what it means?). One member of the International Council on Biblical Inerrancy put it this way: "Biblical authority is an empty notion unless we know how to determine what the Bible means."[45] Hermeneutics dealt with the methodology of how the Bible was interpreted. With their high view of scriptural authority, the evangelicals did not accept interpretive methods that resulted in the rejection of some portions of the Bible, as some liberal scholarship had in the past. So the question became which principles allowed evangelicals to take into account modern scholarship that elucidated the culture and historical setting of the New Testament world and still remain faithful to the words of God?

Evangelical Principles of Interpretation

To help evangelicals decide which principles of biblical interpretation were acceptable to use and still maintain the doctrinal authority of the Bible, the International Council on Biblical Inerrancy met in 1982. At the end of the conference, the council published a statement on biblical hermeneutics, outlining twenty-five articles of traditional, evangelical principles of interpretation, dealing with grammatical context, genre, author's intent, and contextualization.[46] The most vexing question, however, and the one most pertinent to biblical feminists, was how to differentiate universal from culturally limited principles.

Universal principles are those commands in scripture interpreted as being intended for all people, for all time, like Exodus 20:13, "You shall not murder." Culturally limited principles are those confined to a specific time, place, and situation. In the event of a culturally bound instruction, evangelicals believe that the general principle behind the specific directive still needs to be determined and applied. For example, few evangelicals insist that women should not braid their hair or wear jewelry, as is directed in 1 Timothy 2:9: "I want women to adorn themselves with proper clothing, modestly and discreetly, not with braided hair and gold or pearls or costly garments." Bible believers assume that the universal principle being taught is to have the proper attitude of humility in worship, exhibited through modest attire. Women, therefore, do not need to follow the specifics to honor the principle being prescribed. In this way the text is still upheld as inspired because the principle (humility in worship) is timeless, although the specific application (no jewelry or expensive clothes in church) is not.

The question of when a text is culturally limited pertains to more than just superficialities like hair, clothing, and jewels. Conservative evangelicals claim that women cannot teach because Paul told the women in Corinth to keep silent: "Let the women keep silent in the churches" (1 Corinthians 14:34). Biblical feminists claim, however, that the eternal principle behind Paul's time-bound command is that women should keep silent until they have been properly trained in the faith.

In his paper at the International Council on Biblical Inerrancy conference, J. Robertson McQuilkin proposes a solution to determining when a passage is culturally limited, by offering the principle that "every teaching is universal unless Scripture itself treats it as limited."[47] McQuilkin argues that there are several ways that scripture can limit a text. The first is through context, as illustrated in 1 Corinthians 7. In a passage dealing with sexual relations, Paul says: "I wish that all men were even as I myself am. However, each man has his own gift from God, one in this manner, and another in that. . . . I think that this is good in view of the present distress" (vv. 7 and 26). McQuilkin points out that it would be improper to consider Paul's statement as a universal command, since he limits it to "those gifted" and says it was in view of "the present distress."

Next, because all scripture is inspired by God, one text can limit another, such as when passages appear to be in conflict. Cultural background and the clearer passage should then be used to clarify the more obtuse text. Slavery was an issue resolved in this way. Paul's letter to Philemon concerned the occasion of Paul's returning a runaway slave to his owner. By studying the culture surrounding the institution of slavery in New Testament times, scholars discovered that slavery was very different then. In many instances, after several years a slave earned his or her freedom. According to most evangelicals, although this did not make slavery any more acceptable, it explained why Paul would have returned a slave to his master, especially when compared with Paul's other writings. To the Galatians, Paul writes that there is "neither Jew nor Greek, there is neither slave nor free. . . . And if you belong to Christ, then you are Abraham's offspring, heirs according to promise" (Galatians 3:28–29). Paul continues, explaining that Christians should not use their freedom for license but to serve one another. Many scholars have used this passage in Galatians to suggest that Paul was not condoning the institution of slavery by returning Philemon. Rather, it indicated only that Paul was following the culture of his day by permitting slavery for a period of time.

Finally, McQuilkin suggests that the reason given for a particular teaching could limit a text. In 1 Thessalonians 4:11, Paul urges the Christians to work with their hands: "But we urge you, brethren to excel still more, and to make it your ambition to lead a quiet life and attend to your own business and work with your hands." Evangelicals do not consider this passage normative because the next verse limits it by explaining the purpose for his directive: "so that you may behave properly toward outsiders and not be in any need." Today, scholars contend, there are other ways to maintain a good reputation and meet the basic needs of one's self and family that do not involve physical labor.

New Testament scholar David Scholer was educated at Gordon-Conwell and Harvard and was the dean of Northern Baptist Theological Seminary in 1983 when he published his guidelines for determining cultural relativity of a passage. Scholer points out that in one way, cultural relativity could be applied to the entire Bible. In this sense, cultural relativity is an affirmation of the non-docetic character of biblical revelation. Its spiritual message cannot be separated from the lives of the people who wrote it. "The Bible, as God's Word, is representative of the fact that God's communication was in history, not above or apart from it."[48] Of course, the more common understanding of the phrase, he acknowledges, is that some biblical texts pertained to their own cultural setting and therefore do not make transcultural, normative claims.

To help distinguish culturally relative from normative texts of scripture, Scholer offers eight guidelines: (1) Determine the central core of the gospel message. The further away a passage is from the core, the greater the likelihood is that it is culturally relative. For example, the injunction to "greet one another with a holy kiss" is more apt to be a limited instruction than are the teachings on the resurrection of Jesus. (2) The frequency of a topic indicates the emphasis placed on it. Foot washing is mentioned infrequently and thus should not be considered a core, normative message. Conversely, baptism is mentioned more often, and so it is more likely to be a universal teaching. (3) Descriptive passages should be distinguished from didactic ones. Descriptive passages should to be related to normative teachings in order to be authoritative. Several passages in the gospels describe giving away all one's wealth to take care of the poor. Such illustrations must be combined with pedagogical lessons on the same topic for them to be normative. (4) Notice when the New Testament has a consistent witness on a particular point and when there are differences. When there are differences, the teaching may not be universal. There is, for example, consistently uniform witness on the subject of Jesus' deity, but New Testament writers are less consistent on women's role as a teacher. (5) One must also discern the difference between principle and application. The former may be absolute, whereas the latter is variable. The example of women's adornment in church, mentioned earlier, illustrates this principle. (6) Ask whether any other passages of scripture specifically limit a text. In Matthew 10:5–6, Jesus tells his disciples to avoid preaching to the Samaritans and Gentiles. Yet in his great commission to them preceding his ascension, Jesus sends them into the world to make disciples of all the nations. (7) The more cultural options that are open to the writer, the greater is the likelihood of cultural relativity. For example, there were few alternatives in the New Testament culture for women or slaves to alter their lowly status. Christians in this culture, therefore, would assume these perspectives. In contrast, on issues in which it is possible to hold more than one view (e.g., belief in the resurrection of the body), the writers' teaching is more likely to be normative. Last, (8) it is important to compare the cultural setting of New Testament times with that of one's own time. Significant differences may uncover limited applications. The education of women and the institution of slavery are examples of such a revelation in modern times, according to Scholer.

The shift from inerrancy to hermeneutics as the theological key to setting evangelical boundaries allowed biblical feminists, like those in the CBE, to help establish those boundaries. Biblical feminists focused most of their energy on providing detailed interpretations of scriptural passages, using these methods of analysis, to prove that the Bible teaches egalitarianism. This effort allowed them to participate in the specialized debates about the methodology of interpretation, for example, as in Gretchen Gaebelein Hull's participation in the third International Council on Biblical Inerrancy summit. In addition, their associations with evangelical leaders and institutions gave them a platform to air their views, as well as some respectability. Finally, their topic of interest—women's equality at home and in the church—also helped push the boundaries on a social issue of great importance to postwar evangelicals. In his study of evangelical beliefs and practices, Hunter documented that evangelicals had come to view the Victorian model of family as the model of a "traditional" (meaning "biblical") family.[49] According to his study, support of the traditional family had become the "highest priority on the evangelical social agenda" and a "cause célèbre."[50] The more traditional biblical feminists' connections in the evangelical coalition, their special interest in women's rights, which affected the traditional family, and their emphasis on biblical interpretation all positioned Christians for Biblical Equality to make a significant impact on contemporary evangelicalism.

The Evangelical Women's Caucus and the Daughters of Sarah

The fallout from the turbulent 1986 conference in Fresno continued for a number of months, and even years, in the Evangelical Women's Caucus. Friendships were strained to the breaking point; women who had been leaders in the organization left or faded away; individuals discontinued their membership; and chapters withdrew. The result was organizational disruption as volunteer and financial support lagged.

Organizational and Identity Crisis

Between the end of 1986 through 1987, individual memberships in the Evangelical Women's Caucus fell to half their earlier number, and the number of chapter memberships also declined. In addition to Minnesota, Portland withdrew out of disagreement with the new direction that the EWC was taking. At the same time, in 1987, the Albany chapter downgraded its status to affiliate. According to its leaders, it was simply unable to generate enough interest to maintain the necessary ten members for a full chapter; it had nothing to do with what happened at the Fresno business meeting. A year later, the summer 1988 *Update* echoed the problems of the Albany group on a larger scale. The Atlanta, Boston, and Southwest chapters all reported similar struggles to maintain prior levels of activity as old leaders left their positions and local chapters had difficulty recruiting others to fill their spaces. The Southwest chapter switched its format from biannual retreats to monthly meetings, hoping to attract more people, but only six to fifteen came. By 1990, only four women were meeting together as the Indiana chapter and the Seattle chapter disbanded. Down to two women, the Delaware chapter applied for affiliate status in 1992. Again, reasons for the attrition were said to be job pressures and "simply running out of steam." In general, between 1987 and 1990, individual memberships averaged 250 during the conference years and fewer than 200 in the other years. Half the local chapters saw attendance fall by 50 percent.[51]

When the chapters' activities and memberships began to decline, the impact was widespread. First, finances became tight. Income dropped because of the fewer chapters and individual memberships. Since the money for the national budget came from membership fees, it also was adversely affected. But the national budget now had to pick up some of the chapters' expenses. For example, in the past the chapters had paid the cost for their representatives to attend national council meetings. With fewer chapters but an ongoing need for volunteers to run the organization, the national council found itself paying for more of its leaders to gather to plan meetings. At times, the EWC did not know where the funds to cover the next edition of *Update* would come from.

Second, the drop in membership affected the EWC's conferences. Whereas the attendance at the earlier conferences was as high as 800 in 1978, 700 in 1982, and 600 in 1986 at Fresno, attendance dropped precipitously in 1988 when only 150 people attended the "Journey in Peace-making" at Northpark. Although these biennial events had traditionally been hosted and planned by a local chapter, when the Minnesota chapter resigned and other chapters lagged in volunteer energy, the EWC had to find another way to staff these gatherings. The 1988 meeting, scheduled for Minnesota, was moved to North Park College and Theological Seminary, close to the origins of biblical feminism and the Daughters of Sarah collective. Various national council members were assigned coordinating roles. Later conferences followed a similar pattern, with the national organization giving primary oversight to the event, local individuals playing coordinating roles, and attendance hovering around 150.

The 1990 conference helped the EWC's financial situation for a time by making a profit. Even then, however, the council was borrowing money from local chapters to pay for brochures to advertise the 1992 conference. Thus, partly to redirect the flow of much needed dollars to the national organization, the council changed the EWC from an organization based on chapters to one based on individual memberships. This meant that membership fees would no longer be shared with a local chapter. Still, by the time of the 1992 gathering in San Francisco, the EWC was again in difficult financial straits, having only enough money to print the next issue of *Update*. The 1992 conference only made the financial situation worse. The coordinators had contracted with the University of San Francisco to accommodate 150 people. But when only 100 needed housing, the EWC found itself forced to pay $5,300 for unused rooms. The EWC's administrator reported at the end of the conference that the event had consumed all of its assets.

In sum, the meeting in San Francisco failed to meet the two most critical expectations of an Evangelical Women's Caucus convention: recruiting volunteers and replenishing the coffers. The EWC's rhythm revolved around the biennial gatherings of "the sisters of summer." Membership and involvement dropped off during nonconference years. Then the conventions energized the committed members, and money flowed into the bank as large donations came in and a few new members joined. In anticipation of the low attendance numbers and dismal financial situation, the national council discussed ways of scaling down the organization at their executive meeting in the days leading up to the gathering in San Francisco. Three ideas surfaced: to merge with Daughters of Sarah, to become inactive for two years (until the next conference), or to cease to exist altogether. Council members were unsure about the correct course of action. They decided to be honest about the caucus's financial situation and present their options to the larger membership at the San Francisco business meeting a few days later. In the end, although much was left unclear, it was decided that there would be a conference in 1994, cosponsored by the Daughters of Sarah, which would be a twentieth-anniversary commemoration of it and the EWC. If the EWC were to disband, its members wanted it to go out in a celebration of all they had accomplished.

All the financial and manpower difficulties caused an identity crisis within the EWC. In 1988, the outgoing national coordinator, Britt Vanden Eykel, wondered in print, "What do members want and expect from this organization?"[52] The article was entitled "NOT a Swan Song," in an apparent reference to her ending her tenure at the helm of the EWC. An astute reader, however, would also be led to wonder whether the caucus was in danger of going under. Vanden Eykel was concerned that even though many women supported the EWC in concept, few were willing to attend a meeting, much less volunteer. She proposed that the EWC accept its role of nurturing women to use their gifts. This also meant recognizing that as their constituents' lives became busier—juggling homes, families, volunteer activities, and careers—they would have little time to participate in the ministry that had first nurtured them. Anne Eggebroten agreed. In 1989, Eggebroten argued that short-term memberships were a sign of the Evangelical Women's Caucus's strength:

> The women who are healed by our ministry go on to live lives rooted in biblical feminism. . . . Let's face our identity as an organization that provides short-term therapy. Rather than worry because our paid membership is down, let's rejoice that the total number of those who have been members in the past and present comes to more than 2,400.[53]

Not everyone agreed with Eggebroten and Vanden Eykel's analysis, however. In response to Vanden Eykel's editorial, letters to the editor focused on the change in the EWC since the Fresno business meeting. Some writers indicated that they remained in the group because the resolutions made it a more open, welcoming place that pursued broader feminist concerns. Other readers said they intended to leave, or had left, the EWC because the resolutions indicated that it was taking an unbiblical stance on homosexuality and failing to support women in evangelical churches. None of these writers indicated that they simply had outgrown the EWC's ministry. Their response does not invalidate Vanden Eykel and Eggebroten's theory, but it does indicate that events at Fresno had more of an impact on the EWC's ministry than its leaders wanted to admit.

Solving the Crisis

Whether or not it was a clear-cut strategy, the Evangelical Women's Caucus managed to find a way out of its organizational malaise by resolving its financial and numerical problems and, most important, by settling on a new purpose.

First, the caucus tightened its fiscal management by cutting its conference expenses. Prior to the San Francisco conference, the EWC had been operating on a limited budget but had remained solvent. San Francisco taught the council that they needed to choose a less expensive location. North Park Theological College and Seminary, where the earlier 1988 and 1990 conferences had been held, fit the bill. The midwestern location made travel cheaper, and all the site fees were lower. In addition, active Evangelical Women's Caucus and *Daughters of Sarah* groups provided volunteer labor to coordinate the event. Because the attendance in San Francisco in 1992 was 100, that was the breakeven figure set by coordinators for the 1994 conference at Northpark. This time, though, instead of 100 to 150, approximately 200 women attended the twentieth anniversary gathering. Featured speakers included feminist theologian Rosemary Skinner Keller, a professor in the joint Ph.D. program at Northwestern University and Garrett-Evangelical Theological Seminary (where several EWC members studied, including Sue Horner, its former coordinator), Methodist Bishop Ann Sherer, Nancy Hardesty, and Virginia Mollenkott. Seventy-six new members joined the EWC as a result of that conference, and new life—financially and numerically—was infused into the fading organization. Ironically, the *Daughters of Sarah*, the organization that the EWC had looked to for help in pulling out of its own crisis, did not survive long after its twentieth anniversary. The final issue of the magazine was published in the winter of 1996, before the next EWC conference.

Second, the EWC scaled back its activities to what was most important to its members: the biennial conferences and *Update*. It learned from the success of the 1994 convention, just as it had learned from earlier mistakes. The anniversary conference convinced the group that the EWC was not ready to die. There remained a desire to gather with far-flung friends and like-minded feminists who had battled together during the 1970s and 1980s for the passage of the equal rights amendment and basic equal opportunity rights for women. In addition, the women in the EWC believed that there was still much work to be done, especially in changing the consciousness of the conservative Protestant American community. Thus, Letha Scanzoni and Rebecca Bowers, both residents of Norfolk, Virginia, volunteered to host the 1996 conference at Old Dominion University in Norfolk. They arranged cosponsorship of the event with the Women's Center at the university. Later years saw the event return to the Midwest, in 1998 at Aquinas College in Grand Rapids, Michigan, and again at North Park in 2000. At all three conferences, attendance was around 150 to 200, and none broke the EWC's budget. Workshop topics addressed themes of loss, midlife passages, and stress reduction for "women who achieve," as well as social activism and feminist theology.

Update remained the other nucleus of the EWC. The newsletter continued to give members news of their friends, reporting when someone moved, was promoted, finished a program of study, or published a book. With increasing frequency, however, obituaries, prayer requests for those who were ill, and retirement notices also appeared in its pages. Like the topics of midlife passages and stress reduction, these themes highlighted the aging membership of the EWC. A couple of issues specifically addressed why members' daughters were not interested in feminist issues.[54]

Update continued to introduce women to new books on topics of interest to biblical feminists. The books reviewed covered therapeutic topics, such as domestic abuse and child rearing, but they now also addressed more liberal feminist theologies, like that of liberation theologians Rosemary Radford Ruether and Elisabeth Schüssler Fiorenza and womanist theologian Delores Williams. Reviews of these books were not intended as endorsements for their theologies; rather, Scanzoni commented that their purpose was to stretch women's minds. This willingness to open the minds of its audience, though, reveals the caucus's increasing inclusiveness and willingness of its members to consider more liberal theologies and methodologies.

Another writer whose work was reviewed was Kwok Pui-lan. In *Discovering the Bible in the Non-Biblical World*, Pui-lan, a Chinese feminist, rejected the idea of a closed canon of scripture as imperialistic and patriarchal. Instead, she drew upon Buddhist, Dao, Hindu, and Confucian texts to help her discern spiritual principles. Her guideline for judging a theological model was whether and how it helped relieve human suffering. This was a line of reasoning more akin to the direction taken in contemporary philosophy than to that in orthodox Christianity. The reviewer of Pui-lan's book, former *Update* editor Deborah Jang, admitted that "for those who regard the Bible as the inspired word of God, the gist of Kwok Pui-lan's convictions would raise many an evangelical eyebrow."[55] Still, Jang's review elicited no critical response by readers, unlike earlier positive views of books with questionable evangelical credentials (such as the second edition of Scanzoni and Hardesty's *All We're Meant to Be* had, with Hardesty's endorsement of homosexual Christians).

In addition to greater theological diversity, *Update* also began to reflect the growing diversity of sexuality within the EWC. One issue that reflected this began with a poem Virginia Mollenkott wrote after the end of "what she had expected to be a lifelong relationship with a beloved partner."[56] Following the poem was an interview with Mollenkott on the topic of friendship. Mollenkott stated in the interview that she now believed that friendship, rather than marriage, should be the normative model for human relationships. When asked why, Mollenkott replied: "Friendship is an inclusive model that reaches out in solidarity to the entire planet and the universe and all the creatures in it. By contrast, marriage has functioned as an excluding model that tends to shut out the rest of the world." Mollenkott's last few books also emphasized the inclusivity of the Christian message.

Other activities besides biennial conferences and the publishing of *Update* did take place. For example, one year after the 1994 conference, ten caucus members living in California and Oregon gathered on the West Coast for a time of sharing and encouragement. But increasingly, the EWC promoted events of interest to its constituents that were sponsored by other groups. In 1993, the center spread of *Update* advertised the upcoming "Re-Imagining" and "Women-Church" conferences. The purpose of "Women-Church: Weavers of Change" was to unify women from diverse socioeconomic, racial, ethnic, and cultural backgrounds around their "sense of the sacred," in hopes that the resulting harmony would be the starting point of collective action for both personal and structural transformation.

As important as fiscal solvency, achieved by scaling back the organization to what it did best, was finding a solution to the EWC's identity crisis. This came not through concerted effort but by the natural changes that were already occurring in the organization. Socially and theologically, it was becoming more diverse and inclusive, particularly as more traditional evangelicals drifted away owing to discomfort with the EWC's growing inclusivity and its inability to witness to conservative churches.

The result was an organization more uniformly accepting of a broad array of social and theological diversity. Debbie Jang's pilgrimage, which appears at the beginning of this chapter, illustrates the kind of changes occurring among members of the EWC. So whereas at the 1988 conference the reviews of a plenary session on sexuality were mixed—some participants complained that the lecture served solely to promote homosexuality, others expressed appreciation of the openness toward gay and lesbian Christians—almost every participant commented positively on the openness and inclusiveness toward lesbians at the EWC's 1990 conference. Nor did anyone complain at later conferences about Ruether (in 1990) or Williams (1992) as plenary speakers, as some did about Schüssler Fiorenza in 1986, and theologians like David Scholer were no longer invited even to lead workshops.[57]

In response to the obviously increasing diversity, in 1988 the national council recommended changes in the EWC's name and statement of faith. The suggested new name was the "Ecumenical Women's Caucus." The initials of the organization would remain the same, but many felt that "ecumenical" better described the group. "Evangelical" seemed "too narrow and confining." In summarizing the pros and cons of this change, Letha Scanzoni wrote that some members "do not wish to be identified with fundamentalist interpretations of scripture and a right-wing social/political agenda."[58] The council recommended changes in the statement of faith for similar reasons. Sue Horner, the national co-coordinator, explained both the changes and the rationale behind them:

> These proposed changes to our Statement of Faith . . . reflect the Council's desire to remove hierarchical and androcentric language (e.g., the word Ruler changed to Sustainer). The change in definition of the Bible from the infallible guide to a central guide is in response to a broader understanding of God's witness. That is, God is made known to us not only through the written words of the Bible, but also in the broader historical traditions of the church and in the workings of the Holy Spirit. Terms like infallible and final seem limiting, and the Council wanted to affirm the multiplicity of perspectives that our membership represents.[59]

The council needed the approval of the membership at large to make these kinds of adjustments. Thus, mail-in ballots were sent to every member of the EWC. On the first ballot, the vote was almost evenly split between those who wanted to keep the name "Evangelical Women's Caucus" and those who wanted a change. Without an overwhelming mandate, the council decided not to change the name at that time. In addition, the changes suggested for the statement of faith were invalidated because the wording of the ballot confused people and a number of women did not respond to the council's revisions, instead writing in their own changes.

Some members of the EWC, even those who approved of the move toward more inclusivity, did not want to relinquish the term *evangelical* in their name. Mollenkott and Scanzoni were among them, pointing out that the EWC's heritage was evangelical. It began in the neo-evangelical movement, and many of its members had been nurtured in their love of the scripture by that movement. But they also recognized that "evangelical" was a confining image. Thus, by the 1990 business meeting at the biennial gathering in North Park, a compromise solution was reached, and members voted to change their name to the "Evangelical and Ecumenical Women's Caucus" (EEWC).[60] Later that year, 89 percent of the members who responded to another mail-in ballot approved the changes to the statement of faith.

The Evangelical and Ecumenical Women's Caucus and the Religious Establishment

Referring to the broadening conception of authority, the former *Update* editor Virginia Hearn described the Evangelical and Ecumenical Women's Caucus's revisions in the statement of faith as "a monumental change." According to Kaye Cook's survey, after 1992 most EEWC members held a more liberal view of biblical authority and the interpretation of scripture. In response to questions about biblical authority, Cook found that the women were split between positions of limited inerrancy and neo-orthodoxy:

> No Evangelical and Ecumenical Women's Caucus member agreed with strict inerrancy ("The Bible is the inspired Word of God, not mistaken in its statements and teachings, and is to be taken literally, word for word."); 31 percent believed in limited inerrancy ("The Bible is the inspired Word of God, not mistaken in its teachings, but is not always to

be taken literally in its statements concerning matters of science, history, etc."); 28 percent agreed with a neo-orthodox statement ("The Bible becomes the Word of God for a person when he or she reads it in faith"); and 2 percent agreed that the Bible is not the Word of God ("The Bible is an ancient book of legend/history/moral precepts recorded by men").[61]

Cook concluded from comparing these figures with those from the CBE (86 percent of whom agreed with a strict or limited inerrancy position) that "attitudes toward the inerrancy of Scripture do not adequately differentiate between these groups. It may be that, although members of both groups believe in some form of inerrancy, one group sees Scripture as having less authority in their lives."

Given that just under one-third of the EEWC members (versus more than four-fifths of CBE members) accepted some form of inerrancy, it seems that when combined with an analysis of the theology and social positions of the Evangelical and Ecumenical Women's Caucus, Cook's study indicated that attitudes toward inerrancy and scripture did differentiate the Evangelical and Ecumenical Women's Caucus from Christians for Biblical Equality. And this difference was crucial, because even though both groups of evangelical feminists claimed that their identity was formed by a relationship to the text of scripture that viewed it as authoritative, only one of them acknowledged the presence of constraints on how and what they should read, as well as on the kinds of conclusions that they could properly draw from their reading.[62]

Members of the EEWC claimed to take the Bible seriously. This meant they read it for meaning and to undercover its suggestions and imperatives for action. However, as one theologian observed, relating to scripture as authoritative also involves "the presence of some acknowledged constraints upon what and how religious readers should read . . . as well as (by entailment) upon the kinds of conclusions that can properly be drawn and taught from this reading."[63] As such, it must take place in a community that establishes the constraints. Yet the Evangelical and Ecumenical Women's Caucus did not recognize the social, hermeneutical or textual limits of the evangelical community. Although it wanted to continue to be known as evangelical, it did not accept those aspects by which evangelicals defined their movement: the inerrancy of scripture, particular methods of biblical interpretation, and appropriate social conclusions that could be drawn. Instead, the EEWC's growing inclusivity, acceptance of homosexuality, and changing its statement of faith convinced the evangelical community that it no longer belonged.

It was not the text of scripture alone that constrained progressive biblical feminist action. Particularly in their arguments that homosexuality was compatible with scripture, progressive biblical feminists were seen as elevating reason, science, personal revelation and experience, and even non-Christian texts to the same level as God's revealed Word. Yet deciding what to read is "the most basic decision religious readers can make; from it flows almost everything of importance about the religious accounts they offer."[64] Mollenkott's book *Omnigender: A Trans-Religious Approach*—in which she uses Christian, Jewish, Buddhist, Hindu, Muslim, and other sources to argue for the acceptance of all forms of sexuality—exemplifies the importance of text and methodology to the conclusions reached.

Mollenkott's work also shows that what began in Fresno in 1986 as a desire for recognition and acceptance of homosexual persons led to demands for political rights in the church and society. Thus some of the women in the Evangelical and Ecumenical Women's Caucus left their evangelical churches when those congregations could not meet their pleas for justice and joined denominations that were more open to homosexuality. Virginia Mollenkott and, for a while, Nancy Hardesty joined the Protestant Episcopal Church in the U.S.A. (commonly known as the Episcopal Church).[65] At one point, Hardesty even considered becoming ordained as an Episcopalian priest but left when it, too, refused to ordain openly homosexual persons. Others joined the Universal Fellowship of Metropolitan Community Churches (known as the Metropolitan Community Church, or MCC), which describes itself as an evangelical church that serves lesbian, gay, bisexual, and transsexual believers.[66] Founded with just twelve congregants in 1968, the MCC claimed more than 42,000 members in sixteen countries in 2000.

Even though the overwhelming majority of American evangelicals do not recognize the MCC as evangelical, its presence illustrates that the struggle for acceptance of homosexuality within the evangelical community has made an impact on evangelicalism. Progressive biblical feminists have helped convince some people in the conservative Protestant community that rejecting someone because of her or his sexual orientation is unjust and therefore not Christian, regardless of the truth claims of scripture on this topic. Consequently, evangelical and conservative Protestant churches have found it more difficult to maintain a publicly acceptable moral position against homosexuality. In this way, the issue of homosexuality and the progressive evangelical feminists have helped move American culture toward a declining acceptance of moral arguments, on any subject, that are founded primarily on the biblical witness.

So why have many progressive feminists insisted on retaining the label of "evangelical?" Mollenkott was even embarrassed by aspects of evangelical culture, like its conservative politics and the confusion of Christian lifestyle with suburban materialism.[67] There are many, likely conflicting, reasons. Certainly one reason, already mentioned, was that "evangelical" describes the heritage of Evangelical and Ecumenical Women's Caucus and many of its members. Their faith began and was nurtured in the evangelical church, and they wanted to recognize this. In this historical sense, many of the women in Evangelical and Ecumenical Women's Caucus indeed were evangelical. They came out of the historical tradition of American revivalism, and held some of its beliefs (the importance of a transformed life, scripture, and a type of evangelism), though not all. They also shared characteristics with historical evangelicalism, especially the lack of respect for tradition, authority and institutions, and the tendency to follow charismatic teachers, argue, splinter, and form new groups.

In addition, it was through evangelicalism that progressive biblical feminists learned to love and value scripture. They still insisted that "when wholistically interpreted, the Bible teaches the full equality and mutual responsibility of women and men in the church, in the family, and in society as a whole."[68] For these women, even if not read within the constraints of the evangelical community, the Bible still informed their feminist beliefs. As Scanzoni put it: "I could not just make up my feminism on my own. It would not have the same authority. It [the Bible] gives me guidance."[69]

Another reason that some progressive evangelical feminists retained the label of evangelical was their desire to resymbolize American evangelicalism in light of their own presumptions about diversity and pluralism. Mollenkott, in particular, seemed to have this perspective. She indicated that one reason she wanted to continue to keep "evangelical" in Evangelical and Ecumenical Women's Caucus's name was that by using the language of conservative Protestants, Mollenkott believed she could keep the lines of communication open between herself and conservative evangelicals. She responded to a critique from Carter Heyward about Mollenkott's apparent belief that Jesus was the Messiah by conceding that "perhaps I have not always been as explicit about that [Christology] as I should have been. If so, my timidity has stemmed from my efforts to preserve communication with evangelical women and men."[70] The ability to communicate in the language of the evangelical milieu was thus why Mollenkott still used the exclusive language of Christianity, although she would describe her theology as inclusive, even panentheistic.

Mollenkott thinks it is important to maintain a conversation with evangelicals, for two reasons. First, by keeping the traditional Christian language, Mollenkott hopes that biblical feminism will continue to appear as a viable option for women who find the male patriarchy in the evangelical church unbearably oppressive. She calls it "putting up a flag" for women to rally to when they otherwise might abandon the Christian faith altogether.

Second, Mollenkott wants to remain in conservative Protestantism at least symbolically in order to transform it. She understands that transformation must come from within the culture. Mollenkott advocates what she calls "subversion." In *Sensuous Spirituality*, Mollenkott describes herself (and all oppressed minorities) as living in enemy-occupied territory: heteropatriarchy.[71] To overcome oppression, people should be willing to use subversion, defined as the "systematic attempt to overthrow or undermine a political system by persons who work secretly with the system involved."[72] Mollenkott sees herself as covertly working to transform traditional evangelicalism by being open by about her views, lifestyles, theology, and values all the while using the theological language of evangelicalism. Being known as an "evangelical feminist," then, may allow her inclusive beliefs to be heard within the conservative Protestant community. It was for exactly this reason that evangelicals fought so tenaciously to determine their boundaries, in order to filter out "impurity." The battle about the right to name oneself was in reality a battle for power, the power to transform or maintain the purity of the evangelical movement.

Some people might wonder why some progressive biblical feminists like Mollenkott bothered remaining Christians at all. After all, Mollenkott admittedly held pluralistic beliefs. One feminist theologian asked Mollenkott why, like Mary Daly, she did not leave Christianity entirely. Mollenkott responded that when convinced that something really matters, faithful people will stick to it.[73] Underlying her answer was Mollenkott's belief that scripture does matter. It also reveals that she understood the power of religious language and convictions to influence society, particularly that of evangelicalism. Thus if she could influence it, she could move society further toward her pluralistic, inclusive vision.

For some progressive biblical feminists, thus, the name "evangelical" highlights their commitment to biblical teachings as a rule of faith and practice. However, it also serves, unconsciously or not, to obfuscate the more progressive manner in which they interpret the Bible's teachings. By remaining symbolically in evangelicalism, progressive biblical feminists have retained the possibility of making the evangelical community and, through it, American society more inclusive.

Because progressive biblical feminists have become inclusive in their theological methods, conclusions, and sources of authority, they have not maintained close ties with evangelical organizations, seminaries, and leaders. For example, the members of the Evangelical and Ecumenical Women's Caucus are involved not with the National Association of Evangelicals but most often with the National and World Council of Churches (e.g., the World Council sponsored the Re-Imagining Conference and Mollenkott's work on its Inclusive Language Lectionary). Academically, progressive biblical feminists interact most often with nonevangelical feminist theologians. Evangelical and Ecumenical Women's Caucus conference speakers more often are liberal theologians, like Elisabeth Schüssler Fiorenza, than evangelicals. In addition, by the later years of biblical feminism, progressive biblical feminists and liberal theologians had discussions in journals, such as the exchange between Mollenkott and Carter Heyward in the *Journal of Feminist Studies in Religion* or between Mollenkott and Schüssler Fiorenza. Members of the Evangelical and Ecumenical Women's Caucus and the Evangelical Theological Society did not have such discussions.

The national council of the Evangelical and Ecumenical Women's Caucus also voted at their meeting after the 2000 biennial conference to house their archives at the Union Theological Seminary Library. They had previously arranged for the archives to go to Wheaton College, which has a large archival collection on evangelicalism. The reason for the change was that Union was establishing the Archives of Women in Theological Scholarship, in which the Evangelical and Ecumenical Women's Caucus's papers would be held. This location would "place Evangelical and Ecumenical Women's Caucus's material in historical dialogue with that of other religious women's organizations and with the work of feminist theologians."[74] This again showed that progressive evangelical feminists' primary community of accountability was feminist, not evangelical.

Despite the progressive biblical feminists' attempts to place themselves symbolically within evangelicalism—by continuing to describe themselves as such and using traditional evangelical language—there did not appear to be any widespread recognition by either the Evangelical and Ecumenical Women's Caucus or the broader evangelical coalition that the EEWC and many of the women in it were accepted members of the evangelical community. In other words, to the American evangelical community, even though the Evangelical and Ecumenical Women's Caucus's roots were in historic evangelicalism, progressive biblical feminists were no longer evangelicals.

For the most part, the members of the Evangelical and Ecumenical Women's Caucus agreed. When the 1994 council asked them at the biennial business meeting to reflect on "who we are; whom do we serve; and how do we serve," their responses focused on the EEWC's inclusiveness, particularly of lesbian Christians, and its ecumenical nature, not on its strict adherence to the Bible. To the question of whom they served, women answered: "mainstream liberal feminist Christians," "Christian feminists and lately (as of three conferences ago) lesbians of faith," "women who are finding their own voices and need to be energized by womenspiritpower." "We are inclusive and welcoming," wrote one woman, "you don't have to be a member of church first or afterward. Marginalized are welcome—lesbians, Roman Catholics, African/Asian Americans, emerging ex-fundamentalists, Pentecostals. Inclusivity and diversity." Members said that the Evangelical and Ecumenical Women's Caucus served them by allowing them to "experiment with female God language in a loving atmosphere" and by "push[ing] people to think about their faith and feminism without telling them that they have to do it in any one way (like CBE might do) . . . it's okay to be inclusive of all sorts of messages." The question "who are we" was summed up by one member: "We are, I believe, a radically feminist group—more inclusive than some, more biblically oriented than others."[75]

By the end of the millennium, the description of Evangelical and Ecumenical Women's Caucus in *Update* proclaimed:

> We are inclusive: EEWC is evangelical because it was rooted in the belief that the gospel is good news for all persons. EEWC is ecumenical because we recognize that faith is expressed through a rich diversity of traditions and forms of spirituality. We offer a community of safety for all who have experienced abuse, marginalization, or exclusion by Christian

churches. We have discovered that the expansiveness of God calls us to be an inclusive communtiy.[76]

In the summer 2000 *Update* the national council of the Evangelical and Ecumenical Women's Caucus listed its new goals, one of which is to "increase our visibility as a welcoming community for lesbian, gay, bisexual, and transgendered persons by exchanging ideas, newsletters and communication with their organizations and caucuses." Another goal is to "maintain our ecumenical identity and to continue our dialogue with persons of other faiths."[77]

Evangelicalism and American Culture

Traditionalist biblical feminists, conversely, do accept the constraints of the evangelical community on how to interpret scripture and on what texts are authoritative and thus are accepted into the evangelical community. They adhere to the belief that the Bible is the sole source of authority for determining the content of their faith and moral values. They believe that the Bible was given by God as an inspired, reliable, external witness, "the final authority in faith and practice," as the CBE's statement of faith indicates. In addition, traditionalist biblical feminists faithfully follow strictly outlined methods of biblical interpretation, particularly in regard to determining the transcultural or normative nature of a text, unlike progressive biblical feminists for whom a more abstract measure (love and justice) determines what is normative. Using such methods of interpretation, traditionalist biblical feminist doctrine remains within the boundaries of orthodox evangelicalism in virtually every area: theology proper, the Trinity, the Holy Spirit, Christology, atonement, salvation, sin, and grace. Even their anthropology has remained orthodox in their belief in the essential dignity of all persons as created equally in the image of God, and in heterosexual marriage as the proper channel for human sexuality.

Thus, the conclusions these biblical feminists have reached about how the scripture commands them to live are aligned with those of the younger evangelical community. They strongly support the family (CBE's marriage seminar and its statement of faith with the affirmation of "faithful heterosexual marriage" illustrate this), maintain that men and women have essential gender differences, do not favor the use of inclusive language for God, and oppose same-sex relationships and abortion. Unlike progressive feminists, traditionalist biblical feminists see justice as related to moral righteousness, not as an individual right. Therefore, abortion, rather than homosexuality, is an issue of justice for them. For these reasons, traditionalist biblical feminists have remained within the community standards set by the evangelical community regarding how to read the text of scripture and what are acceptable conclusions to draw about how to act.

This kind of religious reading of the text of scripture by traditionalist biblical feminists may be one of the principal reasons that contemporary American evangelicalism has been able to survive and grow in a world marked by pluralism and inclusivity. According to sociologist Christian Smith, American evangelicalism "thrives on distinction, engagement, tension, conflict, and threat. Without these, evangelicalism, we suggest, would lose its identity and purpose and grow languid and aimless."[78] The emphasis on particular ways of reading and specific conclusions drawn from the text of scripture to establish boundaries have helped evangelicals promote a strong identity and satisfy its members' need for "stability, assurance, and truth" in a pluralistic environment.[79]

Certainly American culture today is changing. Ours is an increasingly therapeutic, consumerist society that, instead of basing morality on the internalization of reveal, external truths, bases it on the perceived needs and desires of the individual. American culture has become a society in which faith is a powerless authority.[80] Instead of being a transcendent authority that teaches one how to live rightly through disciplining the self, religion has been transformed into "personal faith" or "spirituality," something to assist each individual to "find himself or hersellf" and achieve his or her potential.[81] Exclusive faith beliefs, which insist on authority higher than the individual and limit behavior, do not fit into such an environment. It is just this exclusivity, however, according to Smith, that sets evangelicalism apart from its culture and makes it resilient.[82]

If the exclusive claims of evangelicalism enable it to survive in contemporary culture, this implies that progressive biblical feminism will fare less well in a pluralist environment. Since progressive feminists are identified by their inclusivity, this fact fails to set them apart from the rest of contemporary culture, and their faith provides fewer reasons for its adherents to remain bound to it. This may be one reason that many members of the Evangelical and Ecumenical Women's Caucus found it as a place of transition, a place that provided "short-term therapy."[83] They participated for a while but then moved on. Nor is it a surprise that when its membership was asked to reflect on whom it served, one answer included evangelicals, a few mentioned Christianity more broadly, and several failed to mention religion at all.[84] Two women stated that they did not see the EEWC as a religious organization at all. To them it was just a good feminist organization, no different from its secular feminist counterparts, particularly with the rise of ecofeminism and goddess worship, with their spiritual foundations.

Arguably, then, American evangelicalism has not been left unaltered by its encounter with the modern world. Although it may remain strong at its core, it is fraying at the edges. Statistically its numbers may not be declining, but it has lost members as they come into contact with contemporary American culture and values—as the women of the Evangelical and Ecumenical Women's Caucus illustrate—by losing its ability to bind members to its key tenets.

Traditionalist feminists, by contrast, have remained exclusive in their faith beliefs and the authority of scripture, though they have stretched the limits of the evangelical social agenda. In doing so, traditionalist evangelical feminists actually have provided a robust, alternative theory to secular feminism. Although both secular and traditionalist evangelical feminism have sought equality for women, secular feminism has had no external foundation on which to base their calls for equality. Secular feminism, instead, demands equality for women based on women's own experience and, in doing so, has played a role in the disestablishment of external moral demands. The feminist movement has therefore had difficulty in settling competing moral claims. How, for example, is one to judge behaviors in another culture, such as the wearing of head scarves or clitoridectomy? Secular feminists (such as Susan Moller Okin) have used Western women's experience to judge the treatment of women in other cultures.[85] Traditionalist evangelical feminists, however, have located their feminist ideals in a preestablished moral order that provides an external means for settling such questions.

Traditionalist evangelical feminists have not been left unaffected, however, by the changes in American culture, although the impact has been subtler. First, like a trend evident more broadly in American evangelicalism, traditionalist evangelical feminism has tended to tailor the message of the gospel to the felt needs of the listener, thus focusing more on the individual faith practitioner than on the Divine. Historian Alister McGrath complained that evangelicalism has been fixated on "the American therapeutic culture of "feel-good-ism," by emphasizing church growth, feel-good preaching, and styles of ministry largely informed by secular psychology.[86] Similarly, sociologist Kimon Howland Sargeant concluded, based on a study of the Willow Creek Church, that the current religious environment of much of American evangelicalism has an expanding "therapeutic ethos" in which religion is more valuable for "its instrumental value in meeting personal needs than for its substantive claims for the truth."[87] As just pointed out, traditionalist biblical feminists have received significant support and have strong ties with the seeker church movement that has resulted in the CBE's strategy to shift priority away from reform of the social order (i.e., a focus on the reinterpretation of scripture) toward marketing its message to individual women and couples, by addressing self-help topics through the marriage conferences and self-help materials.

Second, the emphasis on the ability of individual reason to correctly interpret the words of scripture, without the assistance of an institutional church, shows that the modern ideals of individualism and rationality have made a greater impact on American evangelicalism in general. As we have seen, traditionalist biblical feminists have remained well inside the boundaries of evangelical methods of biblical interpretation. These methods emphasize that through the use of rational, logical methods, individuals can come to correct conclusions about the God's demands on their lives. They do not need to follow the teachings or traditions of a particular institutional form of the church.

Scholars long have argued that American Protestantism, in large part due to its revivalist roots in the soil of democracy, is individualistic.[88] The doctrine of inerrancy only heightens this by assuring all Christians—lay or ordained—that they have an equal ability to understand the text of scripture without any help from the church, its theology, or its institutions. Not surprisingly, then, contemporary Americans evangelicals have been known for their lack of loyalty to any particular church or denomination.[89] Such an individualistic, anti-institutional, and voluntary perspective on the church has led American evangelicals to rely on human reason and ignore the historical tradition of the church and the legacy of its theology as irrelevant, thereby stripping much of the meaning out of the concept of authority. Scripture may be called authoritative, but it is the individual reader, perhaps with the help of his or her favorite preacher or author, who determines what the scripture says and means. This creates, though, a discrepancy between the rhetoric and practice in the evangelical community. Its language emphasizes the authority of the scripture, but in practice, the individual has the authority to reject any interpretation or community with which he or she disagrees. We have seen this in the way traditionalist evangelical feminists have used a variety of theological traditions—Wesleyan, Reformed, Dispensationalist, and the like—to argue for women's equality, as well as in the way that they, along with the majority of the evangelical coalition, have placed great confidence in the capacity of human reason, in the form of particular hermeneutical principles, to judge the truth of revelation.

Future studies of American evangelicalism would do well to seek to learn how such modern trends as scientific rationalism, technological advances, and advanced capitalism have affected even the more conservative aspects of American Protestantism as a way of revealing some of the unintentional consequences of these forces on American culture.

Summary

Lacking authoritative church bodies, evangelicals rely on behavioral norms to control their membership and theological norms as a convenient guide to determine who is a part of their fellowship. By extending both these boundaries through the acceptance of homosexuality and alternate doctrinal authorities and methodologies, the Evangelical and Ecumenical Women's Caucus is no longer regarded by many as a part of evangelical coalition. Cook concluded from her research that

> EEWCers are solidly in the feminist camp and less clearly evangelical (as shown, in part, by their recent name change). They are more likely to question what evangelicalism is and at least a few see themselves as "formerly" evangelical. Although they take their faith seriously, they support prochoice and homosexual agendas, as well as egalitarian principles. . . . EEWC espoused a more homosexual (primarily lesbian) agenda and became less clearly evangelical.[90]

As a result, evangelical theologians no longer bother to discourse publicly with Mollenkott or other feminists in the Evangelical and Ecumenical Women's Caucus. These women are regarded as too extreme to be a threat to traditional evangelical social or theological norms. Instead, progressive biblical feminists' main community of accountability has become the feminist community. They are now less distinguishable from the rest of American culture, thereby helping weaken the appeal of moral arguments based on transcendent authority. At best, the EEWC can be seen as playing a prophetic role in the evangelical coalition in America, by pushing the general Protestant religious ethos in a more inclusive direction and thereby hoping to affect broader American culture. It was this similarity with a more pluralist, individualistic American culture that failed to set it apart from other feminist organizations, combined with its lack of appeal for traditional evangelicals, and that caused progressive evangelical feminism to fare less well than traditionalist evangelical feminism.

Christians for Biblical Equality, however, has remained a part of the American evangelical coalition and sought to change it from within. It has managed to remain in the evangelical community, and by maintaining a strong adherence to scriptural authority and employing methods of interpretation being debated in that community, this organization has participated in the further extension of evangelical boundaries, socially and theologically. Traditionalist biblical feminists, therefore, illustrate that the strength of American evangelicalism lies in its adherence to exclusive truth claims and transcendent authority at the same time that it reveals the extent of inroads on American evangelicalism of modern ideals of pluralism and individualism.

7

Conclusion

In telling the history of evangelical feminism, I have sought to do two things. First, I wanted to tell the story of a group of marginalized yet significant women in the history of American religion. This account is particularly important because evangelicalism has been such a considerable force in American history. Second, I hoped to discover what role, if any, feminists in evangelicalism have played in changes occurring within their own community and beyond. To answer this, I have traced the development of evangelical feminism, focusing on its theology and view of biblical authority and on its leading organizations and their social agenda.

Contrary to the claim of Rosemary Radford Ruether on the opening page of this book, the narrative of evangelical feminism has shown that feminist theology can come from the existing base of the Christian Bible. With a theological rigor that has largely been ignored by theologians and scholars of American religion, evangelical feminists have demonstrated that even in conservative Protestantism, women are more than just the majority of congregants sitting in the pew or serving (male) leaders of the church.

At the center of evangelical feminist theology is the question of biblical authority, its nature, meaning, and scope. From the beginning, biblical feminists addressed this issue because of a desire to convince their fellow evangelicals that the Bible, not just secular society or liberal philosophies, teaches the equality of men and women in the home, church, and society. To do this, they had to take the authority of the Bible seriously and show that those who taught women's subordination had been misinterpreting scripture.

It was as a result of these theological efforts that evangelical feminists helped change the face of American evangelicalism. Since evangelicals do not have the same kind of authoritative bodies that other religious communities have, they have resorted to recognizing informal boundaries regarding how to approach the Bible and social mores, based on particular conceptions of biblical authority and methods of interpretation that restrict the conclusions that can be drawn from the text. In attempting to reinterpret passages traditionally considered to restrict women, evangelical feminists have used modern hermeneutical methods based on a modified definition of inerrancy. Both their social agenda and their methods put them in the vanguard of young evangelicals who helped make acceptable a more culturally relevant, less fundamentalist, style of evangelicalism.[1] Theologically, evangelical feminists helped shift the boundary of evangelicalism away from a strict definition of inerrancy toward the infallibility of scripture and hermeneutics. Socially, evangelical boundaries remain focused on gender roles, but biblical feminists have questioned the traditional definition of family by challenging hierarchialist interpretations that subordinate women to men in the home and church.

The account of evangelical feminism, however, also speaks to larger issues beyond their immediate community, related to the development of two distinct theologies and their concomitant social agendas. These two theologies, one progressive and one traditionalist, are based on competing conceptions of biblical authority. Initially, primarily one organization, the Evangelical Women's Caucus, represented those in the biblical feminist movement. However, as the issue of lesbianism arose in the group, the contested nature of biblical authority became evident and led to the creation of a second organization, the Christians for Biblical Equality. As its name change indicates, the Evangelical and Ecumenical Women's Caucus developed a more inclusive view of biblical authority that rejected the social, hermeneutical, and textual constraints of the evangelical community. In this it reveals the impact of modern ideals such as pluralism, consumerism, and individualism on American religion and in society more broadly. Specifically, as a variety of religious perspectives come in contact with one another in a context in which the authority of the individual has superseded revealed authority, faith no longer makes an exclusive claim on the life of a believer. Faith has become personal, individualistic, and pluralistic. Instead of directing the actions and beliefs of its adherents, traditional religion becomes just one more alternative to serve the needs of the individual, and moral agency is determined by individual preference rather than by a transcendent point of reference.

Furthermore, progressive evangelical feminists illustrate that the nature of religious pluralism in America is changing. Several historians and sociologists of religion have argued that America has long been pluralist, meaning that a diversity of religious views has been tolerated.[2] Although Protestant Christianity may have had a numerical advantage, there always have been alternative religions in America. Quakers, Puritans, Deists, Catholics, Anglicans, Baptists, Jews, and other religious traditions have existed, though not always amicably, alongside one another since the first days of American settlement. Some scholars contend, however, that historians have focused on Protestantism to the exclusion of these other faiths so that America has appeared more uniform than it has been in reality.

Surely, though, there is this truth in the consensus histories: In America's past, although other faiths existed alongside evangelicalism, it is the latter that wielded the dominant influence on American society, and pluralism was defined as the toleration of a wide diversity of religious faiths. Since America's earliest days, religion—particularly that historical strain called evangelicalism, which can be traced from the Puritans through revivalism to modern evangelicalism—has played an influential role in the expression and shaping of American cultural values. Mark Noll has argued that from the very beginning of the American republic, public thought and religious life have influenced each other and moved in tandem, particularly in their stress on individual freedom, confidence in the capacity of human reason, and attentiveness to market realities. Other historians also have documented a similar symbiosis during specific historical periods. Puritan historians detailed the power of religious images to motivate the early colonists to create a "city on a hill," which would have a sacred mission to enlighten other nations with biblical values.[3] Those values included a sense of destiny, "chosenness," the operation of a "higher law," and the opportunity for the free play of the individual. Historian Nathan Hatch pointed out that during the early days of the American republic, the inclusion of the ideal of liberty in religion led to a fundamental reordering of the principles that governed American civil order.[4] William McLoughlin contended that religious awakenings in America from the early eighteenth to the nineteenth century were the shaping power of American culture, acting as the means by which American values could be transferred from one period in American history to another.[5] Because its influence was so pervasive, historian Sydney Ahlstrom described revivalism and evangelicalism as the established religion of America until the contemporary era.[6]

In these earlier periods of American history until today, pluralism was defined as religious people identifying with a particular faith tradition to which they were bound. Thus, in the past, Americans could choose among religions. In contemporary America, however, people no longer choose from a variety of faith alternatives such as between Catholicism and Protestantism, evangelicalism and mainline Protestantism, or Judaism and Christianity. Instead, Americans choose among religious alternatives and come up with their own spirituality. Even those who identify with a particular faith tradition no longer feel bound to its strictures, instead forming their own opinions on social and theological issues. This "pluralization" is substantively different from that in earlier periods in American history.[7]

Traditionalist evangelical feminists have not been left unaffected by modern culture, although less so than their progressive counterparts have. The traditionalist biblical feminists continue to be exclusive in their faith beliefs and the authority of scripture. Accordingly, they remain inside the boundaries of the larger evangelical movement and continue to reach its members with their message of biblical egalitarianism. The exclusivity of traditionalist evangelical feminism also enables it to offer a more robust alternative to secular feminism. For just as the exclusivity of evangelicalism sets it apart from secular American culture, the exclusive nature of traditionalist evangelical feminism sets it apart from a secular feminism that drifts without a foundation outside women's experience on which to ground it. Still, the impact of a consumerist, therapeutic culture can be seen in the way that traditionalist evangelical feminism focuses on using the Bible to meet the perceived needs of the individual and in its reliance on individual reason to judge the truth of scripture, without the assistance of an institutional and historical church. This trend, which emphasizes individual preference and rationality, indicates that even in evangelicalism, religious authority has been minimized. The irony, of course, is that American evangelicals base their identity on the concept of transcendent authority and have fought against American individualism and pluralism.[8]

The history of evangelical feminism reveals that although American evangelicalism will undoubtedly continue to survive and grow in its modern, even postmodern, environment expressly because it has kept its symbolic theological and social boundaries largely intact and remained exclusive in its faith claims, it is nonetheless eroding. The trends among evangelical feminists that emphasize individual preference and rationalism indicate that modern ideals of pluralism and individualism have made a greater impact on American religion than previously acknowledged, thereby reducing the scope and force of religious authority in American society.

What is more, the story of evangelical feminism suggests that evangelicalism may have inadvertently contributed to the loss of its own dominance in contemporary American society, by not challenging its culture when it was the dominant religious perspective, but by fitting into it so well. Owing to its voluntary nature, democratic tendencies, anti-institutionalism, and dominance of the American scene, evangelicalism is quite compatible with an increasingly individualized, commodified culture. For this reason, evangelicalism has helped shape a new pluralization in which individual choice and preference are fundamental and individuals choose among a variety of faith perspectives. It is pluralization, not evangelicalism, that is now the dominant fact of American religion. Religion and faith are not at risk of being destroyed by modernism in American society; however, the binding nature of those faiths are at risk, and evangelicalism, despite its own apparent health, has participated in the destruction of the acceptance of faith (of all kinds) as binding.

This conclusion gives reason for both hope and caution in regard to American religion and society: historically, the Christian faith, if not its institutions, has often thrived when it has been persecuted or been in the minority. The weakening of traditional, institutional faith portends, however, a weakening of community ties and moral commitments based on more than personal preference, which bodes ill for the practice of civil life in America today. Future studies would do well to consider in greater depth how forces of modernity, such as scientific rationalism, technology, and advanced capitalism, have unintentionally affected American religion and society.[9]

Notes

NOTES TO CHAPTER 1

1. Anne Eggebroten reported this incident in the third person in *Green Leaf* 6 (winter 1982/83): 11. Some details about Eggebroten come from a later testimonial, "Metamorphosis," *Update* 9 (winter 1985/86): 6–7.

2. In the beginning of this book, I use the terms *biblical feminism* and *evangelical feminism* interchangeably, for both stylistic reasons and because the women who made up this movement also use these terms interchangeably.

3. Revivalism, fundamentalism, and evangelicalism have long been plagued by accusations of anti-intellectualism. For an early argument of this kind, see, for example, Sidney Mead's *The Lively Experiment: The Shaping of Christianity in America* (New York: Harper & Row, 1963). More recent historians largely have discredited this thesis, but not in regard to women in American evangelicalism, who have been depicted as the bulwark of the church because of their activism and piety not because of their intellectual contributions. For an exception to this kind of depiction of American women, see Catherine A. Brekus, *Strangers and Pilgrims: Female Preaching in America, 1740–1845* (Chapel Hill: University of North Carolina Press, 1998).

4. See Wade Clark Roof, *Spiritual Marketplace: Baby Boomers and the Remaking of American Religion* (Princeton, N.J.: Princeton University Press, 1999); and Robert Wuthnow, *After Heaven: Spirituality in American since the 1950s* (Berkeley: University of California Press, 1998).

5. See Jon Butler, *Awash in a Sea of Faith: Christianizing the American People* (Cambridge, Mass.: Harvard University Press, 1990), for an account of the diversity of religious expression in colonial America to the time of the Civil War.

6. Sandeen, *The Roots of Fundamentalism*; Marsden, *Fundamentalism and American Culture and Reforming Fundamentalism*; Brereton, *Training God's Army*; Carpenter, *Revive Us Again*.

7. For a history of American evangelicalism and how it has been shaped by, and helped shape, American culture and systems of individualism, democracy, and capitalism, see Mark A. Noll, *America's God: From Jonathan Edwards to Abraham Lincoln* (New York: Oxford University Press, 2002).

8. George Marsden suggested a similar definition: evangelicals are those who come from the same historical pattern. See Marsden's "Introduction: The Evangelical Denomination," in *Evangelicalism and Modern America*, edited by George Marsden (Grand Rapids, Mich.: Eerdmans, 1984), vii–xix. Historians have disagreed, however, over which traditions to include, in particular the Holiness Churches. Such a historical definition, while imprecise, is nonetheless necessary, particularly because it gives a sense of the similarity of characteristics—not just beliefs—over time between current and earlier faith adherents.

9. My first "historical" definition of evangelicalism combines two definitions (historical pattern and beliefs), which George Marsden identified separately. I do not think that these two definitions can be disconnected, however, since the common beliefs were a primary link between these denominations and movements in every historical period.

10. My second definition is similar to Marsden's third definition, which includes all people who are consciously evangelical. By his definition, evangelicalism is a community or coalition rooted in its commitment to a transdenominational infrastructure of institutions, including radio programs, Bible schools, Christian colleges, parachurch organizations, and publishing houses.

11. Christian Smith, *American Evangelicalism: Embattled and Thriving* (Chicago: University of Chicago Press, 1998).

12. R. Marie Griffith, *God's Daughters: Evangelical Women and the Power of Submission* (Berkeley: University of California Press, 1997). This difference may be in part due to methodological as well as denominational issues. By nature, ethnographic studies reveal more of the emotions of day-to-day life, whereas intellectual history uncovers thought processes rather than emotions.

13. Jon R. Stone, *On the Boundaries of American Evangelicalism: The Postwar Evangelical Coalition* (New York: St. Martin's Press, 1997).

14. For the early history of fundamentalism as it separated from or, as he suggests, "reformed" fundamentalism, see George Marsden, *Reforming Fundamentalism: Fuller Seminary and the New Evangelicalism* (Grand Rapids, Mich.: Eerdmans, 1987).

15. Virginia R. Mollenkott, "Evangelicalism: A Feminist Perspective," *Union Seminary Quarterly* 32 (1977): 97.

16. Richard Quebedeaux, "We're on Our Way, Lord!: The Rise of 'Evangelical Feminism' in Modern American Christianity," in *Women in the World's Religions, Past and Present*, edited by Ursala King (New York: Paragon House, 1987), 141.

17. Evangelical Women's Caucus changed its name to the Evangelical and Ecumenical Women's Caucus in 1990. I refer to the organization as the Evangelical Women's Caucus in most of the book and begin referring to it as the Evangelical and Ecumenical Women's Caucus in chapter 6.

NOTES TO CHAPTER 2

1. Letha Scanzoni, preface to *All We're Meant to Be*, by Letha Scanzoni and Nancy Hardesty, 1st ed. (Waco, Tex.: Word Books, 1974), 8.

2. Nancy Hardesty, preface to *All We're Meant to Be*, by Letha Scanzoni and Nancy Hardesty, 1st ed. (Waco, Tex.: Word Books, 1974), 9.

3. Some of these were John Alexander (editor of the journal *The Other Side*), Myron Augsburger (president of Eastern Mennonite College), Rufus Jones (general director of the Conservative Baptist Home Mission Society), William Pannell (the first African American to be elected a trustee of Fuller Seminary, in 1970, and the soon-to-be first African American member of the regular faculty, 1974), and Lewis Smedes (professor of theology and ethics at Fuller).

4. Nancy Hardesty to Ronald Sider, August 29, 1973, Evangelicals for Social Action Papers, box 1, folder 11.

5. Ibid.

6. According to *Christian Century*, it was Hardesty's tenaciousness that resulted in this challenge to biblical scholars. See *Christian Century*, December 19, 1973, 1245.

7. Ronald Sider, ed., *The Chicago Declaration* (Carol Stream, Ill.: Creation House, 1974), 2.

8. According to Hardesty, she volunteered to send out the invitations in order to invite more women. See Karen Kidd, "Nancy A. Hardesty and the Evangelical Women's Caucus: An Oral History." Oral History, Claremont Graduate University, Claremont, Calif., 1988. As a member of the editorial staff at *Christianity Today*, Forbes also had contacts with several Christian women who had written for that periodical, including Patricia Ward, Virginia R. Mollenkott, and Ruth Schmidt.

9. Ronald Sider to Evangelicals for Social Action conference invitees, June 18, 1973, Evangelicals for Social Action Papers, box 1, folder 11.

10. Just what was included in "the fundamentals" varied, but a basic list would include the inerrancy of scripture, the virgin birth, Jesus's substitutionary atonement, his bodily resurrection, his second coming, and a belief in miracles.

11. Martin E. Marty first made this observation in the 1970s in the midst of the inerrancy debates; see Marty, "Tensions within Contemporary Evangelicalism," in *The Evangelicals: What They Believe, Who They Are, Where They Are Changing*, edited by David F. Wells and John D. Woodbridge (Nashville, Tenn.: Abingdon Press, 1975), 170–88.

12. Marty, "Tensions," 182.

13. See the introduction for a brief explanation of the difference among evangelicalism, fundamentalism, and neo- (or new) evangelicalism. I use the term *evangelical* primarily to refer to contemporary American evangelicalism. But

when discussing events between the mid-1950s and 1970s, I also use *neo-evangelical* or *new evangelical* to highlight the distinction between fundamentalists and evangelicals. Finally, when discussing the internecine struggles over definitions of inerrancy within neo-evangelicalism, I refer to those with a less stringent view of inerrancy as *progressive evangelicals.*

14. Since the fundamentalist-modernist debates, fundamentalists had retreated into their own degree-granting institutions, such as Westminster Theological, founded by Greshem Machen, and Dallas Theological Seminary, the leading dispensationalist seminary.

15. A letter from Fuller's mother reveals both the conservative evangelical hesitancy and logic for attending what was now a suspect institution:

We are praying so earnestly for you that God will give you a crystal clear vision to detect the error and also to see and cling to the truth. . . . Do you feel that you should leave Princeton? Do you feel by being there that you are endorsing the college for other young men? Dad has felt that if you could come through Princeton, which is good in many ways, a strong conservative like [Harold J.] Ockenga and [Robert Boyd] Munger and many, many others, it would widen your field of influence and open many doors to you. . . . It may be God's plan to have this large group of ultra conservative students there to raise their voices and "fight like cats" if necessary for the truth and it may check Princeton and open [President John] McKay's [Mackay's] eyes and act as a purge.

Grace Payton Fuller to Daniel Fuller, September 17, 1946, quoted in George Marsden, *Reforming Fundamentalism: Fuller Seminary and the New Evangelicalism* (Grand Rapids, Mich.: Eerdmans, 1987), 23.

16. Ann Moor, "Is Evangelical Theology Changing?" *Christian Life*, March 1956, 16–19.

17. Bernard Ramm, *The Christian View of Science and Scripture* (Grand Rapids, Mich.: Eerdmans, 1954). A "high" view of scripture is one that takes seriously the authority of the Bible and its accuracy.

18. Edward J. Carnell, *The Case for Orthodox Theology*, vol. 3 (Philadelphia: Westminster Press, 1959). Dispensational theology holds that God deals with humanity differently in each of approximately six different epochs, or dispensations. Most American dispensationalists are also "premillennial." This means they believe that Christians will be removed from the earth before a time of persecution prior to the ushering in of God's thousand-year reign on earth. Thus many dispensationalists focus on the spiritual urgency of converting people rather than on social problems.

19. Letter from Daniel Fuller to Charles and Grace Fuller, February 25, 1960, quoted in Marsden, *Reforming Fundamentalism*, 201.

20. Marsden, *Reforming Fundamentalism*, 113.

21. See Marsden, *Reforming Fundamentalism*, for a complete history of the inerrancy struggle at Fuller.

22. Letha Scanzoni, "Woman's Place: Silence or Service," *Eternity* 17, no. 2 (1966): 14–16. In a later address at the first EWC meeting, Scanzoni stated that *Eternity*'s editors had deleted portions of her article addressing interpretations of 1 Timothy in which she suggested that women were no more prone to false doctrine than men were. She pointed out that many cults were led by men and that every seminary that had strayed from orthodoxy was led by a man. See the printed address in Roberta Hestenes and Lois Curley, eds., *Women and the Ministries of Christ* (Pasadena, Calif.: Fuller Theological Seminary, 1979), 126–34.

23. Contemporary feminism in 1973 was still, however, a fairly young movement. After the ratification of the Nineteenth Amendment to the Constitution in 1920, which gave women the right to vote, the concentrated political activity of the early American women's movement diffused into several issues, and the battle for women's rights seemed to die out or go underground before blossoming in the 1960s.

24. These churches recognized abilities based on the gifting of the Holy Spirit rather than on prescribed gender roles (Assemblies of God, Church of the Nazarene, Salvation Army). Some of these churches later reversed their views of women in leadership, perhaps because of the backlash against the contemporary feminist movement in the 1980s.

25. The United Methodist Church began ordaining women in 1924 as local preachers, and in 1956 women were granted membership in the annual conferences, thereby signifying their full ecclesiastical equality with men. In *All We're Meant to Be*, 1st ed., Scanzoni and Hardesty list many of these dates on p. 226, n. 2.

26. Rosemary R. Ruether, *Liberation Theology: Human Hope Confronts Christian History and American Power* (New York: Paulist Press, 1972); Letty M. Russell, *United Presbyterian Women, and the Young Women's Christian Association's U.S. National Board, Women's Liberation in a Biblical Perspective. A Six-Session Study Guide* (Lancaster, Pa.: United Presbyterian Women, 1971); Letty M. Russell, *Human Liberation in a Feminist Perspective—A Theology* (Philadelphia: Westminster Press, 1974); and Mary Daly, *The Church and the Second Sex* (New York: Harper & Row, 1968).

27. Scanzoni, "The Feminists and the Bible," *Christianity Today*, February 1973, 10–15. Scanzoni's earlier article, "Woman's Place: Silence or Service." *Eternity* 17, no. 2 (1966): 14–16, received quite a bit of criticism from readers. Letters to the editor in a later issue (17, no. 4) ran two to one against her argument, and every letter chastising Scanzoni's view referred to 1 Timothy 2 ("let a women keep silent") and implied or stated that her position would lead to a rejection of biblical authority.

28. Most of the quotations from scripture are from the New International Version, Inclusive Language edition, unless otherwise stated. This translation best illustrates the exegesis of evangelical feminists. In this instance, however, it is traditional exegesis with which I am concerned, so I use a more traditional translation. Issues of biblical translation are considered in greater detail in chapter 5.

29. In 1974 and 1975, Donald W. Dayton wrote a series in the *Post-American* on recovering an evangelical social heritage. As part of this series, he often wrote about the early women's movement in America and evangelical feminism. For his argument on the influence of Neoplatonism, see in particular his article "Dialogue on Women, Hierarchy and Equality: An Egalitarian View," *Post-American*, May 1975, 8–15.

30. Scanzoni and Hardesty, *All We're Meant to Be*, 1st ed., 17.

31. Ibid., 156. With such a statement, Hardesty left open the possibility that the biblical text might not condemn those who are homosexual in orientation. Instead it prohibits homosexual acts by heterosexuals.

32. C. E. Cerling, review of *All We're Meant to Be*, by Letha Scanzoni and Nancy Hardesty, *Journal of the Evangelical Theological Society* 18 (fall 1975): 29–95.

33. Gerald T. Sheppard, "Biblical Hermeneutics: The Academic Language of Evangelical Identity," *Union Seminary Quarterly* 32, no. 2 (1977): 91.

34. Marsden, *Reforming Fundamentalism*, 227.

Notes to Chapter 3

1. *Daughters of Sarah* 1, no. 1 (November 1974): 1.

2. *Daughters of Sarah* 4, no. 1 (January/February 1978): 1. The Northpark collective that published *Daughters of Sarah* initially offered a one-year subscription to their newsletter for $1. The group thought that everything they had to share would be exhausted by that time. They were forced to continue, however, when fifty of the two hundred initial respondents sent in payment for a two-year subscription. See *Daughters of Sarah* 6, no. 1 (January/February 1980): 9.

3. *Daughters of Sarah* 2, no. 3 (May 1976): 6–7.

4. An exact comparison cannot be made of the age group between twenty-three and forty-five in the two polls because in 1978 this group consisted of one category, whereas in 1976 there were two categories. See *Daughters of Sarah* 2, no. 3 (May 1976); and *Daughters of Sarah* 4, no. 4 (July/August 1978): 15. A comparison of the two surveys shows that the number of readers aged eighteen to twenty-two fell from 7 to 3 percent and the number aged forty-six to sixty-four rose from 10 to 15 percent. This hints at an aging readership.

5. The 1980 survey results can be found in *Daughters of Sarah* 7, no. 2

(March/April 1981): 20; and the 1984 survey results can be found in *Daughters of Sarah* 11, no. 2 (March/April 1985): 16–19.

6. According to the U.S. Census Bureau, the median household income in 1983 was $32,941.

7. These data fit with the findings of Jason Schnittker, Jeremy Freese, and Brian Powell in "Who Are Feminists and What Do They Believe? The Role of Generations," *American Sociological Review* 68, no. 4 (August 2003): 607–22. Using the 1996 *General Social Survey*, the authors suggested that one explanation for such data is that historical events (the feminist movement of the 1960s and 1970s) shared by cohorts can leave a lifelong influence on beliefs about the world and self. This can help explain why the same age group of women was attracted to the EWC, even though younger women failed to join them.

8. In 1985/86, Hearn was coeditor with Sharon Gallagher.

9. Virginia K. Hearn, *Our Struggle to Serve: The Stories of Fifteen Evangelical Women* (Waco, Tex.: Word Books, 1979).

10. Ann Ramsey Moor, *Green Leaf* 6, nos. 1 & 2 (spring/summer 1982): 8.

11. The accounts of Eggebroten's life are taken from autobiographical accounts in "Metamorphosis," *Update* 9, no. 4 (winter 1985/86): 6–7; *Green Leaf* 8, no. 1 (winter 1984): 4–7; and chapter 9 and appendix 3 of Hearn, *Our Struggle to Serve*, 109–19 and 184–88. Appendix 3 originally was anonymous, but in her *Update* story, Eggebroten acknowledged authorship.

12. Anne Eggebroten, "Choices/Changes," *Green Leaf* 8, no. 1 (winter 1984): 5.

13. The *Ms.* ad alone received seventy-five responses, only one of which was negative. Others replied: "Your presence is a sign of hope to all feminists of faith"; "Congrats on being different"; and "I . . . would like to be part of any movement that would seek to discredit the extreme right." See *Update* 6, no. 1 (January/February 1980): 3.

14. Membership in the EWC was set up on both an individual and a chapter basis. For an annual fee of $10 (or $5 hardship or student), anyone who agreed with the caucus's purpose could become an individual member. Chapters were composed of at least ten individual members and were required to meet at least twice a year. Before the EWC gained nonprofit status, funds were contributed through *The Other Side*, a journal with which many biblical feminists had a close relationship.

15. Karin Granberg Michaelson (on behalf of the Planning Committee) to invitees, 1 September 1975, Evangelicals for Social Action Papers, box 4, folder 14.

16. Ann Moor, editorial, *Update* 4, no. 1 (January/February 1978): 2.

17. For the inside stories of "the sisters of summer," see S. Sue Horner, *Born Again: A History of the Contemporary Evangelical Feminist Movement* (Peabody, Mass.: Hendrickson Publishers, forthcoming).

18. Roberta Hestenes and Lois Curley, eds., *Women and the Ministries of Christ* (Pasadena, Calif.: Fuller Theological Seminary, 1979), 11.

19. Ibid., 12.

20. Ibid., 278. This egalitarian paradigm derived from the same tradition seen in Wesleyan Methodism and the Holiness movement. As far back as the eighteenth-century British revivals, women had been preachers and leaders in these movements. Many considered Phoebe Palmer, a woman, to be the founder of the Holiness movement through the popularization of her modification of John Wesley's doctrine of perfectionism at the Bible studies she led in New York, in her writing and in her preaching.

21. Articles by one or all these authors appeared in the August/September 1974 issue of the *Post-American* dedicated to the modern women's movement, as well as in other publications. See the bibliography for a list of some of these.

22. In *The Grounding of Modern Feminism* (New Haven, Conn.: Yale University Press, 1987), Nancy F. Cott agreed that the Protestant faith was foundational to the establishment of the women's movement but that it was only one of three traditions that nourished its growth. The other two were Enlightenment rationalism and socialist critiques of capitalism.

23. Nancy Hardesty, *Women Called to Witness* (Nashville, Tenn.: Abingdon Press, 1984).

24. Nancy Hardesty, *Your Daughters Shall Prophesy: Revivalism and Feminism in the Age of Finney*, vol. 5 of Chicago Studies in the History of American Religion (Brooklyn, N.Y.: Carlson, 1991).

25. Hestenes and Curley, eds., *Women and the Ministries of Christ*, 9.

26. I use the terms *conservative* and *liberal* in regard to Gundry's and Mollenkott's theologies following the conclusions of Ina Kau, who studied evangelical feminists in her 1977 master's thesis ("Feminists in the American Evangelical Movement") from the Pacific School of Religion. Since I use these terms primarily to indicate distinctions within biblical feminist theology at this time and not to indicate what was generally considered liberal theology at that time, I enclose the terms in quotation marks.

27. Quotation is from Russ Williams, "Truth . . . and Consequences: How Pat Gundry Discovered Biblical Feminism," *The Other Side*, October 1980, 16.

28. Bill Gothard led seminars that taught women to be submissive to men. Marabel Morgan wrote *The Total Woman* (Old Tappan, N.J.: Revell, 1973), a book in which she encouraged Christian women to manipulate their husbands to get their way, but never to directly usurp male authority.

29. Much of this account is taken from Williams, "Truth . . . and Consequences."

30. Williams, "Truth . . . and Consequences," 15.

31. Ibid., 16.

32. Aileen Kraditor, ed., *Up from the Pedestal: Selected Writings in the His-*

tory of American Feminism (New York: Quadrangle / New York Times Book Company, 1968), 50. Quoted in Patricia Gundry, *Woman Be Free!* (New York: Zondervan, 1977), 29.

33. Ann Douglas, *The Feminization of American Culture* (New York: Knopf, 1977).

34. Betty DeBerg, *Ungodly Women: Gender and the First Wave of American Fundamentalism* (Minneapolis: Fortress Press, 1990); and Margaret L. Bendroth, *Fundamentalism and Gender, 1875 to the Present* (New Haven, Conn.: Yale University Press, 1993).

35. Gundry, *Woman Be Free!* 37.

36. Ibid., 38.

37. Ibid., 84.

38. Ibid.

39. Bernard Ramm, *Protestant Biblical Interpretation* (Boston: Wilde, 1956).

40. Richard Clark Kroeger and Catherine Clark Kroeger, "St. Paul's Treatment of Misogyny, Gynephobia, and Sex Segregation in First Corinthians 11:2–6," Society of Biblical Literature, seminar paper no. 17, 1979, 214.

41. Ibid., 216.

42. Hearn, *Our Struggle to Serve*, 154.

43. Ibid., 156.

44. Virginia R. Mollenkott, *Speech, Silence, Action!: The Cycle of Faith, Journeys in Faith* (Nashville, Tenn.: Abingdon Press, 1980), 18.

45. John Alexander, "How to Seek the Truth That Wants to Set You Free: A Conversation with Virginia Mollenkott," *The Other Side*, May/June 1976, 24.

46. Ibid., 28.

47. Virginia R. Mollenkott, "Women and the Bible: A Challenge to Male Interpretation," *Sojourners*, February 1976, 25.

48. Sharon Gallagher, "More on Women and Biblical Authority," *Sojourners*, March 1976, 36–37.

49. Alexander, "How to Seek the Truth," 73.

50. Ibid., 75.

51. Virginia R. Mollenkott, "An Evangelical Feminist Confronts the Goddess," *Christian Century*, October 1982, 1043–46.

52. Reta Halteman Finger, "Men, Women and the Bible: A Review," *Daughters of Sarah*, May 1977, 7.

53. Philip Siddons, "Paul's View of Women." *Christianity Today*, February 1978, 40–42.

54. Virginia R. Mollenkott, *Women, Men, and the Bible* (Nashville, Tenn.: Abingdon Press, 1977), 96.

55. Virginia K. Hearn, "A Liberating Word: Feminist Theology as a Theology of Liberation," in *Liberation Theology: North American Style*, edited by Deane William Ferm (New York: International Religious Foundation, 1987), 191.

56. Quebedeaux based his appraisal of evangelical feminism on the research by Ina Kau in her master's thesis at the Pacific School of Religion. He also made clear that he agreed with Kau's conclusions.

57. Richard Quebedeaux, *The Worldly Evangelicals* (New York: Harper & Row, 1978), 178, n. 4.

58. Ibid., 122.

59. For a few of these, see Stephen B. Clark, *Man and Woman in Christ* (Ann Arbor, Mich.: Servant Books, 1980); Elisabeth Elliot, *Let Me Be a Woman: Notes to My Daughter on the Meaning of Womanhood* (Wheaton, Ill.: Tyndale House, 1976); Susan T. Foh, *Women and the Word of God: A Response to Biblical Feminism* (Grand Rapids, Mich.: Baker Book House, 1979); Thomas Howard, "A Dialogue on Women, Hierarchy and Equality," *Post-American*, May 1975, 10; James B. Hurley, *Man and Woman in Biblical Perspective* (Grand Rapids, Mich.: Zondervan, 1981); and George Knight III, *The New Testament Teaching on the Role Relationship of Men and Women* (Grand Rapids, Mich.: Baker Book House, 1977).

60. Letha Scanzoni, "Marching On!" in Hestenes and Curley, eds., *Women and the Ministries of Christ*, 130.

61. Roberta Hestenes, "Culture, Counterculture and Christian Transformation," in Hestenes and Curley, eds., *Women and the Ministries of Christ*, 278–82.

62. Ibid., 115.

63. The ten essays in *Christianity Today* were published in the same year as a book: see Carl F. H. Henry, *Evangelicals in Search of Identity* (Waco, Tex.: Word Books, 1976), 22.

64. Henry, *Evangelicals*, 54.

65. Harold Lindsell, *The Battle for the Bible* (Grand Rapids, Mich.: Zondervan, 1976), 30–31.

66. Ibid., 24.

67. Jack B. Rogers and Donald K. McKim, *The Authority and Interpretation of the Bible: An Historical Approach* (San Francisco: Harper & Row, 1979).

68. For theological refutations of Lindsell, see Dewey M. Beegle, *Scripture, Tradition, and Infallibility* (Grand Rapids, Mich.: Eerdmans, 1973); and Donald G. Bloesch, *God, Authority, and Salvation*, vol. 1 of The Essentials of Evangelical Theology series (San Francisco: Harper & Row, 1978). In *The Debate about the Bible: Inerrancy versus Infallibility* (Philadelphia: Westminster Press, 1977), Stephen T. Davis makes a philosophical critique of Lindsell's book.

69. In *New Review of Books and Religion*, September 1976, 7.

70. Harold Lindsell, *The Bible in the Balance* (Grand Rapids, Mich.: Zondervan, 1979), 311.

71. Jon R. Stone, *On the Boundaries of American Evangelicalism: The Postwar Evangelical Coalition* (New York: St. Martin's Press, 1997), 171; George

Marsden, *Reforming Fundamentalism: Fuller Seminary and the New Evangelicalism* (Grand Rapids, Mich.: Eerdmans, 1987), 227.

72. Carl F. H. Henry, "Revolt on the Evangelical Frontiers," *Christianity Today*, April 1974, 4–8.

73. Henry, *Evangelicals*, 61.

74. Bylaws of the Evangelical Women's Caucus, International (adopted June 17, 1978), Evangelical and Ecumenical Women's Caucus records.

75. Letha Scanzoni and Nancy Hardesty, *All We're Meant to Be: Biblical Feminism for Today*, 2nd ed. (Nashville, Tenn.: Abingdon Press, 1986), 18. Hardesty was explaining why she chose to call her theology "biblical feminism." Notice, too, the change in subtitles between the first and second editions; the first edition was subtitled "A Biblical Approach to Women's Liberation." It would appear that Scanzoni and Hardesty wanted to use the secular language of the day.

76. June S. Hagen, ed., *Rattling Those Dry Bones: Women Changing the Church* (San Diego: LuraMedia, 1995).

77. Mollenkott, "An Evangelical Feminist," 1045.

78. Ibid.

79. Alvera Mickelsen and Berkeley A. Mickelsen, "Does Male Dominance Tarnish Our Translations?" *Christianity Today*, October 1979, 23–29.

80. Ibid., 24.

81. Alexander, "How to Seek the Truth," 25.

82. For an overview of different types of secular feminism, see Rosemarie Tong, *Feminist Thought: A Comprehensive Introduction* (Boulder, Colo.: Westview Press, 1989).

83. Virginia R. Mollenkott, "The Women's Movement Challenges the Church," *Journal of Psychology and Theology* 2, no. 4 (1974): 298–310.

84. Mollenkott concluded by acknowledging the pressing problem of racism but stated that racism was a symptom of the "deeper problem" of sexism; hence sexism must be solved before racism could be ("The Women's Movement," 308). This was in direct contrast to the opinion of Delores Williams, author and professor, who later complained that white feminists were exclusive and imperialistic for giving visibility solely to white, middle-class feminist women. See Delores Williams, "The Color of Feminism," *Christianity and Crisis*, April 29, 1985, 164–65.

85. Nonwhite, less privileged feminists also complained that white women assumed that all women were the same, that the priority of all women was for upwardly mobile, equal-opportunity legislation, like equal pay for equal work. Yet women in the lower classes and non-Caucasian women often needed more basic needs addressed. For example, whereas liberal and radical feminists sought the right to control their reproductive lives through access to birth control and abortion on demand, women in poverty wanted access to basic medical services. See

Jennifer Nelson, *Women of Color and the Reproductive Rights Movement* (New York: New York University Press, 2003).

86. Letha Scanzoni and Virginia R. Mollenkott, *Is the Homosexual My Neighbor?* 1st ed. (San Francisco: Harper & Row, 1978).

NOTES TO CHAPTER 4

1. Letha Scanzoni and Virginia R. Mollenkott, *Is the Homosexual My Neighbor?* 1st ed. (San Francisco: Harper & Row, 1978), ix.

2. 1978 Conference files, Evangelical and Ecumenical Women's Caucus records. See also Karen Kidd, "Nancy A. Hardesty and the Evangelical Women's Caucus: An Oral History," oral history, Claremont Graduate University, 1988, 35–36.

3. Don Williams, "Shall We Revise the Homosexual Ethic?" *Eternity*, May 1978, 46–48.

4. Scanzoni and Mollenkott, *Is the Homosexual My Neighbor?* 1st ed., 55.

5. Derrick S. Bailey, *Homosexuality and the Western Christian Tradition* (London: Longman, Green, 1955).

6. Letha Scanzoni and Virginia R. Mollenkott, *Is the Homosexual My Neighbor?* 2nd ed. (San Francisco: HarperSanFrancisco, 1994), 57 and 206, n. 1.

7. Scanzoni and Mollenkott, *Is the Homosexual My Neighbor?* 1st ed., 59–60.

8. See Williams, "Shall We Revise the Homosexual Ethic?" 47.

9. John Boswell, *Christianity, Social Tolerance, and Homosexuality* (Chicago: University of Chicago Press, 1980), 99.

10. Scanzoni and Mollenkott, *Is the Homosexual My Neighbor?* 2nd ed., 63 and 207, n. 16.

11. Evangelicals who disagreed with Scanzoni and Mollenkott on this point include Tim Stafford, Don Williams, John Stott, and Richard B. Hays. Both Stafford, writing in *Christianity Today*, "Issue of the Year," May 1978, 36–40, and Williams suggested that prohibitions on homosexuality were based on the order of creation.

12. George R. Edwards, *Gay/Lesbian Liberation: A Biblical Perspective* (New York: Pilgrim Press, 1984).

13. Theologians have struggled for a long time to interpret Paul on this issue. For example, in his commentary on Romans, Karl Barth assumed that Paul indeed was condemning homosexuality. His interpretation of Romans 1: 24–28 was that the sins Paul outlined show the end result of those who abandon God and are, therefore, abandoned by God. Immorality "follow[s] automatically." Eugene Rogers, though, argued that Barth changed his mind about this interpretation. Instead of identifying the idolatry of Romans 1 with homosexuality,

Barth would have associated it with an excessive concern for procreation and family. See Eugene F. Rogers Jr., ed., *Theology and Sexuality: Classic and Contemporary Readings* (Malden, Mass.: Blackwell, 2002), 114–21.

14. Richard B. Hays, "Relations Natural and Unnatural: A Response to John Boswell's Exegesis of Romans 1," *Journal of Religious Ethics* 14, no. 1 (1986): 211, n. 3. Hays wrote: "Boswell's influence was particularly important in shaping the discussion of biblical texts in John J. McNeill, S.J. (1976). Though his book appeared in print four years earlier than *Christianity, Tolerance, and Homosexuality*, McNeill explicitly acknowledged his dependence on Boswell's then unpublished research, describing it as one of his 'principal sources'" (200, n. 39). McNeill in turn received a great deal of attention in the theological community and influenced the exegetical work of other writers such as James B. Nelson (1978) and Letha Scanzoni and Virginia Ramey Mollenkott (1978).

15. Bailey, in *Homosexuality and Western Christian Tradition*, as quoted in Hays, "Relations Natural and Unnatural," 201.

16. Robin Scroggs, *The New Testament and Homosexuality* (Philadelphia: Fortress Press, 1983), 130.

17. Scanzoni and Mollenkott, *Is the Homosexual My Neighbor?* 1st ed., 71.

18. Mary S. van Leeuwen, ed., *Gender and Grace* (Downers Grove, Ill.: InterVarsity Press, 1990), 213.

19. Ibid., 224.

20. Ibid., 225.

21. Kay Lindskoog, review of *Is the Homosexual My Neighbor?* by Letha Scanzoni and Virginia R. Mollenkott, *Wittenburg Door*, October/November 1977, 35–36.

22. Don Williams, *The Bond That Breaks: Will Homosexuality Split the Church?* (Los Angeles: BIM Publishing, 1978), 110.

23. Helmut Thielicke, *The Ethics of Sex*, translated by John Doberstein (New York: Harper & Row, 1964).

24. Ibid., 285.

25. Lewis Smedes, "Homosexuality: Sorting out the Issues." *Reformed Journal*, January 1978, 9–12.

26. Lewis Smedes, *Sex for Christians* (Grand Rapids, Mich.: Eerdmans, 1976), 73.

27. Lewis Smedes, "Shall We Revise the Homosexual Ethic?" *Eternity*, May 1978, 47.

28. For a full description of his typology, see Robert K. Johnston, *Evangelicals at an Impasse: Biblical Authority in Practice* (Atlanta: John Knox Press, 1979), chap. 5.

29. Nancy Hardesty, e-mail, March 15, 2000.

30. Reta Halteman Finger, "Loving Women, Loving Men," *Daughters of Sarah*, September/October 1982, 9.

31. Sharon Gallagher, e-mail, October 5 and 7, 1999. Letha Scanzoni did not recall any disagreements over biblical authority but did recall that Mollenkott's opening address, in which she denounced the misuse of the Bible by Total Woman and other groups that attempted to justify women's submission through scripture taken out of context, may have caused a stir. Letha Scanzoni, e-mail, July 2, 2003.

32. Kidd, "Nancy A. Hardesty and the Evangelical Women's Caucus," 34.

33. Nancy Hardesty to Evangelical Women's Caucus "sisters," April 8, 1976, Evangelical and Ecumenical Women's Caucus records.

34. Kidd, "Nancy A. Hardesty and the Evangelical Women's Caucus," 35–36.

35. Ibid., 37.

36. *Update*, September 1984 / February 1985, 14.

37. Dorothy V. Meyer, "At Wellesley, We Were 'Free Indeed': Reliving Our Sixth Plenary Conference," *Update*, September 1984 / February 1985, 10–11.

38. Kaye Cook (on behalf of the National Council) to Workshop Leaders, December 1, 1983, Evangelical and Ecumenical Women's Caucus records.

39. Sharon Gallagher, "What Does Our Diversity Mean?" *Update* 9 (summer 1985): 2.

40. "Results of the EWCI Membership Poll (1984)," Evangelical and Ecumenical Women's Caucus records.

41. Virginia K. Hearn to "Council Sisters," August 7, 1986, Evangelical and Ecumenical Women's Caucus records.

42. Ballot from Gretchen Gabelein Hull to EWCI executive council, n.d., Evangelical and Ecumenical Women's Caucus records.

43. Gallagher, "What Does Our Diversity Mean?" 3.

44. Council Minutes, Bass Lake, Calif., June 28–30, 1985, Evangelical and Ecumenical Women's Caucus records.

45. Nancy Hardesty, "More on the Resolutions Debate," *Update* 9, no. 3 (fall 1985): 7.

46. The following accounts are taken from a talk by Karen Berns at EWCI's 1992 conference, personal interviews, letters in the Evangelical and Ecumenical Women's Caucus archives, Evangelical Women's Caucus's newsletter *Update*, and articles in the Christian press.

47. Accounts of the lesbians and friends gathering come from Anne Eggebroten, "Handling Power," *The Other Side* (December 1986): 20–25. Details of the business meeting and its aftermath come from personal interviews with several of the participants as well as articles in *Update*, *Green Leaf*, *Christianity Today*, and *The Other Side*.

48. As co-coordinators of the EWC, Britt Vanden Eykel and Barbara Gifford chaired the bulk of the business meeting, but Hardesty led the new business portion. According to Hardesty, this was because no one else was brave enough, for

fear that a resolution on lesbianism would be raised. Kidd, "Nancy A. Hardesty and the Evangelical Women's Caucus," 38–39.

49. Eggebroten, "Handling Power," 22.

50. Beth Spring, "Gay Rights Resolution Divides Membership of Evangelical Women's Caucus," *Christianity Today*, October 1986, 41.

51. Ibid., 43.

52. Nancy Hardesty, e-mail to me, July 7, 2000. Hardesty indicated that the EWC had continued to pass resolutions at several subsequent conferences, but the records show otherwise. Certainly, she was correct that the EWC had supported other political causes, such as the ordination of women and better treatment of women in Christian institutions.

53. Virginia Hearn, "Fresno Conference Report," *Green Leaf* 10, no. 3 (fall 1986): 12–13. Mollenkott later wrote to Hearn complaining about the report of her (Mollenkott's) address.

54. Margaret A. Faud, letter to the editor, *Update* 11, no. 1 (spring 1987): 10.

55. Patrick Wall, letter to the editor, *Update* 11, no. 1 (spring 1987): 11.

56. Spring, "Gay Rights Resolution," 43.

57. Hearn now believes that perhaps those more fundamentalist/evangelical churches really are unreachable. Virginia K. Hearn, e-mail, March 4, 2000.

58. Olive R. Anstice, letter to the editor, *Update* 11, no. 1 (spring 1987): 10.

59. Britt Vanden Eykel to Evangelical Women's Caucus sisters, July 23, 1986, Evangelical and Ecumenical Women's Caucus records.

60. Hearn, "Fresno Conference Report," 13.

61. Christiane Carlson-Thies, Letter to the editor, *Green Leaf* 10, no. 4 (winter 1986/87): 10–11.

62. Christiane Carlson-Thies wrote in her letter to the editor of *Green Leaf*: "I found Nancy Hardesty's leadership during that portion of the meeting to be simply unacceptable."

63. *Update* correspondence, October 1986, Evangelical and Ecumenical Women's Caucus records.

64. Kidd, "Nancy A. Hardesty and the Evangelical Women's Caucus," 38–39.

65. Patricia Ward, telephone interview, August 5, 1999.

66. Both Eggebroten and Mollenkott wrote about their roles in the conflict, and Hardesty talked about her role to an interviewer from the Claremont Graduate University. Hannay, Ward, and others have denied any clandestine meetings at Wellesley, and I could find no evidence of such an event taking place.

67. Margaret Hannay to Evangelical Women's Caucus, n.d., Evangelical and Ecumenical Women's Caucus records.

68. Ina Kau, "Feminists in the American Evangelical Movement," master's thesis, Pacific School of Religion, 1977.

69. Alice Echols, *Daring to Be Bad: Radical Feminism in America, 1967–75*

(Minneapolis: University of Minnesota Press, 1989), 215. See her book for an extensive history of the radical feminist movement. For a history of the larger feminist movement, see also Ginette Castro, *American Feminism: A Contemporary History*, translated by Elizabeth Loverde-Bagwell (New York: New York University Press, 1990).

70. Virginia R. Mollenkott, "Becoming Sin for Others," *Daughters of Sarah*, May/June 1987, 25.

71. Virginia R. Mollenkott, *Sensuous Spirituality: Out from Fundamentalism* (New York: Crossroad, 1992), 11–12.

72. Kidd, "Nancy A. Hardesty and the Evangelical Women's Caucus," 33.

73. Nancy Hardesty, "The Communion of Saints and Sinners," in *Rattling Those Dry Bones: Women Changing the Church*, edited by June S. Hagen (San Diego: LuraMedia, 1995), 34–42. Mollenkott wrote of her experience as a lesbian Christian in "The Closet and the Classroom" and "Surviving the Second Great Reformation," in Hagen, ed., *Rattling Those Dry Bones*, 183–92.

74. Letha Scanzoni, *Sex Is a Parent Affair* (Glendale, Calif.: G/L Regal Books, 1973).

75. Letha Scanzoni and Nancy Hardesty, *All We're Meant to Be: A Biblical Approach to Women's Liberation*, 1st ed. (Waco, Tex.: Word Books, 1977), 156.

76. Ibid., 157.

77. Letha Scanzoni and Nancy Hardesty, *All We're Meant to Be: Biblical Feminism for Today*, 2nd ed. (Nashville, Tenn.: Abingdon Press, 1986), 183–84.

78. Letha Scanzoni and Nancy Hardesty, *All We're Meant to Be: Biblical Feminism for Today*, 3rd ed. (Grand Rapids, Mich.: Eerdmans, 1992), 230–34.

79. Echols, *Daring to Be Bad*, 18.

80. Ibid., 240.

81. See Suzanne Wemple, *Women in Frankish Society: Marriage and the Cloister, 500–900* (Philadelphia: University of Pennsylvania Press, 1981). Also, Elaine Pagels argued in *Adam, Eve, and the Serpent* (New York: Random House, 1988), that as Christianity shifted from a persecuted sect to a protected religion of the state, the view of sexuality changed from one in which humans were believed to have individual moral freedom by God to one in which human beings needed government to control their baser instincts.

82. For an introduction to issues related to the body and theology from patristic to modern times, particularly as it relates to debates on homosexuality, see Rogers, ed., *Theology and Sexuality*.

83. For a survey of the theological, social, and political ideas of the Protestant Reformation, see Alister E. McGrath, *Reformation Thought* (Cambridge, Mass.: Blackwell, 1988).

84. Two of the most famous examples of this are Luther's *Lesser Catechism* and Calvin's *Institutes*.

85. See Sidney Mead, "Denominationalism: The Shape of Protestantism in America," in *The Lively Experiment: The Shaping of Christianity in America*, edited by Sidney Mead (New York: Harper & Row, 1963): 103–33.

NOTES TO CHAPTER 5

1. From the invocation used before each address, Re-Imagining Conference tapes, Minneapolis, November 4–7, 1993. Words and music for the invocation can also be found on p. 11 of the conference packet.

2. Chung Hyun-Kyung, "Re-Imagining God," plenary address, Re-Imagining Conference, Minneapolis, November 4–7, 1993, tape 2-2, side A.

3. Delores Williams, "Re-Imagining Jesus," question and answer session, Re-Imagining Conference, tape 3-2, side B.

4. Virginia R. Mollenkott, "Re-Imagining Church as Worshipping Community," plenary address, Re-Imagining Conference, tape 11-1, side B.

5. Reta Halteman Finger, "Feminist Reflections on the Trinity," *Update* 12, no. 1 (spring 1988): 3.

6. See chapter 3 for this discussion.

7. Virginia R. Mollenkott, *The Divine Feminine* (New York: Crossroad, 1983), 97.

8. Rebecca Merrill Groothuis, *Good News for Women: A Biblical Picture of Gender Equality* (Grand Rapids, Mich.: Baker Books, 1997), 99.

9. Karen Torjesen and Leif Torjesen, "Inclusive Orthodoxy: Recovering a Suppressed Tradition," *The Other Side*, December 1986, 15–16.

10. Ibid., 16.

11. Groothuis, *Good News*, 115.

12. Ibid., 56, 245, n. 16.

13. Ibid., 58, 246, n. 24. A more recent monograph on this question is Kevin Giles's *The Trinity and Subordinationism: The Doctrine of God and the Contemporary Gender Debate* (Downers Grove, Ill.: InterVarsity Press, 2002).

14. Catherine Clark Kroeger, Mary Evans, and Elaine Storkey, eds., *Study Bible for Women: The New Testament* (Grand Rapids, Mich.: Baker Books, 1995), 570–76.

15. Torjesen and Torjesen, "Inclusive Orthodoxy," 16.

16. June O'Connor, "Feminism and The Christ," in *Concepts of the Ultimate*, edited by L. Tessier (Basingstoke: Macmillan, 1989), 70.

17. Cornelius Plantinga Jr., letter to the editor of *Christianity Today*, February 1991, 8.

18. Susan Cady and Hal Taussig, "Jesus and Sophia," *Daughters of Sarah*, November/December 1988, 7–11. Also by Susan Cady and Hal Taussig, with

Marian Ronan, *Sophia: The Future of Feminist Spirituality* (San Francisco: Harper & Row, 1986), and *Wisdom's Feast: Sophia in Study and Celebration* (San Francisco: Harper & Row, 1989).

19. Tina J. Ostrander, "Who Is Sophia?" *Priscilla Papers* 8, no. 2 (spring 1994): 1–3.

20. Reta Halteman Finger, "How Can Jesus Save Women?" *Daughters of Sarah*, November/December 1988, 14–18.

21. Williams, "Re-Imagining Jesus."

22. Finger, "How Can Jesus Save Women?" 16.

23. Ibid., 18.

24. Virginia R. Mollenkott, *Sensuous Spirituality: Out from Fundamentalism* (New York: Crossroad, 1992), 52.

25. Virginia R. Mollenkott, "An Unfinished Symphony of Liberation" (reply to C. Heyward), *Journal of Feminist Studies in Religion* 2, no. 2 (fall 1986): 107–8.

26. Letty M. Russell, *Human Liberation in a Feminist Perspective—A Theology* (Philadelphia: Westminster Press, 1974).

27. Rosemary Radford Ruether, *Sexism and God-Talk: Toward a Feminist Theology* (Boston: Beacon Press, 1983), 54.

28. Elisabeth Schüssler Fiorenza, *Bread Not Stone: The Challenge of Feminist Biblical Interpretation* (Boston: Beacon Press, 1984), 35.

29. Elisabeth Schüssler Fiorenza, *In Memory of Her: A Feminist Theological Reconstruction of Christian Origins* (New York: Crossroad, 1983), 30.

30. For a discussion of Schüssler Fiorenza's hermeneutic principles, see her *Bread Not Stone*, 15–22.

31. Schüssler Fiorenza, *Bread Not Stone*, xiii.

32. Virginia R. Mollenkott, *Godding: Human Responsibility and the Bible* (New York: Crossroad, 1987), 2.

33. In her book *Sensuous Spirituality*, Mollenkott explains that the term *godding* was coined by Carter Heyward. Mollenkott inadvertently borrowed it without attribution in her earlier work because she could not remember where she first heard it.

34. Mollenkott, *Godding*, 80.

35. Ibid., 7.

36. Mary J. Evans, *Woman in the Bible* (Downers Grove, Ill.: InterVarsity Press, 1983), 33.

37. Phyllis Trible, "Depatriarchalizing in Biblical Interpretation." *Journal of the American Academy of Religion*, March 1973, 30.

38. Leonard Swidler, "Jesus Was a Feminist," *Catholic World*, January 1971, 178.

39. Ruether, *Sexism and God-Talk*, 95–98.

40. Mary Hayter, *New Eve in Christ* (Grand Rapids, Mich.: Eerdmans, 1987), 100.

41. Phyllis Trible, *God and the Rhetoric of Sexuality* (Philadelphia: Fortress Press, 1978), quoted in Hayter, *New Eve in Christ*, 100.

42. Hayter, *New Eve in Christ*, 92.

43. Trible, *God and the Rhetoric of Sexuality*, 17.

44. Gilbert Bilezekian, *Beyond Sex Roles* (Grand Rapids, Mich.: Baker Books, 1985).

45. Ibid., 46. This point is important to Bilezekian's later interpretations of the Apostle Paul, because it undercuts the possibility of reading 1 Timothy 2:12–14 to mean that women are by nature more culpable than men. Bilezekian interpreted the reference to Eve's temptation as an indication that women need to be instructed so as not to be vulnerable to false teachings.

46. Mary S. van Leeuwen, "The Christian Mind and the Challenge of Gender Relations." *Reformed Journal*, September 1987, 20.

47. Craig S. Keener, *Paul, Women and Wives: Marriage and Women's Ministry in the Letters of Paul* (Peabody, Mass.: Hendrickson Publishers, 1992), esp. chaps. 4–6.

48. Ibid., 169.

49. Ibid., 170. Keener also addresses Paul's use of "head" to describe the husband's role in the marital relationship. He argues that Paul's usage of "Savior" to define what "head" meant, along with Paul's lengthy exhortation of the husband to love and serve his wife, indicates that "head" certainly did not signify "authority over." See p. 168 for his argument.

50. Reta Halteman Finger, "Knitted Together," *Daughters of Sarah*, March/April 1982, 7–8. See also the September/October 1982 issue, which discusses sex and sexuality.

51. Kaye V. Cook, "CBEers: Who Are We?" *Priscilla Papers*, 10, no. 3 (summer 1996): 6–9.

52. Kaye V. Cook, "Negotiating Faith in Context," unpublished essay, June 8, 2000.

53. Letha Scanzoni and Virginia R. Mollenkott. *Is the Homosexual My Neighbor?* 2nd ed. (San Francisco: HarperSanFrancisco, 1994), preface and chap. 1.

54. Cook, "Negotiating Faith," 13.

55. Reta Halteman Finger, "Choosing Life Is a Mutual Decision," *Daughters of Sarah*, September/October 1985, 6.

56. For the range of biblical feminist views on abortion, see *Daughters of Sarah*, September/October 1985.

57. Mollenkott, *Godding*, 84–85.

58. Mollenkott, *Sensuous Spirituality*, 16.

59. Ibid., 15.

60. Throughout *Godding*, Mollenkott uses various terms to describe God. All these titles are used on p. 80 of her book.

61. Cook, "Negotiating Faith," 13.

62. Most evangelicals accept Paul's authorship of 1 Corinthians, 1 Timothy, and Ephesians, even though not all biblical scholars agree, and each of the authors whose work I consider accept Pauline authorship.

63. According to Cook's survey, the majority of CBE members said they were in "transitional churches." Cook defines these as congregations that verbally accept one set of beliefs about women's roles but act otherwise.

64. David M. Scholer, "1 Timothy 2:9–15 and the Place of Women in the Church's Ministry," in *Women, Authority and the Bible*, edited by Alvera Mickelsen, 193–224 (Downers Grove, Ill.: InterVarsity Press, 1986). For more on the historical background, see Catherine Clark Kroeger's response to Scholer's article, "1 Timothy 2:12—A Classicist's View," in Mickelsen, ed., *Women, Authority and the Bible*, 225–44; Catherine C. Kroeger and Richard C. Kroeger, *I Suffer Not a Woman* (Grand Rapids, Mich.: Baker Book House, 1992); and Keener, *Paul, Women and Wives*.

65. Craig Keener agrees with Scholer's overall handling of the passage. See Keener, *Paul, Women and Wives*, 109.

66. See chapter 3 for the earlier discussion of this text and a quotation of this passage in its entirety.

67. Hayter, *New Eve in Christ*, 88.

68. Schüssler Fiorenza, *In Memory of Her*, 228.

69. Hayter, *New Eve in Christ*, 119–26.

70. Gilbert Bilezekian, "Hierarchicalist and Egalitarian Inculturations," *Journal of the Evangelical Theological Society*, December 1987, 423.

71. Hayter, *New Eve in Christ*, 123.

72. Clifford Geertz, "Religion as a Cultural System," in *The Interpretation of Cultures: Selected Essays*, by and edited by Clifford Geertz (New York: Basic Books, 1973), 87–125.

73. Carol P. Christ, "Why Women Need the Goddess: Phenomenological, Psychological, and Political Reflections," in *Womanspirit Rising: A Feminist Reader on Religion*, edited by Carol P. Christ and Judith Plaskow (San Francisco: Harper & Row, 1979), 273–87.

74. Mary Daly, *Gyn/Ecology: The Metaethics of Radical Feminism* (Boston: Beacon Press, 1978).

75. Virginia R. Mollenkott, "The Bible," *The Other Side*, June 1981, 16.

76. For a discussion of these principles, see Nancy Hardesty, *Inclusive Language in the Church* (Atlanta: John Knox Press, 1987), chaps. 4 and 5.

77. Hardesty, *Inclusive Language*, chap. 3.

78. Leslie R. Keylock, "God Our Father and Mother?" *Christianity Today*, November 1983, 50–51; and "O God Our [Mother and] Father," *Time*, October 24, 1983, 56–57. Letters to the editor appeared in *Time*, November 14, 1983, 6.

79. Nancy Hardesty, "'Whosoever Surely Meaneth Me': Inclusive Language and the Gospel," *Christian Scholar's Review* 17, no. 3 (1988): 231.

80. For a fuller history and explanation of bibles and the use of inclusive language, see D. A. Carson, *The Inclusive Language Debate: A Plea for Realism* (Grand Rapids, Mich.: Zondervan, 1998); and Mark L. Strauss, *Distorting Scripture? The Challenge of Bible Translation and Gender Accuracy* (Downers Grove, Ill.: InterVarsity Press, 1998).

81. Strauss, *Distorting Scripture?* 222, n. 34.

82. Susan Olasky, "The Feminist Seduction of the Evangelical Church," *World*, March 29, 1997, 12–15.

83. Doug Leblanc with Steve Rabey, "Bible Translators Deny Gender Agenda," *Christianity Today*, July 1997, 62–64.

84. Carson, *The Inclusive Language Debate*, 35.

85. Ibid., 37.

86. The NIVI remained unpublished in the United States throughout the 1990s, although it was well known that the CBT continued its work to make the NIV gender accurate. In 2001, Zondervan finally published an inclusive-language New Testament in the United States, entitled Today's New International Version. See *The Holy Bible, Today's New International Version* (Grand Rapids, Mich.: Zondervan, 2001). The title is meant to indicate its lineage from, but discontinuity with, the NIV.

87. Hardesty, "'Whosoever Surely Meaneth Me,'" 231.

88. In her first interview with me, Mollenkott indicated that liberation theology was indeed an important turning point in her theology. This was not the case with Nancy Hardesty, however, who maintains that since the early 1970s her interpretation has been informed by the Methodist quadrilateral. Nonetheless, many evangelicals disagree with Hardesty's emphasis on reason and experience, along with tradition and scripture. They also find fault with her social positions, particularly on homosexuality. Nancy Hardesty, e-mail, August 5, 2003.

89. Not all progressive biblical feminists supported these doctrinal changes. Many were more traditional than Virginia Mollenkott, for example. Still, the views of their leading scholars do indicate the inclusive nature of progressive biblical feminist theology, and in general, the group has tended to move in the direction that Mollenkott has "prophesied," by becoming ever more inclusive and less orthodox.

90. Cook, "Negotiating Faith," 17.

91. Ibid., 15.

92. Ibid., 10.

NOTES TO CHAPTER 6

1. This account is taken primarily from two *Update* articles: Debby Jang, "In the Margins, between the Lines," 18, no. 3 (fall 1994): 9; and "Debby Jang: An *Update* Interview," 19, no. 1 (spring 1995): 5–7.

2. "Debby Jang: An *Update* Interview," 5.

3. Jang, "In the Margins," 9.

4. Interview with Catherine Clark Kroeger, Brewster, Mass., July 24, 1992.

5. Catherine Clark Kroeger, e-mail, July 12 and 14, 2003. It was at the 1984 conference that a resolution on the recognition of lesbianism in the EWC was first introduced and tabled.

6. One such note, for example, concerned Shannon Lucid, who had just been named to staff the MIR space station for the United States.

7. Both the Christians for Biblical Equality and the Evangelical Women's Caucus learned that conferences in the Midwest attracted more attendees because their central location made travel cheaper for more people.

8. The Southern Baptist Conference statement is discussed later in this chapter.

9. The CBE also held a conference, "Women, Abuse, and the Bible," in 1994, but there were no plans at that time to make topical events biennial.

10. The first poll was conducted by C. J. Olson Market Research, Minneapolis, and was based on 1,246 responses. It was published in *Priscilla Papers* 6, no. 4 (fall 1992): 15. The second survey was conducted by Kaye Cook and was based on a much smaller sample (120) of members solicited at the CBE's 1995 conference. See Kaye V. Cook, "CBEers: Who Are We?" *Priscilla Papers*, 10, no. 3 (summer 1996): 6–9. The two polls are difficult to compare. My point, however, is merely to suggest the kinds of women in CBE. Later I use the second survey to compare it with the EWC. These two polls are more easily compared, as Cook conducted both, using the same questions, with a similar number of respondents, and at the organizations' conferences.

11. The figure of 25 percent came from the C. J. Olson poll in 1991. Clearly, CBE has continued to have a significant minority of men active in the movement, as indicated by men's involvement on the board of directors, in local chapters, and in attending and leading seminars.

12. Fifty percent of the respondents to CBE's 1995 questionnaire were between the ages of thirty-one and forty-five (a smaller age range than in CBE's earlier survey); 15 percent were between eighteen and thirty; 20 percent were between forty-six and sixty; and 15 percent were between sixty-one and seventy-five. The figures were not available, but anecdotal evidence from *Update* indicated that by the turn of the millennium, the EWC also had begun to attract a younger generation of biblical feminists.

13. Kaye V. Cook, "Negotiating Faith in Context," unpublished essay, June 8, 2000.

14. Cook, "CBEers," 7. The questions are from James Davison Hunter's *Evangelicalism: The Coming Generation* (Chicago: University of Chicago Press, 1987).

15. Cook, "CBEers," 7.

16. Ibid., 8.

17. Interview with Alvera Mickelsen, San Diego, July 16, 1999.

18. Biblical studies is the branch of theology that focuses on issues of inter-pretation. Wheaton is considered to be the premier evangelical college, so Bilezikian's credentials lent added weight to his support of evangelical feminism and Willow Creek.

19. For a concise history and thorough analysis of the Willow Creek Community Church and its association, see Kimon H. Sargeant, *Seeker Churches: Promoting Traditional Religion in a Nontraditional Way* (New Brunswick, N.J.: Rutgers University Press, 2000).

20. Sargeant, *Seeker Churches*, 26–27. The other largest "denomination" in the association is actually not a denomination at all but the constellation of inde-pendent and nondenominational Bible churches prevalent in American evangeli-calism. Of the Baptist churches, two-thirds are Southern Baptist, and although Sargeant does not distinguish among Presbyterian denominations, it would be safe to assume that a more conservative, outreach-minded denomination like the PCA would more likely be drawn to the alliance than would the PC (USA), be-cause of Willow Creek's emphasis on drawing non-Christian "seekers."

21. Bill Hybels, quoted in Sargeant, *Seeker Churches*, 91.

22. Susan Faludi chronicled this conservative reaction to feminism in her book *Backlash: The Undeclared War against American Women* (New York: An-chor Books/Doubleday, 1991).

23. James Davison Hunter and Helen V. L. Stehlin, "Family: Toward An-drogeny," in Hunter, *Evangelicalism: The Coming Generation*, 76.

24. Ibid., 76–92.

25. Craig S. Keener, *Paul, Women and Wives: Marriage and Women's Min-istry in the Letters of Paul* (Peabody, Mass.: Hendrickson Publishers, 1992), 11–12.

26. Baptist Faith and Message, article 18, "The Family."

27. The PCA church was originally named the National Presbyterian Church, but that changed by its second general assembly in 1974. The quotation is from the *Dictionary of Christianity in America*, "Presbyterian Church in America."

28. Ric Perrin and Jeff Taylor, quoted in "Presbyterian Groups Sever CRC Ties," *Christianity Today*, August 1997, 55.

29. "The Danvers Statement," in *Recovering Biblical Manhood and Woman-hood: A Response to Biblical Feminism*, edited by John Piper and Wayne Gru-dem (Wheaton, Ill.: Crossway, 1991), app. 2, 469.

30. Ibid. This statement is on p. 469 of an almost five-hundred-page book

devoted to teasing out the correct, conservative, "apparently plain meaning" of Bible passages that biblical feminists had distorted. It appears that "apparently plain meanings" were not so apparent or plain after all.

Members of the CBMW's board of reference consisted of, among others, Jerry Falwell, Paige Patterson of the Southern Baptist Convention, and Carl F. H. Henry.

31. Piper and Grudem, eds., *Recovering Biblical Manhood and Womanhood*, xiii. The CBMW came into existence around the same time that the CBE was formed. Thus in 1988 when this statement was made, the CBMW was responding to Scanzoni's, Hardesty's, and Mollenkott's earlier, more traditionally evangelical, writings.

32. In opposition to my argument, Gallagher concluded that the evangelical feminist movement has had very little influence among "rank and file" evangelicals because she found very few self-identified evangelical feminists. I disagree that self-identification as an evangelical feminist is the best criterion to determine influence. Our two studies do agree that gender issues are a significant factor in defining evangelical boundaries. (Gallagher argues specifically that male "headship" is the primary requirement for evangelical identity.) See Sally K. Gallagher, *Evangelical Identity and Gendered Family Life* (New Brunswick, N.J.: Rutgers University Press, 2003).

33. Hunter, *Evangelicalism: The Coming Generation*, 111–13.

34. Ibid., 173–75.

35. James Penning and Corwin Smidt, *Evangelicalism: The Next Generation* (Grand Rapids, Mich.: Baker Books, 2002). They did not find, however, the kind of secularization that Hunter anticipated theologically or behaviorally. This shows that these students were, in every other way, traditionally evangelical—a finding that supports my argument that traditionalist biblical feminists were accepted by the evangelical community.

36. Naomi Schaefer, "Women at Religious Colleges—Subordination or Secularization?" *The Public Interest* 152 (summer 2003): 81–101.

37. Joyce Erickson, e-mail, October 17, 2000.

38. Sargeant, *Seeker Churches*, 26–27.

39. Ibid., 91.

40. D. A. Carson and Carl F. H. Henry, eds., *Evangelical Affirmations* (Grand Rapids, Mich.: Zondervan, 1990), 14.

41. For more on this disagreement, see Jon R. Stone, *On the Boundaries of American Evangelicalism: The Postwar Evangelical Coalition* (New York: St. Martin's Press, 1997), 173–78.

42. Carson and Henry, *Evangelical Affirmations*, 97.

43. Ibid., 33.

44. Ibid., 29.

45. Earl D. Radmacher, Robert D. Preus, and the International Council on

Biblical Inerrancy, *Hermeneutics, Inerrancy, and the Bible: Papers from ICBI Summit II* (Grand Rapids, Mich.: Academie Books, 1984), xi.

46. Ibid., 881–87.

47. J. Robertson McQuilkin, "Problems of Normativeness in Scripture: Cultural versus Permanent," in Radmacher et. al., *Hermeneutics*, 217–41.

48. David M. Scholer, "Unseasonable Thoughts on the State of Biblical Hermeneutics," *American Baptist Quarterly*, June 1983, 134–41.

49. James Davison Hunter and Helen V. L. Stehlin, "Family: Toward Androgeny," in Hunter, *Evangelicalism: The Coming Generation*, 76–115.

50. Ibid., 76–77.

51. It is possible that some attrition was due to the lack of strategic focus in the evangelical feminist organization, which was more politically oriented. Still, the equal rights amendment failed in 1982, and if the main cause of attrition was the loss of a cause to promote, more attrition would have been expected earlier.

52. Britt Vanden Eykel, "NOT a Swan Song," *Update* 12, no. 2 (summer 1988): 8a–8b, 8d.

53. Anne Eggebroten, "EWC: Called to Be," *Update* 13, no. 2 (fall 1989): 3.

54. *Update* long had been a forum for personal news, but the nature of the news was changing, indicating the maturing of its audience. Even Nancy Hardesty commented that a weakness of the organization was the lack of younger women. Nancy Hardesty, e-mail, March 15, 2000. Conferences after 2000 were organized to attract younger members and, to some extent, seemed to do so.

55. Deborah Jang, review of *Discovering the Bible in the Non-Biblical World*, by Kwok Pui-lan, *Update* 19, no. 4 (winter 1995/96): 6–7.

56. Virginia R. Mollenkott, "Buoyancy and Splash," *Update* 20, no. 3 (fall 1996): 1. My point is not that all EWC members agreed with Mollenkott's social and biblical positions on homosexuality. Rather, it is the inclusiveness in the EWC that Mollenkott's theological position on sexuality expresses.

57. This was even though Scholer was a longtime friend of numerous EWC leaders and had even taught some of them, like Reta Halteman Finger, in seminary. The last conference at which Scholer addressed the EWC was in 1990 when he was a respondent to Rosemary Radford Ruether's presentation. Letha Scanzoni reported that he has been invited to present a workshop for the 2004 EWC conference. At press time, he had accepted the invitation.

58. Letha Scanzoni, writing in the Council Memos column, "Are We Evangelical or Ecumenical? EWC in Stage II," *Update* 12, no. 3 (fall 1988): 9.

59. Sue Horner, "Are We Evangelical or Ecumenical?" *Update* 12, no. 3 (fall 1988): 10.

60. It was not long before some members suggested dropping both "E's" in Evangelical and Ecumenical Women's Caucus. They felt that "evangelical" connoted "fundamentalism" and that "ecumenical" still hinted at an overdependence on scripture. At the 1992 business meeting, one member put it this way:

"Evangelical has come to mean a fundamentalist who has graduated from an accredited school, and ecumenical sounds like a support group for textual co-dependents." No change has been made, however.

61. Cook, "Negotiating Faith," 10–11. Another 9 percent of the respondents to Cook's survey did not accept any of the categories listed and instead wrote in their own response. Cook did not include these written comments in her article but describes them as supporting some form of limited inerrancy. Even adding this 9 percent to the 31 percent listed earlier means that only 40 percent of EEWC members, fewer than half as many in the CBE, accepted some form of inerrancy. Twenty-two percent of the respondents are not accounted for at all in Cook's article. It may be that 22 percent failed to answer this question at all or wrote in answers that Cook did not correspond to any of her categories of strict inerrancy, limited inerrancy, or neo-orthodoxy.

62. In this argument, I am applying Paul J. Griffiths's argument concerning religious reading from his book *Religious Reading: The Place of Reading in the Practice of Religion* (New York: Oxford University Press, 1999), 41–47.

63. Griffiths, *Religious Reading*, 63.

64. Ibid., 65.

65. The Episcopal Church approved its first openly gay bishop in August 2003. An analysis of the parallels between what happened in the EWC and the Episcopal Church would be fruitful. Unfortunately, this is not the place to do so.

66. The MCC's stated mission is to "embody and proclaim Christian salvation and liberation, Christian inclusivity and community, and Christian social action and justice. We serve among those seeking and celebrating the integration of their spirituality and sexuality." Information obtained from UFMCC, http://www.ufmcc.com (accessed November 28, 2000).

67. Interview with Virginia R. Mollenkott, September 6, 2000.

68. Virginia R. Mollenkott, *Godding: Human Responsibility and the Bible* (New York: Crossroad, 1987), 97.

69. Interview with Letha Scanzoni, Norfolk, Va., July 19, 2000. Nancy Hardesty admits to having mixed feelings about using the term *evangelical*. Although she stated in 1988 that she stopped calling herself an evangelical, she returned to a church (MCC) that calls itself evangelical and has argued in her New Testament classes at Clemson that she takes the Bible "far more literally" than do others who say they are evangelical. Nancy Hardesty, e-mail, August 4, 2003.

70. Virginia R. Mollenkott, "An Unfinished Symphony of Liberation" (reply to C. Heyward), *Journal of Feminist Studies in Religion* 2, no. 2 (fall 1986): 107. Mollenkott went on to explain that she was not excluding Jews, Muslims, post-Christian, or post-Judaic women by her reliance on traditional Christian language and elaborated her universalist view of Christology discussed in chapter 5.

71. See Virginia R. Mollenkott, *Sensuous Spirituality: Out from Fundamentalism* (New York: Crossroad, 1992), 44–50.

72. Ibid., 48.

73. Interview with Virginia R. Mollenkott, September 6, 2000.

74. "Report: Annual Council Meeting," *Update* 24, no. 2 (summer 2000): 10.

75. June Steffensen Hagen, "EEWC Members Free-Write for Our Future," *Update* 18, no. 3 (fall 1993): 6–7. Note, however, that traditional evangelicals are marginalized in the EEWC. Ex-fundamentalists and Roman Catholics may be welcome, but CBE is disparaged.

76. This statement can be found on the inside back cover of every *Update* issue, beginning in the fall of 1999.

77. *Update* 24, no. 2 (summer 2000): 10.

78. Christian Smith, *American Evangelicalism: Embattled and Thriving* (Chicago: University of Chicago Press, 1998), 89.

79. Ibid., 144. Smith admits that American evangelicals have accommodated in some ways to contemporary culture and have been ineffective in their goal of changing that culture. But he concludes that such "'accommodation' . . . appear[s] no more or less cognitively contaminated or ideologically compromised—judged on their own terms—than they were in previous decades" (144).

80. This is Philip Rieff's argument in *The Triumph of the Therapeutic: Uses of Faith after Freud* (New York: Harper Torchbooks, 1966).

81. Numerous studies have chronicled the rise of individualism in religion. Among them are Wade Clark Roof, *Spiritual Marketplace: Baby Boomers and the Remaking of American Religion* (Princeton, N.J.: Princeton University Press, 1999); and Robert Wuthnow, *After Heaven: Spirituality in America since the 1950s* (Berkeley: University of California Press, 1998).

82. On the resilience of religion in times of change, also see Steve Bruce, *Religion in the Modern World: From Cathedrals to Cults* (Oxford: Oxford University Press, 1996), 96.

83. Eggebroten, "EWC: Called to Be," 3.

84. Anonymous comments reported by Hagen in "EEWC Members," 6.

85. Susan Moller Okin, with respondents, "Is Multiculturalism Bad for Women?" in *Is Multiculturalism Bad for Women?* edited by Joshua Cohen, Matthew Howard, and Martha C. Nussbaum (Princeton, N.J.: Princeton University Press, 1999), 7–24. See also Pamela Cochran, "Women and Moral Diversity," *Hedgehog Review*, 3, no. 1 (spring 2001): 117–24.

86. Alister McGrath, *A Passion for Truth: The Intellectual Coherence of Evangelicalism* (Downers Grove, Ill.: InterVarsity Press, 1996), esp. 10–22.

87. Sargeant, *Seeker Churches*, 177–78.

88. Nathan Hatch, *The Democratization of American Christianity* (New Haven, Conn.: Yale University Press, 1989); Mark A. Noll, *America's God: From Jonathan Edwards to Abraham Lincoln* (New York: Oxford University Press, 2002).

89. On the declining significance of denominations, see Robert Wuthnow, *The Restructuring of American Religion: Society and Faith since World War II* (Princeton, N.J.: Princeton University Press, 1988), chap. 5.

90. Cook, "Negotiating Faith," 15, 18.

NOTES TO CHAPTER 7

1. As we saw earlier, several prominent scholars of evangelicalism, including Gerald T. Sheppard from the Union Theological Seminary in New York, Martin E. Marty from the University of Chicago, and Carl F. H. Henry who, along with Billy Graham, could be considered the patriarchs of neo-evangelicalism, suggested at the height of debates on inerrancy that biblical feminists posed a significant threat to the older hermeneutical language of evangelicalism. Sheppard, in fact, called them "the most significant threat." See Gerald T. Sheppard, "Biblical Hermeneutics: The Academic Language of Evangelical Identity," *Union Seminary Quarterly* 32, no. 2 (1977): 91; Martin E. Marty, "Tensions within Contemporary Evangelicalism," in *The Evangelicals: What They Believe, Who They Are, Where They Are Changing*, edited by David F. Wells and John D. Woodbridge (Nashville, Tenn.: Abingdon Press, 1975), 170-88; and Carl F. H. Henry, "Revolt on the Evangelical Frontiers," *Christianity Today*, April 1974, 4–8.

2. Catherine L. Albanese, *America, Religions, and Religion*, 3rd ed. (Belmont, Calif.: Wadsworth, 1999); Jon Butler, *Awash in a Sea of Faith: Christianizing the American People* (Cambridge, Mass.: Harvard University Press, 1990); William R. Hutchison, *Religious Pluralism in America: The Contentious History of a Founding Ideal* (New Haven, Conn.: Yale University Press, 2003); and R. Laurence Moore, *Religious Outsiders and the Making of Americans* (New York: Oxford University Press, 1986).

3. See, for example, Sacvan Bercovitch, *The American Jeremiad* (Madison: University of Wisconsin Press, 1978); Perry Miller, *Errand into the Wilderness* (Cambridge, Mass.: Belknap Press, 1974); and Harry Stout, *The New England Soul* (New York: Oxford University Press, 1986).

4. Nathan Hatch, *The Sacred Cause of Liberty* (New Haven, Conn.: Yale University Press, 1977).

5. William G. McLoughlin, *Revivals, Awakenings, and Reform: An Essay on Religion and Social Change in America, 1607–1977* (Chicago: University of Chicago Press, 1978).

6. Sydney Ahlstrom, *A Religious History of the American People* (New Haven, Conn.: Yale University Press, 1972).

7. Scholars have variously described this new cultural situation, which progressive evangelical feminists illustrate. Sociologist David Lyon called it the "deregulation of religion" and related it to the "sacralization of the self." See David

Lyon, *Jesus in Disneyland: Religion in Postmodern Times* (Malden, Mass.: Blackwell, 2000), 18–19. Philip Rieff concluded that faith had become a "powerless authority" that wore the face of a therapist with no toleration for revealed, eternal, or commanding truths. See Philip Rieff, *The Triumph of the Therapeutic: Uses of Faith after Freud* (New York: Harper Torchbooks, 1966).

I am making a modified argument about the secularization of religion in America. As initially theorized by Peter Berger, this thesis argues that modernity leads to the inevitable secularization of society. Many scholars, including Berger, have concluded, however, that the evidence goes against this initial formulation. In "Globalization and Religion," *Hedgehog Review* 4, no. 2 (summer 2002): 7–20, Berger argues that as people and ideas move freely across cultural borders, modernity fosters pluralism rather than secularization. According to Berger, the impact of pluralism on religion is that people now choose beliefs instead of inheriting them. I contend that the kind of pluralism we have in contemporary America—where people mix and match elements from various belief systems—does indicate a kind of modified secularization, one in which modernity has reduced the scope and force of religious authority. I use the term *pluralization* to describe this, which is from a talk Berger gave at the University of Virginia in the fall of 2001.

8. For discussions about American evangelicalism's opposition to American pluralism, see Grant Wacker's essay, "Uneasy in Zion: Evangelicals in Postmodern Society," in *Evangelicalism and Modern America,* edited by George Marsden (Grand Rapids, Mich.: Eerdmans, 1984), 17–28; and James D. Hunter, *Culture Wars: The Struggle to Define America* (New York: Basic Books, 1991).

9. For an example of the kind of study to which I refer, see Mark A. Noll, *America's God: From Jonathan Edwards to Abraham Lincoln* (New York: Oxford University Press, 2002). He argues that the national culture of commonsense republicanism that developed out of the interweaving of religious and political thought set the stage for the Civil War by imbuing American theologians and clergy with a deep sense of religious purpose and, therefore, conviction that God was on "their" side, both North and South.

Bibliography

ARCHIVAL MATERIAL

Christians for Biblical Equality, Papers. Christians for Biblical Equality Library and Retreat Center, Brewster, Mass.

Evangelical and Ecumenical Women's Caucus. Records. Archives of Women in Theological Scholarship. Burke Library, Union Theological Seminary, New York, N.Y.

Evangelicals for Social Action. Papers. Manuscript Collection no. 37. Archives of the Billy Graham Center for the Study of Evangelicalism. Wheaton College Library, Wheaton, Ill.

JOURNALS OF EVANGELICAL FEMINISM

There have been four primary journals of evangelical feminism. *Daughters of Sarah* was the first and, at its height, the most polished journal. It was published between November 1974 and winter 1996. It can still be found in a number of university libraries and can easily be obtained through Interlibrary Loan. *Update*, the newsletter of the Evangelical and Ecumenical Women's Caucus, began publication in summer 1977 and was still being published at the time this book went to press. *Green Leaf* is the newsletter of the Bay Area chapter of Evangelical and Ecumenical Women's Caucus. Its first issue was in November 1978, and it has continued to be published occasionally up to the time this book went to press. Consult the Archives of Women in Theological Studies at Union Theological Seminary in New York for archival issues of both *Green Leaf* and *Update*. For current issues, go to the Evangelical and Ecumenical Women's Caucus Web site, www.eewc.com. Both the *Priscilla Papers*, which began publication in 1987, and *Mutuality*, which began in the 1990s, are publications of the CBE and are still being published. Current and back issues for both of these newsletters can be found on the CBE's Web site, cbeinternational.org.

SOURCES

Ahlstrom, Sydney. *A Religious History of the American People*. New Haven, Conn.: Yale University Press, 1972.

———. "The Scottish Philosophy and American Theology." *Church History* 24 (1955): 257–72.

Ammerman, Nancy. *Baptist Battles: Social Change and Religious Conflict in the Southern Baptist Convention*. New Brunswick, N.J.: Rutgers University Press, 1990.

Bailey, Derrick Sherwin. *Homosexuality and the Western Christian Tradition*. London: Longman, Green, 1955.

Bendroth, Margaret Lamberts. "Fundamentalism and Femininity: Points of Encounter between Religious Conservatives and Women, 1919–1935." *Church History*, June 1992, 221–33.

———. *Fundamentalism and Gender, 1875 to the Present*. New Haven, Conn.: Yale University Press, 1993.

Bilezikian, Gilbert. *Beyond Sex Roles*. Grand Rapids, Mich.: Baker Books, 1985.

Boswell, John. *Christianity, Social Tolerance, and Homosexuality*. Chicago: University of Chicago Press, 1980.

Brereton, Virginia L. *Training God's Army: The American Bible School, 1880–1940*. Bloomington: Indiana University Press, 1990.

Carpenter, Joel. *Revive Us Again: The Reawakening of American Fundamentalism*. New York: Oxford University Press, 1997.

Carson, D. A. *The Inclusive Language Debate: A Plea for Realism*. Grand Rapids, Mich.: Zondervan, 1998.

Chaves, Mark. "Secularization as Declining Religious Authority." *Social Forces*, March 1994, 749–74.

Christ, Carol P. "Why Women Need the Goddess: Phenomenological, Psychological and Political Reflections." In *Womanspirit Rising, a Feminist Reader on Religion*, edited by Carol Christ and Judith Plaskow, 273–87. San Francisco: Harper & Row, 1979.

Cole, Stewart G. *The History of Fundamentalism*. New York: Harper & Row, 1931.

Cott, Nancy F. *The Grounding of Modern Feminism*. New Haven, Conn.: Yale University Press, 1987.

Countryman, William L. *Dirt, Greed, and Sex: Sexual Ethics in the New Testament and Their Implications for Today*. Philadelphia: Fortress Press, 1988.

Daly, Mary. *The Church and the Second Sex*. New York: Harper & Row, 1968.

Dayton, Donald W. "Dialogue on Women, Hierarchy and Equality: An Egalitarian View." *Post-American*, May 1975, 8–15.

———. *Discovering an Evangelical Heritage*. New York: Harper & Row, 1976.

Dayton, Donald W., and Lucille Sider Dayton. "The Bible among Evangelicals: Evangelical Feminism: Some Aspects of Its Biblical Interpretation." *Explor* 2 (1976): 17–22.

———. "Evangelical Feminism." *Post-American* 3 (1974): 7–9.

———. "Evangelical Roots of Feminism." *Covenant Quarterly* 34 (1976): 41–56.

Dayton, Donald W., Lucille Sider Dayton, and Nancy Hardesty. "Women in the Holiness Movement: Feminism in the Evangelical Tradition." In *Women of Spirit: Female Leadership in the Jewish and Christian Traditions*, edited by Rosemary Ruether and Eleanor McLaughlin, 225–54. New York: Simon & Schuster, 1979.

DeBerg, Betty. *Ungodly Women: Gender and the First Wave of American Fundamentalism*. Minneapolis: Fortress Press, 1990.

Echols, Alice. *Daring to Be Bad: Radical Feminism in America, 1967–75*. Minneapolis: University of Minnesota Press, 1989.

Evans, Mary J. *Woman in the Bible*. Downers Grove, Ill.: InterVarsity Press, 1983.

Furniss, Norman F. *The Fundamentalist Controversy, 1918–1931*. New Haven, Conn.: Yale University Press, 1954.

Gallagher, Sally K. *Evangelical Identity and Gendered Family Life*. New Brunswick, N.J.: Rutgers University Press, 2003.

Groothuis, Rebecca Merrill. *Good News for Women: A Biblical Picture of Gender Equality*. Grand Rapids, Mich.: Baker Books, 1997.

———. *Women Caught in the Conflict: The Culture War between Traditionalism and Feminism*. Grand Rapids, Mich.: Baker Books, 1994.

Gundry, Patricia. *The Complete Woman*. New York: Zondervan, 1981.

———. *Heirs Together*. New York: Zondervan, 1980.

———. *Neither Slave nor Free*. San Francisco: Harper & Row, 1987.

———. *Woman Be Free!* New York: Zondervan, 1977.

Hagen, June Steffensen, ed. *Rattling Those Dry Bones: Women Changing the Church*. San Diego: LuraMedia, 1995.

Hardesty, Nancy. "Evangelical Women Face Their Homophobia." *Christian Century*, August 1986, 768.

———. "Evangelical Women's Caucus Comes of Age." *Christian Century*, September 1982, 959–60.

———. *Great Women of Faith*. Nashville, Tenn.: Abingdon Press, 1980.

———. *Inclusive Language in the Church*. Atlanta: John Knox Press, 1987.

———. "Reflections." In *The Chicago Declaration*, edited by Ronald J. Sider, 123–26. Carol Stream, Ill.: Creation House, 1974.

———. "'Whosoever Surely Meaneth Me:' Inclusive Language and the Gospel." *Christian Scholar's Review* 17, no. 3 (1988): 231–40.

———. "Women and Evangelical Christianity." In *The Cross and the Flag*, edited by R. Clouse, 65–79. Carol Stream, Ill.: Creation House, 1972.

———. *Women Called to Witness*. Nashville, Tenn.: Abingdon Press, 1984.

———. *Your Daughters Shall Prophesy: Revivalism and Feminism in the Age of Finney*. Vol. 5 of Chicago Studies in the History of American Religion. Brooklyn, N.Y.: Carlson, 1991.

Hatch, Nathan. *The Democratization of American Christianity*. New Haven, Conn.: Yale University Press, 1989.

———. *The Sacred Cause of Liberty*. New Haven, Conn.: Yale University Press, 1977.

Hayter, Mary. *New Eve in Christ*. Grand Rapids, Mich.: Eerdmans, 1987.

Hearn, Virginia K. "Christian Feminists in North America: The Experience of Evangelical Feminists." *Dialogue and Alliance* 2, no. 3 (fall 1988): 57–75.

———. "A Liberating Word: Feminist Theology as a Theology of Liberation." In *Liberation Theology: North American Style*, edited by Deane William Ferm, 181–206. New York: International Religious Foundation, 1987.

———, ed. *Our Struggle to Serve: The Stories of Fifteen Evangelical Women*. Waco, Tex.: Word Books, 1979.

Henry, Carl F. H. *Evangelical Responsibility in Contemporary Theology*. Grand Rapids, Mich.: Eerdmans, 1957.

———. *Evangelicals in Search of Identity*. Waco, Tex.: Word Books, 1976.

———. *God, Revelation, and Authority*. Waco, Tex.: Word Books, 1976.

———. "Revolt on the Evangelical Frontiers." *Christianity Today*, April 1974, 4–8.

———. *The Uneasy Conscience of Modern Fundamentalism*. Grand Rapids, Mich.: Eerdmans, 1947.

Hestenes, Roberta, and Lois Curley, eds. *Women and the Ministries of Christ*. Pasadena, Calif.: Fuller Theological Seminary, 1979.

Hewitt, Nancy A. "The Perimeters of Women's Power in American Religion." In *The Evangelical Tradition in America*, edited by Leonard I. Sweet, 233–56. Macon, Ga.: Mercer University Press, 1984.

Horner, S. Sue. *Born Again: A History of the Contemporary Evangelical Feminist Movement*. Peabody, Mass.: Hendrickson Publishers, forthcoming.

Hull, Gretchen Gaebelein. *Equal to Serve: Women and Men in the Church and Home*. London: Scripture Union, 1989.

Hunter, James Davison. *American Evangelicalism*. New Brunswick, N.J.: Rutgers University Press, 1983.

———. *Culture Wars: The Struggle to Define America*. New York: Basic Books, 1991.

————. *Evangelicalism: The Coming Generation.* Chicago: University of Chicago Press, 1987.

————. "The New Class and the Young Evangelicals." *Review of Religious Research*, December 1980, 155–69.

Hunter, James Davison, and Kimon Howland Sargeant. "Religion, Women, and the Transformation of Public Culture." *Social Research* 60, no. 3 (fall 1993): 545–70.

Hutchison, William R. *The Modernist Impulse in American Protestantism.* Cambridge, Mass.: Harvard University Press, 1976.

Ingersoll, Julie. *Evangelical Christian Women: War Stories in the Gender Battles.* New York: New York University Press, 2003.

Jewett, Paul. *Man as Male and Female.* Grand Rapids, Mich.: Eerdmans, 1975.

Kau, Ina. "Feminists in the American Evangelical Movement." Master's thesis, Pacific School of Religion, 1977.

Keener, Craig S. *The IVP Bible Background Commentary: New Testament.* Downers Grove, Ill.: InterVarsity Press, 1993.

————. *Paul, Women and Wives: Marriage and Women's Ministry in the Letters of Paul.* Peabody, Mass.: Hendrickson Publishers, 1992.

Kidd, Karen. "Nancy A. Hardesty and the Evangelical Women's Caucus: An Oral History." Oral history, Claremont Graduate University, 1988.

Kroeger, Catherine Clark. "Ancient Heresies and a Strange Greek Verb." *Reformed Journal*, March 1979, 12–15.

————. "The Apostle Paul and the Greco-Roman Cults of Women." *Journal of the Evangelical Theological Society*, March 1987, 25–38.

————. "Are Gay Unions Christian Covenants." In *Caught in the Crossfire*, edited by Sally B. Geis and Donald E. Messer, 132–40. Nashville, Tenn.: Abingdon Press, 1994.

————. "1 Timothy 2:12—A Classicist's View." In *Women, Authority and the Bible*, edited by Alvera Mickelsen, 225–44. Downers Grove, Ill.: InterVarsity Press, 1986.

Kroeger, Catherine Clark, Mary Evans, and Elaine Storkey, eds. *Study Bible for Women: The New Testament.* Grand Rapids, Mich.: Baker Books, 1995.

Kroeger, Catherine Clark, and Richard Clark Kroeger. "An Enquiry into Evidence of Maenadism in the Corinthian Congregation." *Society of Biblical Literature: Seminar Papers* 14 (1978): 331–38.

————. *I Suffer Not a Woman.* Grand Rapids, Mich.: Baker Book House, 1992.

————. "May Women Teach? Heresy in the Pastoral Epistles." *Reformed Journal*, October 1980, 14–18.

————. "Pandemonium and Silence at Corinth." *Reformed Journal*, June 1978, 6–10.

————. "Sexual Identity in Corinth: Paul Faces a Crisis." *Reformed Journal*, December 1978, 11–15.

———. "St. Paul's Treatment of Misogyny, Gynephobia, and Sex Segregation in First Corinthians 11:2–6." *Society of Biblical Literature: Seminar Papers* 17 (1979): 213–21.

———. "What Does the Bible Say about Homosexuality." In *Caught in the Crossfire*, edited by Sally B. Geis and Donald E. Messer, 48–56. Nashville, Tenn.: Abingdon Press, 1994.

———. "Why Were There No Women Apostles?" *Equity* (1982): 10–12.

Lindsell, Harold. *The Battle for the Bible*. Grand Rapids, Mich.: Zondervan, 1976.

McFadden, Carol Prester. "Christian Feminists: 'We're on Our Way, Lord!'" *Christianity Today*, December 1975, 36–37.

Marsden, George. *Fundamentalism and American Culture: The Shaping of Twentieth-Century Evangelicalism: 1870–1925*. New York: Oxford University Press, 1980.

———. *Reforming Fundamentalism: Fuller Seminary and the New Evangelicalism*. Grand Rapids, Mich.: Eerdmans, 1987.

———, ed. *Evangelicalism and Modern America*. Grand Rapids, Mich.: Eerdmans, 1984.

Marty, Martin E. "Tensions within Contemporary Evangelicalism." In *The Evangelicals: What They Believe, Who They Are, Where They Are Changing*, edited by David F. Wells and John D. Woodbridge, 170–88. Nashville, Tenn.: Abingdon Press, 1975.

McKim, Donald K. *A Guide to Contemporary Hermeneutics: Major Trends in Biblical Interpretation*. Grand Rapids, Mich.: Eerdmans, 1986.

———. "Hearkening to the Voices: What Women Theologians Are Saying." *Reformed Journal*, January 1985, 7–10.

McLoughlin, William G. *Revivals, Awakenings, and Reform: An Essay on Religion and Social Change in America, 1607–1977*. Chicago: University of Chicago Press, 1978.

McNeill, John J. *The Church and the Homosexual*. Kansas City, Kans.: Sheed Andrews and McMeel, 1976.

Mickelsen, Alvera. "Can Homosexual Sex Be Sanctified?" *The Standard*, October 1988, 12–15.

———. "Does Order of Creation, Redemption, and Climax Demand Female Supremacy?" In *Equal to Serve*, edited by Gretchen Gabelein Hull, 245–50. Old Tappen, N.J.: Revell, 1987.

Mickelsen, Alvera, ed. *Women, Authority and the Bible*. Downers Grove, Ill.: InterVarsity Press, 1986.

Mickelsen, Alvera, and Berkeley A. Mickelsen. "Does Male Dominance Tarnish Our Translations?" *Christianity Today*, October 1979, 23–29.

———. "The Head of the Epistles." *Christianity Today*, February 1981, 20–23.

Mollenkott, Virginia R. "The Bible and Linguistic Change." *The Other Side* 117 (1981): 14–19.

———. "The Closet and the Classroom; Reflections of an Aging Lesbian Professor." In *Twenty-first Century Challenge: Lesbians and Gays in Education*, edited by Sue McConnell-Celi, 21–26. Red Bank, N.J.: Lavender Crystal Press, 1993.

———. *The Divine Feminine.* New York: Crossroad, 1983.

———. "An Evangelical Feminist Confronts the Goddess." *Christian Century*, October 1982, 1043–46.

———. "Evangelicalism: A Feminist Perspective." *Union Seminary Quarterly* 32, no. 2 (1977): 95–103.

———. "Female God-Imagery and Wholistic Social Consciousness." *Studies in Formative Spirituality*, November 1984, 345–54.

———. "Feminism and the Kingdom: From Machismo to Mutuality." *Sojourners* 6 (1977): 28–30.

———. *Godding: Human Responsibility and the Bible.* New York: Crossroad, 1987.

———. *Omnigender: A Trans-Religious Approach.* Cleveland: Pilgrim Press, 2001.

———. "Reproductive Choice: Basic to Justice for Women." *Christian Scholar's Review* 17, no. 3 (1988): 286–93.

———. *Sensuous Spirituality: Out from Fundamentalism.* New York: Crossroad, 1992.

———. *Speech, Silence, Action!: The Cycle of Faith, Journeys in Faith.* Nashville, Tenn.: Abingdon Press, 1980.

———. *Women, Men, and the Bible.* Nashville, Tenn.: Abingdon Press, 1977.

———. *Women of Faith in Dialogue.* New York: Crossroad, 1987.

———. "The Women's Movement Challenges the Church." *Journal of Psychology and Theology* 2, no. 4 (1974): 298–310.

Niebuhr, H. Richard. "Fundamentalism." In *Encyclopedia of the Social Sciences*, vol. 6, pp. 526–27. New York: Macmillan, 1931.

———. *The Social Sources of Denominationalism.* New York: Meridian Books, 1957.

Noll, Mark A. *America's God: From Jonathan Edwards to Abraham Lincoln.* New York: Oxford University Press, 2002.

———. *Between Faith and Criticism: Evangelicals, Scholarship, and the Bible in America.* Society of Biblical Literature Confessional Perspectives Series. San Francisco: Harper & Row, 1986.

———. "Common Sense Traditions and American Evangelical Thought." *American Quarterly* 37 (summer 1985): 216–38.

———. *The Princeton Defense of Plenary Verbal Inspiration.* New York: Garland, 1988.

———. *The Princeton Theology, 1812–1921: Scripture, Science, Theological Method from Archibald Alexander to Benjamin Breckinridge Warfield.* Grand Rapids, Mich.: Baker Books, 1983.

O'Brien, William. "Handling Conflict: The Fallout from Fresno." *The Other Side*, December 1986, 25–41.

Olasky, Susan. "The Battle for the Bible." *World*, April 19, 1997, 14–15, 18.

———. "The Feminist Seduction of the Evangelical Church." *World*, March 29, 1997, 12–15.

Piper, John, and Wayne Grudem. *Recovering Biblical Manhood and Womanhood: A Response to Evangelical Feminism.* Westchester, Ill.: Crossway, 1991.

Quebedeaux, Richard. "We're On Our Way, Lord!: The Rise of 'Evangelical Feminism' in Modern American Christianity." In *Women in the World's Religions, Past and Present*, edited by Ursala King, 129–44. New York: Paragon House, 1987.

———. *The Worldly Evangelicals.* New York: Harper & Row, 1978.

———. *The Young Evangelicals.* New York: Harper & Row, 1974.

Radmacher, Earl D., Robert D. Preus, and the International Council on Biblical Inerrancy. *Hermeneutics, Inerrancy, and the Bible: Papers from ICBI Summit II.* Grand Rapids, Mich.: Academie Books, 1984.

Rogers, Eugene F. Jr., ed. *Theology and Sexuality: Classic and Contemporary Readings.* Malden, Mass.: Blackwell, 2002.

Rogers, Jack Bartlett. *Biblical Authority.* Waco, Tex.: Word Books, 1977.

Rogers, Jack Bartlett, and Donald K. McKim. *The Authority and Interpretation of the Bible: An Historical Approach.* San Francisco: Harper & Row, 1979.

Ruether, Rosemary Radford. *Liberation Theology: Human Hope Confronts Christian History and American Power.* New York: Paulist Press, 1972.

———. *Sexism and God-Talk: Toward a Feminist Theology.* Boston: Beacon Press, 1983.

Russell, Letty M. *Human Liberation in a Feminist Perspective—A Theology.* Philadelphia: Westminster Press, 1974.

Sandeen, Ernest R. *The Roots of Fundamentalism: British and American Millenarianism 1800–1930.* Chicago: University of Chicago Press, 1970.

Sargeant, Kimon Howland. *Seeker Churches: Promoting Traditional Religion in a Nontraditional Way.* New Brunswick, N.J.: Rutgers University Press, 2000.

Scanzoni, Letha. "Conservative Christians and Gay Civil Rights." *Christian Century*, October 1976, 857–62.

———. "The Feminists and the Bible." *Christianity Today*, February 1973, 10–15.

———. "The Great Chain of Being and the Chain of Command." *Reformed Journal*, October 1976, 14–18.

———. "On Friendship and Homosexuality: Antidotes for Homophobia." *Christianity Today*, September 1974, 11–16.

———. *Sex Is a Parent Affair*. Glendale, Calif.: G/L Regal Books, 1973.

———. *Sexuality*. Philadelphia: Westminster Press, 1984.

———. "Woman's Place: Silence or Service." *Eternity* 17, no. 2 (1966): 14–16.

Scanzoni, Letha, and Nancy Hardesty. *All We're Meant to Be: A Biblical Approach to Women's Liberation*. 1st ed. Waco, Tex.: Word Books, 1974.

———. *All We're Meant to Be: Biblical Feminism for Today*. 2nd ed. Nashville, Tenn.: Abingdon Press, 1986.

———. *All We're Meant to Be: Biblical Feminism for Today*. 3rd ed. Grand Rapids, Mich.: Eerdmans, 1992.

Scanzoni, Letha, and Virginia R. Mollenkott. *Is the Homosexual My Neighbor?* 1st ed. San Francisco: Harper & Row, 1978.

———. *Is the Homosexual My Neighbor?* 2nd ed. San Francisco: HarperSanFrancisco, 1994.

Scanzoni, Letha, and John H. Scanzoni. *Men, Women, and Change: A Sociology of Marriage and Family*. New York: McGraw-Hill, 1976.

Schmidt, Ruth A. "Second-Class Citizenship in the Kingdom of God." *Christianity Today*, January 1971, 13–14.

Scholer, David M. "1 Timothy 2:9–15 and the Place of Women in the Church's Ministry." In *Women, Authority and the Bible*, edited by Alvera Mickelsen, 193–224. Downers Grove, Ill.: InterVarsity Press, 1986.

———. "Unseasonable Thoughts on the State of Biblical Hermeneutics." *American Baptist Quarterly*, June 1983, 134–41.

———. *Women in Early Christianity*. Vol. 14 of *Studies in Early Christianity*. New York: Garland, 1993.

Schüssler Fiorenza, Elisabeth. *Bread Not Stone: The Challenge of Feminist Biblical Interpretation*. Boston: Beacon Press, 1984.

———. *In Memory of Her: A Feminist Theological Reconstruction of Christian Origins*. New York: Crossroad, 1983.

Scroggs, Robin. *The New Testament and Homosexuality*. Philadelphia: Fortress Press, 1983.

Siddons, Philip. "Paul's View of Women." *Christianity Today*, February 1978, 40–42.

Sider, Ronald, ed. *The Chicago Declaration*. Carol Stream, Ill.: Creation House, 1974.

Smedes, Lewis. "Homosexuality: Sorting out the Issues." *Reformed Journal*, January 1978, 9–12.

———. *Sex for Christians*. Grand Rapids, Mich.: Eerdmans, 1976.

———. "Shall We Revise the Homosexual Ethic?" *Eternity*, May 1978, 46–48.

Spencer, Aida Besançon. *Beyond the Curse*. Nashville, Tenn.: Nelson, 1985.

———. "Eve at Ephesus." *Journal of the Evangelical Theological Society*, fall 1974, 215–22.

Spring, Beth. "Gay Rights Resolution Divides Membership of Evangelical Women's Caucus." *Christianity Today*, October 1986, 41–43.

Stone, Jon R. *On the Boundaries of American Evangelicalism: The Postwar Evangelical Coalition*. New York: St. Martin's Press, 1997.

Strauss, Mark L. *Distorting Scripture? The Challenge of Bible Translation and Gender Accuracy*. Downers Grove, Ill.: InterVarsity Press, 1998.

Tong, Rosemarie. *Feminist Thought: A Comprehensive Introduction*. Boulder, Colo.: Westview Press, 1989.

Trible, Phyllis. "Depatriarchalizing in Biblical Interpretation." *Journal of the American Academy of Religion*, March 1973, 30–48.

———. *God and the Rhetoric of Sexuality*. Philadelphia: Fortress Press, 1978.

Van Leeuwen, Mary Stewart, ed. *After Eden: Facing the Challenge of Gender Reconciliation*. Grand Rapids, Mich.: Eerdmans, 1993.

———. "Between the 'F' Word and the 'R' Word." *Reformed Journal*, June 1990, 3–5.

———. "The Christian Mind and the Challenge of Gender Relations." *Reformed Journal*, September 1987, 17–23.

———. "The Contradictions of Headship." *Reformed Journal*, May/June 1990, 21–28.

———. "Does God Listen to Girls?" *Reformed Journal*, June 1986, 7–11.

———. "The End of Female Passivity." *Christianity Today*, January 1986, 121–31.

———. *Gender and Grace*. Downers Grove, Ill.: InterVarsity Press, 1990.

———. "Muscular Christianity." *Radix* 19, no. 1 (1989): 20–21, 31.

Williams, Delores S. *Sisters in the Wilderness: The Challenge of Womanist God-Talk*. Maryknoll, N.Y.: Orbis Books, 1993.

Williams, Don. *The Bond That Breaks: Will Homosexuality Split the Church?* Los Angeles: BIM Publishing, 1978.

Wuthnow, Robert. *The Restructuring of American Religion: Society and Faith since World War II*. Princeton, N.J.: Princeton University Press, 1988.

Yamane, David. "Secularization on Trial: In Defense of a Neosecularization Paradigm." *Journal for the Scientific Study of Religion*, January 1997, 113–15.

Index

Abortion, 159; in *All We're Meant to Be*, 29; Nancy Hardesty on, 12–13; Virginia Mollenkott on, 75; views in CBE on, 133, 152, 185; views in EWC on, 94, 134–135, 147–148

Ahlstrom, Sydney, 192

All We're Meant to Be (Scanzoni and Hardesty), 14, 34, 62, 75, 91, 98, 104–105, 126, 175; history of, 25–26; reception of, 29; summary of, 26–29; writing of, 11–12

Ammerman, Nancy, *Baptist Battles*, 158

Androcentrism, 23, 60, 111, 122, 130, 176; in biblical interpretation, 49, 58

Aquinas, Thomas, 126

Aristotle, 131

Atonement: models of, 119–120; substitutionary, 147

Augustine, Saint, 46, 107, 126

Authority: and civil society, 107–108; moral, 147. *See also* Biblical authority; Inerrancy, biblical

Bailey, D. S., 80–81

Baly, Jeanne, 97

Barth, Karl, 86, 206n. 13

Bendroth, Margaret, 47

Berkouwer, G. C., 26–27, 88

Biblical authority, 190–191; debates over, 17–21; definition of, 2–3, 29–32; and evangelical feminist interpretation, 26–27, 42, 45, 48; and evangelical hermeneutics, 165–169; EWC and, 177–179; Carl F. H. Henry on, 66–67; homosexuality and, 77, 89–91; and inerrancy, 108; sexuality, and civil society, 106–107. *See also* Inerrancy, biblical

Bilezekian, Gilbert, 140, 154–155, 160, 213n. 45; on the creation accounts, 128–129; and Willow Creek Church, 155

Bonhoeffer, Dietrich, 26

Borba, Michelle, 97, 101

Boswell, John, *Christianity, Social Tolerance, and Homosexuality*, 80, 81, 82, 83, 84, 90

Brown, Antoinette, 44

Cady, Susan, on *sophia*, 117–118

Calvin, John, 46, 126

Campus Crusade for Christ, 1, 16–17

Carlson-Theis, Christiane, 100, 102

Carnell, Edward J., and inerrancy, 19–20

Carson, D. A., 164; and the NIVI, 145–147

Chicago declaration, 14, 18, 69

Christ, Carol, 142
Christian Century, 60, 62, 72
Christianity Today, 18, 21, 24, 62, 72, 158, 161; on inclusive language, 144; and inerrancy debates, 67; review of *All We're Meant to Be*, 29; review of *Is the Homosexual My Neighbor?* 87
Christians for Biblical Equality (CBE): and the evangelical coalition, 154–156; founding of, 103; on inclusive language, 144; marriage conference, 159; member surveys, 133, 151–152; organization of, 150–151; statement of faith, 152–153. *See also* Traditionalist evangelical feminism
Christology: Jesus' maleness, 60, 116–117; Jesus and *sophia*, 117–119; Jesus' treatment of women, 124–126; as male savior, 124; Virginia Mollenkott on the incarnation, 61. *See also* Atonement; Salvation; *Sophia* (wisdom)
Cook, Kaye, surveys of CBE and EWC, 133–134, 137, 144, 147, 152, 154, 177–178, 188
Cott, Nancy, *The Grounding of Modern Feminism*, 202n. 22
Council on Biblical Manhood and Womanhood, 115, 146, 160–161; complementarianism, 146, 160
Countryman, William, 105; *Dirt, Greed, and Sex*, 83
Creation accounts: in *All We're Meant to Be*, 27–28; and anthropology, 126–127; and homosexuality, 82–83; and male and female relationships, 128–130; Virginia Mollenkott on, 59–60. *See also* Genesis 3:25–26, 27

Daly, Mary, 23, 114, 126, 142, 181; *The Church and the Second Sex*, 49
Daughters of Sarah, 15–16, 62, 72, 117, 119; the end of, 173; and EWC, 171–172; first issue of, 33; surveys of readers, 33–34
Dayton, Donald W., 72, 91; articles on women's equality, 24; and Wesleyan theology, 44–45
Dayton, Lucille Sider, 37; and *Daughters of Sarah*, 15–16; and Wesleyan theology, 44–45
DeBerg, Betty, 47
Dispensationalism, 19, 21, 198n. 18
Dobson, James, 157, 164; and the NIVI debate, 145–146
Douglas, Ann, 47
Dualism, 24, 142; description of, 121–122

Ecclesiology, CBE and EWC on, 136. *See also* Inclusive language; 1 Corinthians 11:2–10; 1 Timothy 2:11–15
Echols, Alice, on radical feminism, 103–104, 106
Edwards, George, *Gay/Lesbian Liberation*, 82, 83
Egalitarianism, 39, 62, 74, 131; in *All We're Meant to Be*, 29; backlash against, 157–158, 160; in CBE, 151–152, 169, 193; among college students, 161–162; versus a traditional paradigm, 42–44; and Willow Creek Church, 162–163. *See also* Equality, women's
Eggebroten, Anne, 14, 149, 172–173; and 1986 Fresno conference, 96, 97, 102; spiritual pilgrimage, 1, 9, 35–37

Episcopal Church: Nancy Hardesty
and, 72, 179; and homosexuality,
220n. 65; and the ordination of
women, 15, 22–23
Equality, women's, 2, 9, 15, 31, 65,
190; in *All We're Meant to Be*,
26–29; backlash against, 156–157;
and the Bible, 32, 46, 61, 72, 115;
and CBE, 103, 150–153, 159,
169; in evangelical feminism,
23–24, 74–75; and EWC, 180; in
EWC's by-laws, 70; and EWC's
purpose, 93, 95, 98–100; and inclusive language, 143; Kenneth
Kantzer on, 154; Luther and
Calvin on, 126; in secular feminism, 22–23, 74, 186; and traditionalist evangelical feminism, 188;
in 1 Corinthians 11, 139. *See also*
Egalitarianism; Traditionalist evangelical feminism
Equal rights amendment, 22, 36, 38,
74; and EWC, 40–41, 93–95
Erickson, Joyce, 39, 162
Eternity: articles on women's equality,
24; Nancy Hardesty editor at, 11;
review of *All We're Meant to Be*,
25; review of *Is the Homosexual
My Neighbor?* 87
Evangelical feminism: backlash
against, 156–160; definition of,
8–9; women of, 32–34. *See also*
Progressive evangelical feminism;
Traditionalist evangelical feminism
Evangelicalism: and American culture,
185–188; boundaries of, 30 161,
163–165, 169, 181, 185, 191, 193;
definitions of, 6–8, 12, 164; neo-,
18–19; progressive, 20, 64–65, 69,
108, 161, 197n. 13; young, 19–22,

24, 26, 184. *See also* Evangelical
feminism
Evangelicals for Social Action, 35, 37,
69, 101; Thanksgiving Day workshops, 12–16
Evangelical Theological Society, 182;
*Journal of the Evangelical Theo-
logical Society*, 29
Evangelical Women's Caucus (EWC),
12; Bay Area EWC, 36–38, 97,
100; and biblical authority,
177–179; by-laws and statement
of faith, 70; changes to statement of faith and name,
176–177; and the evangelical
coalition, 180–181, 183–184;
founding of, 16; inclusivity of,
175–176; and inerrancy,
177–178; membership survey of,
133; organizational decline,
170–172; organizational recovery,
173–174; organization of, 37.
See also Evangelical Women's
Caucus national conferences; Progressive evangelical feminism
Evangelical Women's Caucus national
conferences: and homosexuality,
92–93; 1975 in Washington, D.C.,
37; 1978 in Fullerton, 39–40; 1980
in Saratoga Springs, 40; 1982 in
Seattle, 40; 1984 in Wellesley,
93–94; 1986 in Fresno, 96–103,
169, 172; 1988 in Northpark,
170–171; 1990 in Northpark, 171,
177; 1992 in San Francisco,
171–172; 1994 in Northpark, 173;
1996 in Old Dominion University,
174; 1998 in Grand Rapids, 174;
2000 in Northpark, 174
Evans, Mary, *Study Bible for Women*,
116

Faludi, Susan, 156
Family: and civil society, 106–107; guidelines for, 131–132; "traditional," 156–157, 169
Feminism, secular, 22, 71; backlash against, 156; and comparisons with evangelical feminism, 74–76, 103–104, 106; evangelical accommodation to, 64–65, 90; liberal, 74, 103; and progressive evangelical feminism, 188–189; radical, 75, 103–104, 106; and traditionalist evangelical feminism, 186
Finger, Reta, 116; on abortion, 134–135; on the atonement, 119–120; on lesbianism, 91; on the Trinity, 112
Finney, Charles, 44
Fuller, Charles, 18, 19
Fuller, Daniel, 18, 24; and inerrancy, 19–21
Fuller Theological Seminary, 18, 21, 68, 73, 79, 154
Fundamentalism, 6, 18–19; fundamentals of the faith, 6, 17; and neoevangelicalism, 30–31

Gallagher, Sally, 161, 218n. 32
Gallagher, Sharon, 12, 37, 63, 92; on Virginia Mollenkott's hermeneutics, 57–58
Gay rights, 107, 109; Stonewall riots, 107
Geertz, Clifford, 142
Gender: roles, 2, 26, 75, 191; of God, 111–115; and inerrancy, 161; of Jesus, 117; Virginia Mollenkott on, 123, 134; and sin, 129–130. *See also* Christology; Equality, women's; Inclusive language
Gilligan, Carol, 102, 129–130
Gnosticism, 118, 140

Green Leaf, 100; women's stories in, 34–35
Grimké, Angelina, 44
Grimké, Sarah, 44
Groothuis, Rebecca Merrill: on functional subordination, 115–116; on the Trinity, 114
Grudem, Wayne, 145, 160; on functional subordination, 115–116
Gundry, Patricia, 63, 127, 160; *Heirs Together*, 48–49; *Woman Be Free!* 45–48
Gundry, Stanley, 46, 52

Hannay, Margaret, 72, 101–102, 209n. 66
Hardesty, Nancy, 9, 37, 54, 72, 92, 160, 173, 179, 208n. 48; and *All We're Meant to Be*, 25–29, 105, 126–127; collaboration with Letha Scanzoni, 11–12; coming out, 104; on evangelical feminism, 71; and the Fresno conference, 94, 96–98, 101–102; on homosexuality, 106; on inclusive language, 143–144; on lesbianism, 75; Thanksgiving Day conferences, 12–16; on Wesleyan theology, 44–45, 91; and women's equality, 24. See also *All We're Meant to Be*
Hatch, Nathan, 164, 192
Hays, Richard, 90; on homosexuality, 84–85
Hayter, Mary, on 1 Corinthians 11, 139–141
"Headship" (*kephale*), 43–44, 51
Hearn, Virginia, 9, 64, 94; and the Bay Area EWC, 36–37; on the EWC name change, 177; on the Fresno conference, 102; and *Green Leaf*, 34–35; on the resolution on homosexuality, 98–100, 133

Henry, Carl F. H., 99, 164; on biblical authority, 66–67

Hermeneutics: and *All We're Meant to Be*, 26–27; and biblical authority, 29–30; definition of, 2; and early evangelical feminist methods, 45, 63–64; evangelical, 165–169; Patricia Gundry and, 48; higher criticism, 20–21, 63; and inerrancy, 162; Virginia Mollenkott and, 56–58; and the Pauline passages, 62–63; principles for cultural limitation, 26, 131, 139–140, 142, 166–169; of suspicion, 122; and women's equality, 24

Hestenes, Roberta, 21, 162; and early evangelical feminist interpretation, 41–43; on evangelical feminist accommodation to secular feminism, 65–66

Heyward, Carter, 180, 182, 212n. 33

Holy Spirit, as feminine aspect of the Trinity, 113–114

Homosexuality, 179–180; CBE member survey on, 133; and CBE's statement of faith, 153; and Christian ethics, 88–89; and civil society, 106–107; and evangelical theology, 147–148; in EWC, 176; EWC resolution on, 93–95; in Genesis 19, 78–80; and human sexuality, 82–83; and *Is the Homosexual My Neighbor?* 77–89; and levitical law, 80–82; orientation versus acts, 29, 84–86, 90; in the Pauline passages, 83–85; scientific evidence concerning, 86–87. *See also* Gay rights; Lesbianism

Horner, Sue, 173, 176

Hubbard, David, 21, 154

Hull, Gretchen Gaebelein, 102, 154–155, 160, 169; on resolution on homosexuality, 95

Hunter, James Davison, 152, 156–157, 161–162, 169

Hybels, Bill, 154–155, 163–164

Hyun-Kyung, Chung, 110

Inclusive language: and Bible translation, 143–144; lectionary, 144, 182; Alvera and Berkeley Mickelsen on, 73; Virginia Mollenkott on, 72–73; in the NIVI, 144–147

Individualism: in American religion, 194; in American society, 108; in evangelical feminism, 4–5; in evangelicalism, 187, 191; sexuality, and the family, 106. *See also* Pluralism

Inerrancy, biblical, 32; and American culture, 187; and authority, 108; definition of, 2, 17; and evangelical boundaries, 71, 161, 169; and evangelical identity, 66–69; and EWC, 71, 177–178; Patricia Gundry on, 47; Carl F. H. Henry on, 69; and hermeneutics, 163; International Conference on Biblical Inerrancy (ICBI), 155, 165–166, 169; limited, 3–4, 29–30; and Virginia Mollenkott, 58; survey questions on, 152; and traditionalist evangelical feminism, 137, 148, 153; younger evangelical views on, 19–20; 1989 conference on, 164. *See also* Biblical authority

International Bible Society (IBS), 144–145

Is the Homosexual My Neighbor? (Scanzoni and Mollenkott), 76–77; reviews of, 87; summary and analysis of, 78–89

Jang, Deborah, 175–176; spiritual pilgrimage, 149–150

Jewett, Paul K., 39, 72, 127, 130; influence on evangelical feminism, 26, 54, 74, 160; *Man as Male and Female*, 24–25, 29–30

Johnston, Robert, on homosexuality, 89–90

Kantzer, Kenneth, 67, 154–155, 164

Keener, Craig, 154, 155, 213n. 49; on Ephesians 5, 131–132; and inerrancy, 157–158

Keller, Rosemary Skinner, 173

Kroeger, Catherine Clark, 9, 118, 127, 154; and founding of CBE, 102–103, 150; at the Fresno conference, 97; on pederasty, 85; on the resolution on homosexuality, 99; *Study Bible for Women*, 116; on 1 Corinthians 11, 50–51

Kroeger, Richard Clark: on pederasty, 85; on 1 Corinthians 11, 50–51

Lee, Luther, 44

Lesbianism: in *All We're Meant to Be*, 29; evangelical feminism and, 75; in EWC, 97; Nancy Hardesty and, 104; lesbian and friends caucus, 93, 96–97, 101, 104; Virginia Mollenkott and, 104; in Romans 1, 84. *See also* Homosexuality

Liberation theology, 23, 121–122, 135, 147

Lindsell, Harold, 21; and inerrancy debates, 67–69

Luther, Martin, 46, 126

Marsden, George, 30; on the definition of evangelicalism, 6–8, 196nn. 8–10

Marty, Martin, 18, 197n. 11

McLoughlin, William G., 192

McNeil, Father John, *The Church and the Homosexual*, 78, 80, 84, 87

McQuilkin, J. Robertson, 166–167

Mellado, Jim, 156

Metropolitan Community Church, 179, 220n. 6

Mickelsen, Alvera, 9, 40, 160; on equality and the founding of CBE, 102, 152–153, 154; on inclusive language, 73; on *kephale* ("head"), 52; and the resolution on homosexuality, 99, 102

Mickelsen, Berkeley, 40, 160; on the founding of CBE, 154; on *kephale* ("head"), 52

Millet, Kate, 104

Mollenkott, Virginia Ramey, 9, 45, 105, 127, 147, 149, 160; background of, 53–56; and Christianity, 181–182; on Christology, 120–123; coming out, 104; on creation, 59–60; on the crucifixion, 111; on equality of opportunity, 75; at ERA rally, 40; and evangelicalism, 71–74, 180–181, 188; on EWC name change, 177; *The Divine Feminine*, 60, 112–113; at Fresno conference, 96, 98, 101–102; *Godding*, 122–123; on homosexual rights, 106, 133–134; on the incarnation, 60–61; *Is the Homosexual My Neighbor?* 77–89; on lesbianism, 75–76; on marriage, 175; *Omnigender*, 123, 134, 179; principles of interpretation of, 56–58; and racism, 205n. 84; on regeneration, 61–62; response to her theology, 62–63; *Sensuous Spirituality*, 136, 181; on sin, 135–136; on the Trinity, 59–60, 112–113; *Women, Men,*

and the Bible, 56, 58–60, 62–63; at 1978 EWC conference, 37, 92; at 1994 conference, 173. *See also Is the Homosexual My Neighbor?*
Moltmann, Jürgen, 116
Moor, Ann, 35, 38, 39
Ms., 22, 36
Mutuality: in the Bible, 142; in creation, 128–129; in marriage, 131–132; and progressive evangelical feminism, 133; in the Trinity, 116

National Association of Evangelicals, 18, 73, 182
National Council of Churches, 40, 73, 144, 182
National Organization of Women, 1, 22, 37, 103; and the ERA, 40; and EWC, 38; history of, 35; and liberal feminism, 74–75
New International Version Bible (NIV), 144; inclusive language edition, 145–147
Noll, Mark, 192, 195n. 7, 223n. 9

Olasky, Susan, 145
Ordination, women's, 22–23, 137
Ostrander, Tina, on *sophia*, 118
Other Side, 58, 69, 72, 102

Packer, J. I., 67, 145
Panentheism, 136, 147
Patriarchy, 58, 63, 75, 104; and abortion, 135; and the atonement, 119; in the Bible, 24, 37, 54, 60, 72, 122, 126; Jesus and, 125; and language, 143; opposition to, 98, 103; in the Trinity, 111–112
Patterson, Paige, 145, 158
Penning, James, 162
Piper, John, 160, 164

Plantinga, Cornelius Jr., 117, 154, 155
Pluralism: in American society, 5–6, 185, 189; and evangelicalism, 191–193, 194; and progressive evangelical feminism, 180
Post-American, 12, 24
Presbyterian Church in America, 162; women's equality, and inerrancy, 159
Progressive evangelical feminism: and American culture, 185; definition of, 111; and the evangelical coalition, 182–184; theology, 147–148. *See also* Evangelical Women's Caucus
Pui-lan, Kwok, 174–175

Quebedeaux, Richard, 64–65

Ramm, Bernard, 19–20, 48
Re-Imagining Conference, 110–111, 117, 120–121, 143–144, 175
Revivalism, 71, 108, 180. *See also* Evangelicalism, definitions of
Rogers, Jack, 22, 67, 68
Ruether, Rosemary Radford, 23, 174, 176, 190; theology of, 121–122
Russell, Letty, 23, 121

Salvation: as fundamental to evangelicalism, 6, 7, 18; universal, 121, 136, 147; in 1 Timothy 2, 56. *See also* Atonement
Sargeant, Kimon Howland, 187
Scanzoni, Letha, 105, 160; on accommodation to secular feminism, 65; *All We're Meant to Be*, 25–29, 126–127; on biblical authority, 180; collaboration with Nancy Hardesty, 11–12; on EWC name change, 176–177;

Scanzoni, Letha (*Continued*)
on homosexuality, 75–76, 104,
106, 134; *Is the Homosexual My
Neighbor?* 77–89; and Virginia
Mollenkott, 54, 72; and Thanks-
giving Day workshop, 14; and
women's equality, 22, 23; at 1978
EWC conference, 37; and 1996
conference, 174. See also *All
We're Meant to Be*; *Is the Homo-
sexual My Neighbor?*
Schaefer, Naomi, 162
Scholer, David, 52, 154, 155, 176;
on hermeneutics, 167–169; on 1
Timothy 2, 137–139
Schüssler Fiorenza, Elisabeth, 122,
174, 176, 182
Scroggs, Robin, 83, 85, 105
Sheppard, Gerald T., 30
Siddons, Philip, 62–63
Sider, Ronald, 154–155; and the
Chicago declaration, 14; and so-
cial concerns, 16–27; and the
Thanksgiving Day workshop, 12
Smedes, Lewis, 154; on homosexual-
ity, 88–89
Smidt, Corwin, 162
Sophia (wisdom), 110; and Jesus,
117–118; Virginia Mollenkott on,
120–121. See also Christology;
Holy Spirit
Southern Baptist Convention, 145,
151, 162; statement on women,
158–159
Spencer, Aida Besançon, 119, 154,
160; on the Trinity, 112–113
Stafford, Tim, 83, 85, 87, 89
Storkey, Elaine, *Study Bible for
Women*, 116
Stott, John, 103, 154
Strauss, Mark, 145–146
Submission: in marriage, 61,

131–132; mutual, 64–65, 132. *See
also* Mutuality; Subordination of
women
Subordination of women: in the
Apostle Paul's writings, 23, 25,
48, 52, 132, 139, 140; in the
Bible, 29, 111, 351; as cultural
construct, 142; functional,
115–116; in Genesis, 27, 128; in
Western society, 126. *See also*
Submission

Taussig, Hal, on *sophia*, 117–118
Thielicke, Helmut, 26, 87–88
Torjesen, Karen and Leif, 114–115
Traditionalist evangelical feminism:
definition of, 111; on inclusive
language, 144; and secular feminism, 186; theology, 148; theology and social views, 184–185;
on the Trinity, 114. *See also*
Christians for Biblical Equality
(CBE)
Trible, Phyllis, *God and the Rhetoric
of Sexuality*, 127–128
Trinity: Virginia Mollenkott on,
59–60; as patriarchal image,
111–113; sex of, 114–115; subordination and, 115–116. *See also*
Christology; Holy Spirit

Update, 149, 171, 173, 183–184;
changes in, 174–175; content of,
38; on Fresno conference,
100–102; on homosexuality in
EWC, 93–95; and women's pilgrimages, 34–35

Vanden Eykel, Britt, 41, 172–173; on
resolutions on homosexuality, 98
Van Leeuwen, Mary Stewart, 89; on
the fall, 129–130; *Gender and*

Grace, 86; on human sexuality, 132–133

Wallis, Jim, 12, 16–17
Ward, Pat: and founding of EWC, 16; and the Fresno conference, 101–102, 209n. 66
Willard, Francis, 44
Williams, Delores, 110, 174, 176, 205n. 84

Williams, Don: *The Bond that Breaks*, 82; on homosexuality, 79–80, 89; on Virginia Mollenkott's hermeneutics, 83, 87; at 1978 EWC conference, 92
Willow Creek Community Church, 155–156, 187; Willow Creek Association, 162–163
World, 145–146
World Council of Churches, 110, 182

About the Author

Pamela D. H. Cochran is a lecturer in religious studies and the communications director of the Center on Religion and Democracy at the University of Virginia.